March 1999

# VIOLENCE WAS NO STRANGER
## A Guide to the Grave Sites of Famous Westerners

# VIOLENCE
## WAS NO STRANGER

A Guide to the Grave Sites of Famous Westerners

By JAMES A. BROWNING

Barbed Wire Press

P.O. Box 2107, Stillwater, OK 74046
*A Western Publications Company*

Library of Congress Cataloging-in-Publication Data

Browning, James A., 1921-
  Violence was no stranger : a guide to the grave sites of famous westerners / by James
A. Browning. — 1st ed.
       p.    c.m.
  Includes index.
  ISBN 0-935269-11-8
  1. West (U.S.)—Biography—Dictionaries.  2. Tombs—West (U.S.)—Guidebooks.  I.
Title.
F590.5.B76  1993
920.078—dc20                                                                    93-36455
                                                                                    CIP

Cover and book design by L.A. Smith

Published by Barbed Wire Press, P.O. Box 2107, Stillwater, OK 74076
Manufactured in the United States of America. First edition.

# Contents

# Illustrations

# Preface

Not all of the almost one thousand individuals listed in this book were violent people; however, they all had one thing in common. They all lived on the edge of violence. Lawmen and outlaws constantly battled each other for survival. Indians and soldiers were frequently at war. Mountain men and explorers had to contend with the forces of nature and hostile natives. Cattlemen and cowboys faced the dangers of stampedes, swollen streams, and dangerous horses and cattle. Even the missionaries and preachers frequently lived on the brink of violence. To all of those individuals in this work, it can be said, "violence was no stranger."

Each summer for thirty-four years I have spent from three weeks to two months traveling through the United States, Canada, and Mexico. Twenty-five of those trips have been through those states west of the Mississippi River. I have driven more than a quarter of a million miles searching out ghost towns, mining camps, old forts, and historic cemeteries. Old newspaper files, museum and historical society collections, city, county, and state records, and interviews with hundreds of old-timers have resulted in many notebooks filled with information on the people, places, and events relating to the history of the Old West.

As an avid photographer, I have taken more than 34,000 color slides of both scenic and historic interest. Some 2,500 of them are of grave sites of lawmen, outlaws, explorers, fur trappers and traders, Indian leaders, cattlemen, miners, and others known to western historians. Many of my friends, a number of them writers of western nonfiction, have encouraged me to put this material in book form. This work is the result of that encouragement.

The entries are by no means meant as biographies of the individuals; however, every effort has been made to correct errors which have appeared in the literature of the Old West regarding dates of birth and death and the spelling of proper names. More complete biographical sketches of many of these individuals can be found elsewhere. My major purpose has been to pinpoint the location of the burial sites of some one thousand persons. In many instances, specific instructions for locating the graves are given. In some cases no marker is present, but the exact location of the grave has been confirmed through cemetery records. The locations of a few particular burial sites are unknown. A few individuals were cremated and their ashes scattered.

An asterisk (*) following an entry indicates that I have personally located and photographed the grave site. About ninety-six percent of the entries fall into that category. The information pertaining to the remaining four percent was taken from the best sources available, but I have not personally determined that the information is correct.

I would like to thank all of the people who have helped and encouraged me with this work. Although it is impossible to individually list all of the historical societies, archivists, genealogists, city and county records clerks, and newspaper editors who allowed me to search their files, the information they furnished was of tremendous value. Many cemetery directors and other employees unselfishly spent time helping me search for grave sites when the temperature was frequently near 100 degrees.

Some of my most enjoyable moments were those times when I was invited into the homes and offices of knowledgeable individuals who told me stories and gave me information on people and events with which they were familiar.

I am greatly indebted to western historian Chuck Parsons, who took the time to read the manuscript, make several corrections, and furnish relevant information on many of the entries.

Very special "thank you's" go to Art Weinrich of Wood Dale, Illinois; Steve Grimm of Englewood, Colorado; and John W. Briggs of Gurnee, Illinois, who unselfishly shared information which enabled me to locate many gravesites that I might otherwise have missed.

Many individuals took the time to accompany me to cemeteries and remote gravesites. Among them are Ruth Frick of Washington, Missouri, who took me to the newly discovered burial site of John Colter; Ermal Boone of Claremore, Oklahoma; Mary K. Shannon of Fort Stockton, Texas; Della Meadows of Florence, Arizona; Bob Herzog of Ellsworth, Kansas; Jimmy Tewksbury of Globe, Arizona; and the two young Montana cowboys, Gary Casebolt and Brent Voll, who interrupted their work to drive me to the grave sites of Jim Winters and Johnny Logan near Landusky, Montana.

Others who have contributed in one way or another to this publication, listed in alphabetical order, are: Linda Blazer, Las Cruces, New Mexico; Gaston Boykin, Comanche, Texas; Carl Breihan, St. Louis, Missouri; Donaly Brice, Austin, Texas; K.W. Bruner, Independence, Missouri; Eric Cale, Wichita, Kansas; Robert Carlock, Mesa, Arizona; Bob Carlson, Pinedale, Wyoming; Vella Courtney, Trinidad, Colorado; Mrs. Robert Dale, Gallatin, Missouri; Robert K. DeArment, Sylvania, Ohio; Jim Dullenty, Hamilton, Montana; C.F. Eckhardt, Seguin, Texas; Catherine Engel, Denver, Colorado; Leif Ernst, Aalborg, Denmark; Raymond Fisher, Spokane, Washington; Bob Fleming, Albuquerque, New Mexico; Elvis Fleming, Roswell, New Mexico; Patsy Goebel, Cuero, Texas; Dorothy Grothusen, Ellsworth, Kansas; J. Evetts Haley, Midland, Texas; Jane Hoerster, Mason, Texas; Paul Hoylen, Jr., Deming, New Mexico; K.S. Jinkins, Whitewright, Texas; Larry Jochims, Topeka, Kansas; Dave Johnson, Indianapolis, Indiana; Signa Karger, San Antonio, Texas; Cindee Langdon, Austin, Texas; Ester Lehman, Loyal Valley, Texas; Arthur Lewis, Independence, Missouri; Vicki Little, Glendale, California; Gwen McNutt, Paris, Tennessee; Patricia Mallory, Excelsior Springs, Missouri; Julie March, Springfield, Missouri; Priscilla Martin, Loyal Valley, Texas; Rick Miller, Killeen, Texas; John and Edna Nees, Scottsville, Virginia; Gertrude Painter, Alamogordo, New Mexico; Marjorie Parsons, Smiley, Texas; Milton Perry, Kearney, Missouri; David Poston, Fort Worth, Texas; Virginia Probst, Holbrook, Arizona; Shirlene Ricardo, Turlock, California; Margret Roberts, Vernal, Utah; Kent Ruth, Geary, Oklahoma; Mrs. Ralph Sjostrom, Lander, Wyoming; Kathlyeen Sponsler, Humeston, Iowa; Cecelia Stirman, Sanderson, Texas; James W. Tyner, Chouteau, Oklahoma; Henry and Paul Valesquez, Fort Garland, Colorado; Aileen Viles, Portland, Oregon; Ted Wax, Gonzales, Louisiana; John Weber, Portland, Oregon; and Sonny Wells, Liberty, Missouri.

If I have missed anyone, it was unintentional and I apologize. Thank you, one and all.

*James A. Browning*
*Charleston, South Carolina*

# VIOLENCE WAS NO STRANGER
## A Guide to the Grave Sites of Famous Westerners

1. **Adamson, Amanda E.*** (1871-1968). She was the daughter of Joseph Hardin Clements (first cousin to John Wesley Hardin) and his wife, Sarah. She first married Texas Ranger William "Slick" Clements (no relation) and they had four children, one of whom, George (1892–1973), married Bebe Mills, who became a member of the Cowgirl Hall of Fame. When Slick died, Amanda married Carl Adamson who, along with Wayne Brazel, was present when Pat Garrett was killed. Amanda is buried in Block 5, Lot 122, of South Park Cemetery in Roswell, New Mexico. There is a marker. Block 5 is near the office.

2. **Adamson, Carl*** (1856–November 1, 1919). He is best known as one of the two men present when Pat Garrett was killed. The other was Wayne Brazel, who confessed to the killing. Adamson later married Amanda Clements, daughter of Joseph Hardin Clements. Carl is buried in Block 5, Lot 122, of South Park Cemetery in Roswell, New Mexico. His grave is marked and is not far from the cemetery office.

3. **Ado-ette.** See Big Tree.

4. **Allee, Alfred Young*** (May 3, 1855–August 19, 1896). He and his brother, Alonzo R. Allee, were Texas Rangers. Alfred served in Company C. After resigning from the Rangers, he engaged in ranching and also served as a deputy sheriff of Frio County, Texas. While a Ranger, Allee killed outlaw Brack Cornett. On August 19, 1896, he was stabbed and killed in a fight with Marshal A.J.

---

* Indicates the author has visited the grave site.

Bartholomew in Laredo, Texas. Five consecutive generations of Allees have served in the Texas Rangers. Alfred's father was also named Alfred Y. Allee (1810–1870). He, too, was a Texas Ranger and is buried in Goliad County in Christian Church Cemetery near Weesatche, Texas. The brothers, Alfred and Alonzo, are buried in Runge, Texas. To locate the cemetery and grave, see Allee, Alonzo Rolland.

5. **Allee, Alonzo Rolland*** (September 28, 1857–August 18, 1897). He and his brother, Alfred Young Allee, were Texas Rangers. Alonzo also served as sheriff of Goliad County, Texas, from 1890 to 1896. Both he and Alfred are buried in the Runge Cemetery at Runge, Texas. To locate the cemetery and grave: from Highway 72 in Runge, turn north on Highway 81 at the traffic light and go 0.8 mile to four cemeteries on the right. Continue ahead 0.2 mile to the last of the four cemeteries, enter through the arch and take the left-hand drive to the covered shelter on the right. Look left (across the drive from the shelter) to a clump of trees. The Allee graves are to the left of the trees. There is a large marker.

6. **Allemand, Joe.** See Sheepmen's Mass Grave.

7. **Allen, J.C.*** (March 21, 1866–April 19, 1909). He was a Texas and Oklahoma cattleman and was one of four men who were taken from jail and lynched at Ada, Oklahoma, for conspiracy in the murder of Gus Bobbitt. The others were Jim Miller, Jesse J. West, and Berry Burrell. West and Allen supposedly hired Miller to kill Bobbitt, with Burrell acting as a go-between. Bobbitt, an influential rancher and a thirty-second-degree Mason, had political differences with West and Allen, leading to his assassination. After their deaths, Allen and West were taken back to Texas, where they owned a large ranch near Canadian, and buried at Old Mobeetie. Large tree-trunk monuments representing the Woodmen of the World (WOW) mark their graves in the northeastern part of the Mobeetie Cemetery. Allen's wife, Bess (1871–1943), is buried beside him.

8. **Allison, Robert Clay*** (September 2, 1841–July 1, 1887). He was a Texas and New Mexico rancher and gunman who is known to have

killed a number of men. He was killed when he fell beneath a heavily loaded wagon about forty miles from Pecos, Texas. His body was removed from its original grave on the outskirts of Pecos and reburied on the grounds of the Pecos Museum in Pecos, Texas. There is a marker.

9.  **Ames, Jesse\*** (February 4, 1808–December 6, 1894). Captain Ames was a Civil War veteran and Northfield, Minnesota, banker and was active in carrying out Federal Reconstruction policies in the South following the Civil War. Many believe that Ames incurred the enmity of members of the James-Younger Gang during Reconstruction, thus leading to their attempt to rob the bank at Northfield. Ames is buried beside his wife, Martha B. Tolman Ames (May 8, 1813–August 16, 1903), in the Northfield Cemetery, Northfield, Minnesota. There is a very large monument.

10. **Anderson, David L. "Doc"\*** (November 23, 1852–June 4, 1918; NOTE: His headstone gives his year of birth as 1860; the 1900 census for Terrell County, Texas, gives 1852). He rode with Billy the Kid as "Billy Wilson." He was shot and killed by Ed Valentine in Sanderson, Texas. Anderson was Terrell County sheriff at the time. He is buried in St. Mary Magdalena Catholic Cemetery in Brackettville, Texas. The cemetery is north of town. To locate the grave: enter the cemetery from the First Street entrance. The grave is on the right about 100 feet inside the cemetery and about 30 feet before the large statue of the Crucifixion. The plot has a concrete curbing and is covered with gray marble chips. There is a large marble stone. Also in the same plot are his wife, Margaret "Maggie" M. Fitzmaurice Anderson (August 5, 1867–October 20, 1948); his daughter, Ella Mae J. Anderson (October 4, 1905–July 19, 1971; and his father-in-law and mother-in-law, Robert James Fitzmaurice (?–December 26, 1896) and Mary Marie Fitzmaurice (January 29, 1845–December 19, 1894). Robert and Mary Fitzmaurice were both born in Ireland. D.L. and Margaret Anderson were married in 1890.

11. **Anderson, William T. "Bloody Bill"\*** (February 2, 1837–October 26, 1864). Anderson held the rank of captain in the Confederate Army and was a sub-leader in Quantrill's Raiders. He was killed at

the Battle of Old Albany in Ray County, Missouri, and is buried near the rock wall on the south side of the Old Pioneer Cemetery (Mormon) in Richmond, Missouri. A ground-level Confederate States Army headstone marks his grave. The marker incorrectly gives his year of birth as 1840. The grave is in an area away from most of the other graves.

12. **Angus, William Galispie "Red"**\* (November 9, 1849–July 19, 1922). William G. Angus was born in Zanesville, Ohio. He moved to Buffalo, Wyoming, in 1880. He served as sheriff of Johnson County, Wyoming, during the Johnson County War and opposed the Invaders. He is buried beside his wife, Mary E. Bye (1863–1926), whom he had married in 1894, and beside a baby who died as an infant, in Block 4 of Willow Grove Cemetery in Buffalo. Angus had served as a thirteen-year-old drummer boy in the Civil War and later as a soldier during the Indian Wars. There is a large marker.

13. **Antrim, William H.**\* (December 1, 1842–December 10, 1922). He was the stepfather of Billy the Kid. Antrim had married Billy's mother, Catherine McCarty, at Santa Fe, New Mexico, on March 1, 1873. Much of his life was devoted to mining in New Mexico. He died at age eighty at Adelaide, California, and is buried in the San Miguel Cemetery at Paso Robles, California. There is an inscribed headstone.

14. **Applegate, Jesse**\* (July 5, 1811–April 22, 1888). He was an Oregon pioneer and surveyor. He laid out the Applegate Trail, a southern route to Fort Hall, Idaho, following the Rogue and Humbolt rivers. He died of natural causes and is buried in a small private cemetery near Yoncalla, Oregon (not the Yoncalla Cemetery). To locate the cemetery: from the Yoncalla Store, go 2.4 miles north on Oregon 99 to a historical marker. From this point look west. Go through a gate across a cattle guard. Then go through another gate. Do *not* go right where the trail forks. This leads to a ranch house. A few yards beyond the second gate, a mere trace of a road goes left 0.2 mile up the hill to the cemetery in a small clearing in the woods. Both Jesse and his wife, Cynthia Ann (August 15, 1813–June 1, 1882), are buried here. There is a headstone.

15.  **Armstrong, John Barclay** (January 1850–May 1, 1913). He was the Texas Ranger who captured John Wesley Hardin in Florida and returned him to Texas to be tried for murder. He died on his ranch at Armstrong, Texas, and is buried in a small cemetery there. Part of the ranch is currently leased to a mining company and entrance is difficult (1984).

16.  **Arnold, Mason "Mace," alias Winchester Smith\*** (1847–December 27, 1875). He was a friend of Jim Taylor during the Taylor-Sutton Feud in DeWitt County, Texas. Mace, Jim, and A.R. Hendricks were killed by members of the Sutton faction led by Sheriff William Weisiger. He is buried in the Taylor-Bennett Cemetery a few miles south of Cuero, Texas. To locate the cemetery: see Taylor, James "Jim." There is a marker at Arnold's grave.

17.  **Arnold, Philip\*** (November 6, 1823–February 8, 1879). Along with John B. Slack, Arnold perpetrated the "Great Diamond Hoax." They salted an area in northwestern Colorado with diamonds and other precious jewels that were actually rejects from the gem cutters of Amsterdam. They then went to California and sold their rights to the find to a corporation founded by millionaire William C. Ralston and including Horace Greeley and many other famous individuals. The hoax was finally discovered after Arnold and Slack had been paid $600,000. The two men were never tried for their crime but gave back approximately half the money. Arnold settled in Elizabethtown, Kentucky, opened a bank, and a short time later, was shot on the streets of the city by a competitor. He died from the effects of the shooting and pneumonia. His wife and family members are in the Arnold plot. Slack (May 5, 1820–July 26, 1896) went to White Oaks, New Mexico, where he died. His grave is marked. To locate the Elizabethtown Cemetery: from US 62 in town, go east on Dixie East for about three blocks to the cemetery on the right. Enter through the second entrance. The grave is a short distance ahead on the left, marked by a very tall, pink marble shaft.

18.  **Arny, William Frederick Milton\*** (May 1813–September 18, 1881). Born in the District of Columbia, he became Indian agent to

the Utes and Jicarilla Apaches in New Mexico, succeeding Kit Carson. Arny also served as secretary of New Mexico Territory. He died in Topeka, Kansas, and is buried in the Santa Fe National Cemetery, Santa Fe, New Mexico. His grave is behind that of Governor Charles Bent. There is a grave marker.

19.  **Arrington, George Washington**\* (December 23, 1844–March 31, 1923). He was a Texas Ranger, captain of Company C. He was a scout in the Civil War and later was sheriff of Wheeler County, Texas. He was born John C. Orrick, Jr., in Greensboro, North Carolina. After killing Alex Webb, a black man, in 1867, he went to Central America. When he returned to the states, he took the name G.W. Arrington (Arrington was his mother's maiden name). He died at age seventy-nine and is buried beside his wife, Sallie C. Burnett Arrington (May 2, 1862–June 1, 1945), and their son, Gilbert (July 25, 1884–July 5, 1885), in the Mobeetie Cemetery, Old Mobeetie, Texas. There is a large marker.

20.  **Ash, Benjamin Cowden "Ben"**\* (December 19, 1851–April 15, 1946). He was a deputy United States marshal and later Indian agent for the Lower Brulé Sioux Reservation. He died at the state soldiers home in Hot Springs, South Dakota, and is buried in the state veterans cemetery, one of three cemeteries in Hot Springs. The grave is in the eighth row from the entrance; it is the thirty-fourth grave to the left. In 1959, Ash was elected to the National Cowboy Hall of Fame, Oklahoma City, Oklahoma.

21.  **Ashley, William Henry**\* (circa 1778–March 26, 1838). He was a soldier, fur trapper, and trader. He led a group of fur trappers up the Missouri River and into the Northwest in 1822. Ashley served three terms in the United States Congress. He died of pneumonia and is buried near Boonville, Missouri, atop an Indian mound overlooking the Missouri River. To locate the grave: from US 40 (I-70) a few miles west of Boonville, turn north on Missouri Highway 41. Go 4.1 miles to a gravel road. Turn right and go 0.7 mile, then right again for 0.8 mile to a farm lane. Turn left and go 0.3 mile to a one-story white frame farmhouse. The grave is a short distance northwest of the house on the crest of a high bluff. There is a large marker.

(Permission should be obtained at the farmhouse before walking to the grave site.)

22. **Askew, Daniel H.*** (February 28, 1828–April 12, 1875). He was probably killed by the Jesse James Gang. He was a neighbor of the James family and was killed on his front porch a few months after the bombing of the James home. He was suspected of being a spy for the Pinkerton detectives. He is buried in the New Hope Cemetery about two miles southeast of Holt in Clay County, Missouri. The cemetery is west of the New Hope Baptist Church and about one mile east of I-35. The grave is marked by a large marble headstone.

23. **Aten, Ira*** (September 3, 1863–August 6, 1953; NOTE: His headstone gives his year of birth as 1862). He was a Texas Ranger and later, for ten years, was manager of the XIT Ranch in northern Texas, the largest in the United States. He died in Burlingame, California, and is buried in the Aten family plot, Block 7, Lot 2, in Evergreen Cemetery two miles east of El Centro, California. There is a marker. He is buried beside his wife, Imogene B. Aten (May 21, 1867–March 3, 1957); sons Lieutenant A. Boyce and Marion; and daughters Imogene and Eloise. To locate the grave: enter the cemetery from Gillett Street and drive straight ahead past the office on the left to the third cross-lane. Turn right and drive to the small circle at the next cross-lane. Go left on the circle and park. Aten's grave is on the left at the corner.

24. **Aubry, Francois X.** (December 3, 1824–August 18, 1854). He was a freighter on the Santa Fe Trail. He once rode horseback 800 miles from Santa Fe to Independence, Missouri, in four days and twelve hours, averaging 140 miles a day. At age twenty-nine, he was killed in a knife fight in a barroom brawl in Santa Fe, New Mexico. His funeral was in the Catholic Church, the Paroquia, with a large crowd attending. According to the New Mexico Historical Society, the location of his grave is unknown.

25. **Austin, Moses*** (October 4, 1761–June 10, 1821). He was the father of Stephen F. Austin and originated the plan for the Anglo colonization of Texas. He died before he could carry out his plans and is

buried in the Presbyterian Cemetery one block northwest of the courthouse in Potosi, Missouri. The state of Texas tried to obtain his remains, but Missouri would not permit it. There is an inscribed grave marker.

26. **Austin, Stephen Fuller\*** (November 3, 1793–December 26, 1836). He was responsible for the first Anglo settlement in Texas, at San Felipe. He was placed in command of Texas forces when war with Mexico erupted at Gonzales, Texas. In 1836 he was defeated for the presidency of the republic by Sam Houston. He died at his sister's home near West Columbia, Texas, and was originally buried in the Presbyterian Church burial ground at Peach Point, where there is still a marker. In 1910, his remains were reinterred in the state cemetery in Austin, Texas. The large monument marking his grave is at the top of the hill.

27. **Autobees, Charles\*** (1812–June 17, 1882). This name is sometimes spelled "Autobee." He was a fur trapper and mountain man and engaged in several Indian battles. Autobees was a half-brother to Tom Tobin. He lived at Taos, New Mexico, for several years and later settled in eastern Colorado, where he founded a settlement on the St. Vrain Grant beside the Huerfano River a few miles east of Avondale, Colorado. Autobees is buried in the St. Vrain Cemetery. The actual location of his grave has been lost, but there is a large monument in the northern part of the cemetery. To locate the cemetery: in Avondale, go south on Avondale Boulevard for 1.7 miles. Turn left (east) on Olson Road and go 2.8 miles. Then turn right (south) on Fifty-sixth Lane (dirt). Follow this road for one mile as it turns east to the cemetery. Other family members are buried here.

28. **Averell, James "Jim"** (circa 1855–July 20, 1889; NOTE: Some writers give July 21, 1889, as the date of death). This name is sometimes spelled "Averill." He was lynched along with Ella Watson by a group of Wyoming ranchers led by A.J. Bothwell on the pretext that they were stealing cattle, or at least were accepting stolen cattle. Their bodies were buried near the site of the lynching. This spot is now under the waters of a lake near Alcova, Wyoming.

# B

29. **Baca, Cipriano** (1858–September 23, 1936). He was sheriff of Luna County, New Mexico, and was also a deputy United States marshal and later a lieutenant in the New Mexico Mounted Police. He died in 1936 and is buried in Sunset Memorial Park in Albuquerque, New Mexico, Section 8, Plot 19, Grave 1. His grave is not marked.

30. **Baca, Elfego*** (February 10, 1865–August 27, 1945). He was a lawman, politician, and lawyer. He was noted for his battle against eighty cowboys in Frisco, New Mexico, lasting thirty-three hours. Baca died in Albuquerque and is buried there in Sunset Memorial Park, Section 11, Plot 41, Grave 1. There is a ground-level marker.

31. **Baca, Saturnino*** (November 19, 1830–1924). He was sheriff of Lincoln County, New Mexico, at one time and had been a captain in the United States Army, Company E, New Mexico Cavalry. He is buried in the extreme western part of the Lincoln Cemetery. His first name is incorrectly spelled "Saturnio" on his small government headstone.

32. **Bain, George*** (?–October 13, 1896). He also used the aliases George Low and George Harvies. He was killed along with "The Kid" Pearce and Jim Shirley in their attempt to rob the bank at Meeker, Colorado. All three of the outlaws are buried in the southeastern part of the Meeker Cemetery. The graves are marked.

33. **Baird, Moses "Mose"*** (September 25, 1850–September 7, 1875). He was a victim of the Mason County or "Hoodoo" War. He and his

9

brother, John, joined Scott Cooley and John Ringo in opposing Sheriff John Rufus Clark, the Hoersters, John Wohrle (Worley), and other members of the German community. Mose and George Gladden were ambushed by a group led by Sheriff Clark, resulting in the death of Baird and the wounding of Gladden. John later took his brother's body to Burnet, Texas, where he was buried in the Old Burnet Cemetery, which is at the south end of Rhomberg Street. To locate the cemetery and grave: from Highway 29, turn south on Rhomberg until it enters the cemetery and dead ends on Cemetery Street. Turn right and then left at the first lane. Go about sixty feet. On the right are several graves enclosed by wrought iron fences. Baird's grave is beside a corner of one of the fences. The marker is about one foot high and of gray marble. In 1986 this marker replaced one which was broken in half.

**34.** **Baker, Cullen Montgomery\*** (June 23, 1835–January 6, 1869). He was a Texas gunman and outlaw and is said by some historians to have been the first fast-draw artist. He was killed by Thomas Orr in a gunfight and is buried in the Jefferson Cemetery, Jefferson, Texas. The grave is marked and is just inside the main entrance to the cemetery.

**35.** **Baker, James "Jim"\*** (December 19, 1818–May 15, 1898). He was a mountain man and a friend of Jim Bridger. He was later a scout for General Nelson Miles. Jim died in Savery, Wyoming, at the age of seventy-nine and is buried in the Baker Cemetery, which is just west of town on the north side of State Road 70. One of his four wives and some of his children are also buried there. His two-story log cabin is now a museum at Savery. There is a marker at his grave.

**36.** **Baker, Joseph\*** (1804–July 11, 1846). He was one of the founders of the *Telegraph and Texas Register* at San Felipe de Austin, October 10, 1835. Baker was a soldier at San Jacinto, first chief justice of Bexar County, Texas (1836), and a member of the Congress of the Republic (1837). He died at Austin, Texas, and is buried there in Oakwood Cemetery. There is a marker.

**37.** **Baldwin, Lucius M.\*** (February 24, 1869–October 5, 1892). He was killed by the Dalton Gang in their attempt to rob two banks simultaneously in Coffeyville, Kansas. His body was taken to Burlington, Kansas, for burial in Graceland Cemetery. His father and mother, the Reverend D.S. (1841–1889) and Malinda (1842–1917) Baldwin, are beside him. To locate the grave: enter the cemetery and turn right. As the drive curves left, look for the tall obelisk on the right. It is just a few feet from the drive.

38. **Ballard, Charles Littlepage "Charley"\*** (October 11, 1866–April 16, 1950). He was born in Hays County, Texas, but the family moved to Fort Griffin when Charley was ten years old. They later made several moves before settling in Roswell, New Mexico, where Charley worked as a cowhand and then as a deputy sheriff and Roswell city marshal. He helped to bring about the demise of the High Five Gang led by "Black Jack" Christian and also arrested George Musgraves for the murder of George Parker. Musgraves was later found not guilty. When Ballard died in 1950, he was eighty-three years old. He was buried beside his first wife, Araminta "Mintie," in Evergreen Cemetery in El Paso, Texas. After "Mintie" died, he married his second wife, Eunice M. Ballard. Following her death he married Emma Connor, his third and final marriage. Charley's grave is in Section L, Lot 222, Space 7, which is near the curve in the lane adjoining Section L. It is four graves in from the lane.

39. **Ballew, D.M. "Bud"\*** (1877–May 12, 1922). He was undersheriff to Sheriff Buck Garrett in Oklahoma. He was killed in a saloon in Wichita Falls, Texas, by Chief of Police J.W. McCormack in a shootout. He is buried in the Lone Grove Cemetery, one mile north of Lone Grove, Oklahoma (not in the Hewitt Cemetery as most sources say). To locate the cemetery: go north from Lone Grove, Oklahoma, one mile and turn right on a gravel road for 0.2 mile and then left for 0.1 mile to the cemetery. The Ballew grave is on the left, immediately past the first gravel drive after entering the cemetery. There is a large, gray marble marker and a smaller one for his wife, Fannie (1882–1955), and son, Buster (1906–1918).

40. **Barber, Susan McSween\*** (December 30, 1845–January 3, 1931).

She was the wife of Alexander McSween, who was killed in the Lincoln County War in New Mexico. She later married George Barber, a surveyor who was also studying law. They owned a large ranch near White Oaks, New Mexico. She died there and is buried in the White Oaks Cemetery near the cemetery entrance. There is a marker at the grave site. In her later years, Susan was known as the "Cattle Queen of New Mexico."

41. **Barlow, Samuel K. "Sam"\*** (January 24, 1795–July 15, 1867). He was the builder of the "Barlow Trail" in Oregon, from The Dalles, through Barlow Pass, and on to Oregon City, Oregon. He is buried in the Barlow Pioneer Cemetery. To locate the cemetery: leave Oregon City, Oregon, south on Highway 99E. Continue through Canby at 8.6 miles. One and four-tenths miles south of Canby is the Barlow House. It was the home of Sam's son William. One tenth mile south of the Barlow House, turn right toward Barlow for 0.4 mile to the cemetery. It is a small cemetery covered with high grass and thorny bushes. A granite obelisk marks the grave. There is a sign, "Barlow Pioneer Cemetery."

42. **Barlow, William\*** (October 28, 1822–June 13, 1904). He was an Oregon pioneer, the son of Samuel Barlow. He died at Barlow, Oregon, and is buried in Mountain View Cemetery in Oregon City, Oregon. There is a tall monument bearing the Masonic symbol at his grave.

43. **Barter, Richard H. "Rattlesnake Dick"\*** (1833–July 11, 1859). He was a California outlaw who was killed in 1859 under strange circumstances. Barter's body, as well as that of his lover, Mary Eulalie Fee Shannon, were exhumed from their original graves in 1893 and reinterred side by side in the city cemetery in Auburn, California. To locate the cemetery and grave: follow Elm Street west across Highway 49 and bear left on Fulweiler. Enter the cemetery from Fulweiler and immediately turn left. Park at the end of the lane and walk to the left-hand corner of the cemetery to a large, black, inscribed stone.

**44.  Bass Family.**\* The grandparents and other members of the Sam Bass family are buried in the Bass Cemetery about two miles north of Mitchell, Indiana, just west of Indiana Highway 37. The entrance is from "Old Indiana 37" which makes a loop west of Indiana 37. Buried here are:

> William Bass (February 9, 1826–March 3, 1881).
>
> Elizabeth Bass (December 7, 1829–September 14, 1884), William's wife.
>
> John Bass (May 21, 1797–January 9, 1874), Sam's grandfather.
>
> Sarah Bass (January 13, 1802–July 13, 1871), John's wife.
>
> Solomon Bass (September 23, 1823–February 15, 1902), Sam's uncle.
>
> Catherine Bass (April 27, 1824–October 9, 1865), Sam's aunt.
>
> Isom Bass, Company M, Thirteenth Indiana Cavalry.
>
> Augustus Bass (November 18, 1859–December 16, 1935).
>
> Kansas Bass (March 21, 1859–January 17, 1940).
>
> Jonathan Bass (August 20, 1815–October 18, 1887), John's brother.

**45.  Bass, Samuel "Sam"**\* (July 21, 1851–July 21, 1878). He was a Texas and Nebraska outlaw and train robber. Sam was shot in Round Rock, Texas, July 17, 1878, and died July 21, 1878, as a result. He is buried in the extreme western part of Round Rock Cemetery a few feet from the Old Slave Cemetery historical marker. "Sebe" Barnes, a member of Bass's Gang, is buried beside Bass. In 1991, new markers were placed at the graves of both Barnes and Bass. A portion of Bass's original headstone, badly chipped away from souvenir hunters, still remains. Both new markers are inscribed.

**46.  Bassett, Ann "Queen Ann."** See Willis, Ann Bassett.

**47.  Bassett, Charles E.**\* (October 30, 1847–January 5, 1896). He was a Kansas sheriff and a member of the Dodge City Peace Commission. Bassett was a friend of Wyatt Earp. He died in Hot Springs, Arkansas, at age forty-eight and is buried in Forest Hill Cemetery, Kansas City, Missouri. This is no marker, but the grave location is known. A map can be obtained at the office.

**48.   Bassett, Eb\*** (June 22, 1880–November 19, 1925). Eb was the brother of Ann and Josie Bassett. He committed suicide and is buried in the Bassett Cemetery to the west of the old Bassett ranch house site. There is a marker. The cemetery is on private property.

**49.   Bassett, Elizabeth\*** (?–December 11, 1892). She was the wife of Colorado rancher Herbert Bassett, and mother of "Queen Ann." She is buried in the Bassett Cemetery on the hill west of the old Bassett ranch house site. The ranch house no longer stands. There is a grave marker.

**50.   Bassett, Herbert\*** (July 31, 1839–July 20, 1918). Born in New York, Herbert was the husband of Elizabeth and the father of "Queen Ann," Josie, and Eb Bassett. He died in the Illinois Soldiers and Sailors Home at Quincy, Illinois, and was buried there in the Illinois State Home Cemetery. His death certificate lists the cause of death as cerebral hemorrhage and arteriosclerosis. His occupation was listed as farmer.

**51.   Bassett, Josephine "Josie"\*** (January 17, 1874–May 28, 1964). She was the sister of "Queen Ann." Josie married four times, her last husband being a man named Harris. She had two sons by one of her husbands, James F. "Jim" McKnight (1869–1923). Her last years were spent alone in a cabin on Diamond Mountain. She is buried in the Bassett Cemetery on a hill west of the old Bassett ranch house site. There is a marker.

**52.   Baylor, George Wythe\*** (August 23, 1832–March 27, 1916). He became a major in the Texas Rangers before his retirement and took part in several campaigns against the Apache leader Victorio. He died in San Antonio, Texas, and is buried there in the Confederate Cemetery. The large marble headstone is a few feet from the Confederate Cemetery historical marker.

**53.   Bazil\*** (1800–1886). He was the adopted son of Sacajawea. He died in the mountains in the western part of Wyoming and was originally buried there, but on January 12, 1925, his remains were removed and reinterred beside a woman who some people believe was Sacajawea

*Seaborn Barnes and Sam Bass, Round Rock Cemetery, Round Rock, Texas.*

*Roy Bean, Whitehead Memorial Museum, Del Rio, Texas.*

in the Wind River Cemetery near Fort Washakie, Wyoming. There is a marker.

**54.    B'Dam, Molly.** See Hall, Maggie.

**55.    Bean, Roy\*** (circa 1827–March 16, 1903). He was known as "The Law West of the Pecos." Judge Roy Bean was a Texas frontiersman and justice of the peace at Langtry, Texas. He died at Del Rio, Texas, and was originally buried in the Del Rio Cemetery. Later his body was removed to the grounds of the Whitehead Memorial Museum in Del Rio. His grave and that of his son, Sam, are beside the replica of Bean's Jersey Lily Saloon. The graves are marked.

**56.    Bean, Samuel "Sam"\*** (May 16, 1874–May 5, 1907). He was the son of Judge Roy Bean. He was killed in a knife fight in Del Rio, Texas, and is buried beside his father on the grounds of the Whitehead Museum in Del Rio. There is a marker.

**57.    Beaubein, Charles H.** (October 1800–February 10, 1864). He was a famous mountain man and later a judge at Taos, New Mexico. He presided over the trial of the Taos insurrectionists. Beaubein died at Taos and is buried there but the exact site has been lost.

**58.    Beaver, Oscar\*** (1857–August 5, 1892). He was a California deputy sheriff and at the age of thirty-five was killed in a gunfight by the train robbers Chris Evans and John Sontag at the Evans home near Visalia, California. He is buried in the Lemoore Cemetery, Lemoore, California, in Section 1, Block 9, Lot 13. His wife, Jennie (1859–1956), is buried nearby. After Oscar's death she married a man named Beall and lived to age ninety-seven. Oscar's son, John (1889–1954), a sergeant in World War I, is also buried nearby.

**59.    Beck, "Ole."** See Hobek, "Ole."

**60.    Becknell, William\*** (circa 1787–April 30, 1865). He was a freighter and a soldier, and is credited with laying out the Santa Fe Trail. In his later years he settled in Texas and died there near Clarksville. He is buried in a little family cemetery about five miles west of

Clarksville. The grave is about 150 yards south of US Highway 82 in a small clump of trees in the middle of a cultivated field. His headstone incorrectly gives his date of birth as 1797. On the south side of US 82 about three miles west of Clarksville stands a Texas state historical marker dedicated to Becknell. Just beyond the marker (directly south) is the house that Becknell built and in which he died.

61. **Beckwith, Robert "Bob"** (October 10, 1850–July 19, 1878). He was a participant in the Lincoln County War in New Mexico. He was killed by the Regulators and was buried in the post cemetery at Fort Stanton, New Mexico. Most of the bodies were later removed from this cemetery and reburied elsewhere.

62. **Bee, Hamilton P.\*** (July 22, 1822–October 3, 1897). He was secretary of the first Texas senate and speaker of the house, 1854–1856. He served as a lieutenant of cavalry during the Mexican War in 1846 and was made brigadier general of the Texas State Militia in 1861. Bee received the same rank in the Confederate Army in 1862 and was in command of the Western District of Texas. He led a brigade and was wounded in the Red River Campaign of 1864. He is buried in the Confederate Cemetery in San Antonio. His grave is marked by a very tall obelisk as well as a pink marble official Texas historical marker.

63. **Beeson, Chalkley McCarty "Chalk"\*** (April 24, 1848–August 9, 1912). He was sheriff of Ford County, Kansas, from 1892 to 1896 and was a long-time city councilman. Prior to becoming sheriff, he and his partner, W.H. Harris, had operated the COD Ranch and the Long Branch Saloon in Dodge City. He was also the leader of the famous Dodge City Cowboy Band that played at President Benjamin Harrison's inauguration. On December 30, 1892, he led a posse that shot and killed Oliver "Ol" Yantis, a member of the Bill Doolin Gang. "Chalk" died of peritonitis after falling from a horse and is buried in Maple Grove Cemetery in Dodge City, not far from the grave of "Print" Olive. Beeson's wife, Ada M. (1854–1928), and several of their children are buried in the Beeson plot.

**64.  Behan, John Harris "Johnny"*** (October 23, 1845–June 7, 1912).
He was the first sheriff of Cochise County, Arizona, and later
superintendent of Yuma territorial prison. He and Wyatt Earp were
enemies. John died in Tucson, Arizona, and is buried in Holy Hope
Catholic Cemetery, which joins Evergreen Cemetery on the north.
He is in Section B, Row G, Grave 98. A permanent ground-level
marker was placed at the grave site in 1991. Personnel at the
cemetery office can provide a small map and mark the grave so that
it can be found easily.

**65.  Beidler, John X.*** (August 14, 1831–January 22, 1890). He was a
Montana vigilante. He died in Helena, Montana, and is buried in
Forestville Cemetery about three miles north of Helena on McHugh
Drive, which runs at right angles to Custer between Montana
Avenue and Benton Avenue. The cemetery is on the west side of
McHugh. Upon entering the cemetery through the large granite
arch, take the first left-hand drive and then keep right about 150 feet
ahead. The twelve-foot-high obelisk on the right has a metal plaque
dedicated to Beidler.

**66.  Bell, Hamilton Butler "Ham"*** (July 31, 1853–April 4, 1947). He
was a pioneer of Dodge City, Kansas, and served two terms as Ford
County sheriff. He died of natural causes and is buried in Maple
Grove Cemetery, Dodge City. The grave is in Block 3, Lot 77. There
is a marker. His wife, Josephine (1857–1900), is buried beside him.

**67.  Bell, James W.** (circa 1842–April 28, 1881). He was a New Mexico
lawman and was killed, as was Bob Olinger, by Billy the Kid when
the Kid made his escape at Lincoln, New Mexico. Bell's body was
taken to White Oaks Cemetery at White Oaks, New Mexico, for
burial. There is no marker, and the exact location of the grave is
unknown. The Kid later stated that he was sorry he had to kill Bell,
who had been kind to him.

**68.  Beni (Bene, Reni), Jules** (?–circa 1860). He was a frontiersman and
at one time manager of a Russell, Majors and Waddell stage station
on the South Platte River. When division superintendent Jack Slade
fired Jules, a fight ensued. Slade suffered wounds that were at first

thought to be fatal. He recovered, however, and later shot and killed Jules. Slade reportedly cut off Beni's ears and carried one of them for years. Beni is buried in Julesburg, Colorado, which was named for him, but the exact site is unknown.

69.  **Benson, John W., M.D.*** (March 23, 1836–October 6, 1863). He was William Quantrill's regimental surgeon. He is buried at Miami, Missouri, in the old Miami Cemetery beside Highway 41. To locate the grave: from Highway 41 going north, turn left into the cemetery and go to the first large cedar tree. Park and walk up the hill to the second cedar. The two-and-one-half-foot upright marker is just beyond and to the left of the second cedar, about twenty feet from the tree.

70.  **Bent, Charles*** (November 11, 1799–January 19, 1847). Along with his brother, William, he owned and operated frontier trading posts in Colorado. He was the first civil governor of New Mexico Territory and was killed in Taos, New Mexico, during an Indian revolt. He is buried in the Santa Fe National Cemetery, Santa Fe, New Mexico. There is a large marker. To locate the grave: enter the cemetery through the main gate and drive straight ahead to an adobe service building at the back of the cemetery. There, turn right and go about fifty yards to Governor Bent's white marble headstone, which is next to the tall, brown sandstone marker of Lawrence Murphy.

71.  **Bent, George*** (April 13, 1814–October 23, 1847). He was a brother of Charles and William Bent. He died of an unknown disease at Bent's Fort in Colorado and was buried there. Later his remains were removed to St. Louis, Missouri, and reinterred in Bellefontaine Cemetery. Several Bents are buried in Block 103, Lot 322 (the Dorcas-Carr plot). George, Robert, and another brother, John, are all buried in the same grave.

72.  **Bent, Robert S.*** (February 23, 1816–October 20, 1841). He was the youngest of the Bent brothers and was killed and scalped by Comanche Indians. He was first buried just north of Bent's Old Fort in Colorado. Later he was reinterred in Bellefontaine Cemetery in St. Louis, Missouri, in the Dorcas-Carr plot, Block 103, Lot 322.

73. **Bent, Silas*** (1768–1827). He was the father of Charles and William Bent and nine other children. Bent was deputy surveyor of Louisiana, judge of the St. Louis common pleas court, and a justice of the Supreme Court of Missouri Territory. He is buried in Bellefontaine Cemetery, St. Louis, Missouri, in the Dorcas-Carr plot, Block 103, Lot 322.

74. **Bent, William W.*** (May 23, 1809–May 19, 1869). William and his brother, Charles, owned and operated frontier trading posts in Colorado. He died of pneumonia and is buried in the Las Animas Cemetery, Las Animas, Colorado. There is a very large monument at his grave site, which is in the extreme south part of the cemetery. It is on the left about two-thirds of the way down the right-hand (southernmost) drive.

75. **Benton, Thomas Hart*** (March 14, 1782–April 10, 1858). He was a Missouri senator and the father of Jessie Benton, who married John Charles Frémont, "the Pathfinder." He is buried in Bellefontaine Cemetery in St. Louis, Missouri. A map of the cemetery showing the location of Benton's grave, as well as those of many others, is available at the office.

76. **Bernard, Hiram H. "Hi"** (1857–February 3, 1924). He was a Wyoming rancher who ran cattle in the Brown's Park area. At one time he was married to "Queen Ann" Bassett. He is buried in the Rock Springs Cemetery in Rock Springs, Wyoming. The grave is in Block 262, Lot 7. There is no marker.

77. **Berry, George C.*** (December 11, 1826–February 12, 1892). He lived in Tombstone, Arizona, and was wounded when Morgan Earp was shot and killed in a poolroom on March 18, 1882. Berry recovered and lived until 1892. He is buried in the Tombstone Cemetery (not Boothill). To locate the cemetery and grave: follow Allen Street west to the cemetery. The grave is to the right of the central drive and is marked.

78. **Berry, James "Jim"** (?–October 16, 1877). He was a member of the Sam Bass Gang. He was shot in the leg by lawmen; gangrene set in;

*Left: John X. Beidler, Forestville Cemetery, Helena, Montana.*
*Right: Bloody Knife, scout cemetery, White Shield, North Dakota.*

*Dutch Henry Born, Pagosa Springs Cemetery, Pagosa Springs, Colorado.*

21

and he died in Mexico, Missouri. He is buried beside his mother, who coincidentally died a few hours before him, in the Richland churchyard which is near Fulton in Callaway County, Missouri. There is no grave marker.

79. **Berry, William Wiley*** (June 25, 1883–December 22, 1903). Berry was killed, along with fellow sheepman Juan Vigil, by cattlemen John and Zack Booth in 1903. Berry was originally buried at Gisela, Arizona, but his father had his remains reinterred in the Thatcher Cemetery, Thatcher, Arizona, in New Section 1, Lot 36, Site 1. To locate the grave: from US Highway 70 in Thatcher, take Stadium Avenue south to the cemetery. Enter and go to the first cross-lane. Turn left (east) to a wire fence enclosing the Pace plot. Look to the right to the third block of graves. Berry's grave is marked by a three-foot stone carved to resemble a tree trunk.

80. **Biddle, Thomas*** (?–August 30, 1831). He was born in Philadelphia and became an army officer. He was killed in a duel by Congressman Spencer Pettis of St. Louis, Missouri, and is buried in a beautiful tomb in Calvary Cemetery in St. Louis. A map of the cemetery, showing the location of Biddle's grave, along with many others, is available at the cemetery office.

81. **Biddlecome, Joseph "Joe"*** (November 16, 1877–June 16, 1928). He was the father of Pearl Baker (author of *The Wild Bunch at Robbers Roost*) and the founder of the Roost Ranch southeast of Hanksville, Utah. He died at Green River, Utah, and is buried in the Elgin Cemetery which is about one mile east of Green River and a short distance north of US 50 (I-70). Beside him are his wife, Millie (December 4, 1884–January 9, 1976), and other members of his family. To reach the cemetery, take the Green River Exit from I-70, drive through town on "Old US 50," continue across the Green River bridge, and then turn left to the cemetery.

82. **Big Bow "Zepko-ett"*** (circa 1825–October 4, 1901). Big Bow was a Kiowa chief. He killed and scalped many whites and led raids in Texas, New Mexico, Kansas, and Mexico. He took part in the Warren Wagon Train Massacre near Graham, Texas, and generally

was considered one of the most militant of the Kiowas. Big Bow finally surrendered and then enlisted as sergeant of scouts. He died in 1901 and was originally buried in the Rainy Mountain Kiowa Cemetery. In 1964, his body was removed to the post cemetery at Fort Sill, Oklahoma. His grave is on Chief's Knoll near the grave of Quanah Parker.

**83.** **Big Foot "Si-tanka"*** (circa 1825–December 29, 1890). He was a Miniconjou Sioux chief. He was killed in the Battle of Wounded Knee, South Dakota, and is buried there in a mass grave for the Indian victims. A marble marker lists the names of those buried there.

**84.** **Bigford, George*** (February 2, 1855–December 10, 1940). He was a buffalo hunter and later a Texas Ranger. He died at Carrizo Springs, Texas, and is buried there in the Mt. Hope Cemetery. His grave is in the northeast part of the cemetery and is about fifty feet to the right of the easternmost north-south lane. An iron fence surrounds the plot and a large, gray marble monument with the single word, "Bigford," can be seen from the street.

**85.** **Big Tree "Ado-ette"*** (circa 1841–November 13, 1929). He was a Kiowa chief. From the late 1860s until the Kiowas laid down their arms, Big Tree—along with Satanta, Big Bow, Satank, Long Horn, Lone Wolf, Queton, and others—was usually leading forays into Texas, New Mexico, or Mexico. He later adopted Christianity and taught Sunday school in the Baptist church near Rainy Mountain, Oklahoma. When he died at age eighty-eight, he was buried in Rainy Mountain Kiowa Cemetery. Later his remains were taken to Fort Sill, Oklahoma, and reinterred on Chief's Knoll in the post cemetery. There is a marker.

**86.** **Billy Bowlegs "Sonuk Micco"*** (circa 1825–October 30, 1863). He was a Seminole Indian and held the rank of captain in the Union's First Indian Regiment during the Civil War. He is buried in Grave 2109 on Officer's Circle in the national cemetery at Fort Gibson, Oklahoma. There is a marker at the grave site. Several other Seminoles carried the name "Billy Bowlegs."

87. **Bingham, George Caleb\*** (March 20, 1811–July 7, 1879). He was a well known western artist. Bingham is buried in Union Cemetery in Kansas City, Missouri. A map of the cemetery showing the location of graves of famous people can be obtained from the cemetery office. There is a marker.

88. **Bissonette, John P.\*** (1873–1962). He was a member of the United States Army Indian scouts and the son of Joseph Bissonette. He is buried in the national cemetery at Hot Springs, South Dakota. There is a marker.

89. **Bissonette, Joseph** (1818–August 1894). He was a frontiersman and fur trader. He is buried in the Episcopal Cemetery north of Manderson, South Dakota. There is no marker for Joseph, but markers indicate many other members of the Bissonette family. To locate the cemetery: drive north from Manderson on a reservation road about four and one-half miles to a very poor dirt road on the left. Follow this road as it curves back south and then west for about one-half mile to another even worse road which goes to the base of a little hill a short distance away. Park and climb the little hill to the cemetery. Do not attempt to drive these roads in bad weather.

90. **Blachly, Andrew T.\*** (?–September 7, 1893). A bank employee, Blachly was shot and killed by Fred McCarty when the McCarty Gang attempted to rob the Farmers and Merchants Bank of Delta, Colorado. As they fled, outlaws Bill and Fred McCarty were killed by William Ray Simpson, owner of a hardware store in Delta. Tom McCarty escaped and reportedly went to the Northwest, where he lived in the state of Washington for some time. Blachly, who left a wife and eight children, is buried in Block 1, Lot 11, Space 6, of the Delta Cemetery. The grave is in the east-central part of the cemetery and was marked in 1990 by a small, temporary marker.

91. **Black Beaver\*** (1806–May 8, 1880). He was a Delaware scout. He died and was buried at Anadarko, Oklahoma. Later his body was removed to Chief's Knoll in the Fort Sill post cemetery, Fort Sill, Oklahoma.

**92.   Black Kettle\*** (circa 1803–November 27, 1868). He was a Cheyenne chief and was killed by Custer's forces at the Battle of the Washita. His remains are believed to be buried at the Black Kettle Museum in Cheyenne, Oklahoma.

**93.   Blake, William "Tulsa Jack"** (?–April 4, 1895). He was a member of the Bill Doolin Gang. He was killed in a shootout with lawmen west of Dover, Oklahoma, and is buried in the cemetery at El Reno, Oklahoma. No marker can be found.

**94.   Blevins, Andy, alias Andy Cooper\*** (?–September 4, 1887). He was killed in a gun battle by Sheriff Commodore Perry Owens at the Blevins house in Holbrook, Arizona. Killed along with Andy were his brother, Sam Houston Blevins, and Mose Roberts. The three are buried in the Holbrook Cemetery which is at the corner of Navajo Boulevard (Highway 77) and Iowa. To locate the grave: enter the cemetery through the Iowa entrance. The graves are just inside the entrance on the left. A flat, pink sandstone marker bears the names of the three buried here.

**95.   Blevins, Charles\*** (?–September 21, 1887). He was killed by the Tewksbury faction in the Pleasant Valley War in Arizona. He is buried in the Young Cemetery just north of Young, Arizona. The cemetery is on the west side of the road leading to Heber, Arizona. A small, ground-level marker lies among the weeds.

**96.   Blevins, Sam Houston\*** (July 12, 1872–September 4, 1887). He was killed along with his brother, Andy, and Mose Roberts by Sheriff Commodore Perry Owens in a gunfight at the Blevins house in Holbrook, Arizona. Another brother was wounded. For the grave location, see Blevins, Andy.

**97.   Bloody Basin Grave Site\***

> Wilson, William "Billy" (?–August 11, 1888).
> Stott, James "Jim" (September 13, 1863–August 11, 1888).
> Scott, James (?–August 11, 1888).

These three young men were hanged near the Mogollon Rim in Arizona, southwest of Heber, by a group of unknown persons. The lynching occurred near the end of the Pleasant Valley War, which was taking place some miles to the south. The grave site is in the Apache-Sitgreaves National Forest about thirteen miles south of Heber, Arizona, and about two and one-half miles east of Highway 260. To locate the site: from Highway 260 take Forest Service Road 330, marked "Black Canyon Campground." If a campground host is at the campground entrance, ask for directions. If not, drive straight ahead to a circle at the end of a campground (picnic table). Park and walk about 100 feet to a four-wheel-drive road a little to the left of the circle. Do not confuse the poor dirt road with the much better Lake Road to the right. Walk along the very rocky road down a little hill and, as you start uphill, look for a large pine on the right with a cross cut in it many years ago. Turn right at this tree and go to a large stump on the right about forty feet from the tree with the cross. Turn right at the stump on a poor trail and go a short distance to the graves, which are individually marked. A pole fence surrounds the graves. Each stone bears the last name and the date, August 4, 1888. This appears to be an error, as the men died on August 11, 1888.

**98.  Bloody Knife\*** (circa 1840–June 25, 1876). His father was a Hunkpapa Sioux and his mother an Arikara woman. As a youngster, he was never fully accepted by the Sioux, particularly Chief Gall. Bloody Knife took an Arikara woman as his wife, and they had a son who was nine years old when his father was killed. Bloody Knife was first a hunter for the United States Army, and then on May 1, 1868, he and nine other young Arikara men enlisted as scouts for the army. After four years of service, he became a lance corporal. He quickly became Lieutenant Colonel George Custer's favorite scout. At the Battle of the Little Bighorn, Bloody Knife was shot and killed as he rode beside Major Marcus Reno. He was buried in the scout cemetery near White Shield, North Dakota. His grave is in the row of graves next to farthest from State Road 1804.

**99.  Bobbitt, Allen Augustus "Gus"\*** (January 11, 1862–February 27, 1909). He was an Oklahoma rancher who was killed by James "Killing Jim" Miller. This killing resulted in the lynching of Miller and three others at Ada, Oklahoma. Gus is buried in Rosedale

Cemetery in Ada. To locate the grave: turn north off Main Street in Ada onto Oak and continue on Oak to the cemetery. Go straight through the entrance to the office. Turn right at the office, then immediately right again. The grave is on the left, about thirty feet from the last turn, and is marked by a gray marble obelisk. Gus's wife, Tennessee Bobbitt (1865–1951), is buried beside him. Three other Bobbitts are buried in the family plot: Charles I. Bobbitt (December 8, 1896–May 17, 1975); Claude C. Bobbitt (June 2, 1894–August 28, 1965); and Eva S. Bobbitt (February 2, 1899–November 6, 1979). Gus was a Mason and a member of Woodmen of the World.

100. **Bockius, Amanda Jane Billings Tennille\*** (March 9, 1840–April 10, 1916). Amanda was first married to George Tennille who was killed in the Sutton-Taylor Feud in Texas. She then married "Doc" Bockius who had narrowly escaped being killed in the conflict as well. Amanda died in Roswell, New Mexico, and is buried there in South Park Cemetery, Block 21, Lot 59. There is an inscribed marker in the Clements plot near the cemetery office.

101. **Bockius, James Monroe "Doc" or "Dock"\*** (1830–1909). Although he played only a minor role in the Taylor-Sutton Feud in Texas, he narrowly escaped death on one occasion when he was hidden under the raincoat of a friend. Bockius was probably born in Ohio but went to Texas when he was about eighteen years of age. He served as a sergeant in the Texas Rangers under Colonel John S. "Rip" Ford. With the advent of the Civil War, he joined the Confederate forces as a member of the Second Regiment of Texas Mounted Volunteers. He served in various capacities until September 1865. In 1884, Bockius married Amanda J. Billings Tennille, widow of Doc's friend George Tennille, who was killed some ten years earlier in the feud. When Bockius died in 1909, he was buried in Karnes County, Texas, in the Billings Cemetery, which is about three-fourths of a mile north of State Road 108 and one-half mile west of the DeWitt County line. A very poor road, overgrown with weeds, but passable in a car, leads to the cemetery. Shortly after leaving State Road 108, do *not* turn left across a cattle guard. Continue straight ahead and when the road ends, open the gate and

turn left down a lane to a second gate. Go through this gate and keep left to the cemetery, which is fenced. A ground-level, official United States military marker at the back of the cemetery indicates the grave.

102. **Bonneville, Benjamin Louis Eulalie\*** (April 14, 1796–June 12, 1878). He was a general in the United States Army and was also a frontiersman, fur trapper, and explorer. He died at age eighty-two at Fort Smith, Arkansas, and is buried in Bellefontaine Cemetery in St. Louis, Missouri. There is a large marker at his grave site.

103. **Bonney, Billy.** See McCarty, Henry.

104. **Boone, Daniel\*** (November 2, 1734–September 26, 1820). He was a frontiersman and explorer. He died in Missouri at the home of his daughter and was originally buried beside his wife, Rebecca Bryan Boone, near Marthasville, Missouri. Daniel's and Rebecca's remains were supposedly exhumed and reinterred in the Frankfort Cemetery in Frankfort, Kentucky, but there is some doubt as to whether the right bodies were moved.

105. **Boone, Nathan\*** (March 2, 1781–November 16, 1856). He was an army officer and surveyor and was the youngest son of Daniel and Rebecca Boone. He is buried in the family cemetery a short distance from his house, which still stands (1980) in a pasture on private land about two miles northeast of Ash Grove, Missouri. The cemetery is in a little grove of trees and is overgrown with weeds and bushes. There is a marble headstone for Nathan and several smaller stones (some broken) for other family members.

106. **Boone, Rebecca Bryan\*** (1737–1813). She was the wife of Daniel Boone. She was originally buried near Marthasville, Missouri, but her remains, along with those of Daniel, were exhumed and reinterred in Frankfort Cemetery, Frankfort, Kentucky. Whether the right remains were moved is uncertain.

107. **Boone, Squire, Jr.\*** (October 5, 1744–August 5, 1815). He was the brother of Daniel Boone and was a pioneer in Kentucky and Indiana.

He is buried in Squire Boone's Caverns in southern Indiana. Originally buried in a small cave nearby, his bones were later recovered and placed in the large cavern, where his coffin may be seen today on a cave tour. To locate the caverns: from I-64 turn onto Indiana Highway 135 and drive sixteen miles south. Turn east on Squire Boone Cavern Road for three miles to the visitor center. The original burial site is marked and is a short distance east of the visitor center.

**108. Booth, John**\* (March 9, 1855–January 24, 1928). Cattlemen John and Zack Booth both took part in the murder of sheepmen Juan Vigil and Wiley Berry, but since John was married and had children, Zack took the blame and was executed for the crime. John is buried beside his wife, Lovey C. Booth (1849–1927), in the Booth plot of the Gisela Cemetery, Gisela, Arizona. Zack Booth is buried in Phoenix, Arizona, but there is a memorial marker to him in the Booth plot. To locate the Gisela Cemetery, see Vigil, Juan.

**109. Bordeaux, James "Jim"**\* (August 22, 1814–October 11, 1878). He was a trapper, fur trader, and interpreter. He is buried on the Rosebud Indian reservation in the Indian cemetery at St. Francis, South Dakota, along with several other members of the Bordeaux family. There is a marker. A replica of his trading post can be seen at the Fur Trappers Museum a few miles east of Chadron, Nebraska.

**110. Boren, Henry**\* (January 24, 1842–March 18, 1913). He took part in the Lee-Peacock Feud in Texas and is buried in the Old Richards Cemetery near Blue Ridge in Collin County, Texas. His wife, Delila (January 8, 1841–March 19, 1904), is buried beside him. There is a marker.

**111. Boren, Israel**\* (?–?; lived in the nineteenth century). He was the son of Henry Boren and served in Company G, Third Texas Mounted Volunteers in the Mexican War. He also took some part in the Lee-Peacock Feud. Boren is buried in the Old Richards Cemetery near Blue Ridge, Texas. There is a marker.

**112. Born, Henry "Dutch Henry"**\* (July 2, 1849–January 10, 1921). During his earlier life he was an outlaw and horse thief in Arkansas,

Kansas, and other parts of the midwest. He took part in the Battle of Adobe Walls in the Texas panhandle. He later moved to Colorado and lived a clean life. He is buried beside his wife, Ida R. (1867–1949), and two sons, George (1891–1903) and James Henry (1905–1944) who died in World War II. His daughter, Mabel L. Bennett (born 1912), was still living in Pagosa Springs, Colorado, in 1986. The Borns are buried in the Pagosa Springs Cemetery in Block 11, Lot 5 (Born plot). There are markers.

113. **Bostick, Sion Record**\* (December 7, 1819–October 15, 1902). He was a member of the party of young Texans who captured Santa Anna after the Battle of San Jacinto. He is buried in the San Saba Cemetery, San Saba, Texas. There are both a grave marker and a historical marker at his grave.

114. **Boswell, Nathaniel Kimball**\* (November 4, 1836–October 12, 1921). He was a Wyoming lawman most of his life. He died in Laramie, Wyoming, and is buried there in Greenhill Cemetery beside his wife, Martha (September 6, 1837–April 29, 1893). There is a marker.

115. **Boudinot, Elias**\* (1802–June 22, 1839). He was a Cherokee Indian leader and brother of Stand Watie. His real name was Kilakeena "Buck" Watie. He adopted the name Boudinot from his friend, a noted leader in New Jersey. Elias, along with Major Ridge and his son, John Ridge, were killed by Cherokee rivals who considered the three, as well as Stand Watie, traitors for having signed the New Echota Treaty in 1835 which called for the removal of the Cherokees from Georgia and Tennessee to Indian Territory. Boudinot is buried in the Worcester Cemetery not far from Tahlequah, Oklahoma. There is a marker giving information about Elias.

116. **Bowdre, Charles "Charley"**\* (circa 1848–December 23, 1880). He was a member of Billy the Kid's Gang. He was killed by Pat Garrett's posse at Stinking Springs near present-day Taiban, New Mexico. Bowdre is buried beside his two friends, Billy the Kid and Tom O'Folliard, in the old Fort Sumner Cemetery, Fort Sumner, New Mexico. There is a single marker for the three.

**117. Bowers, Lemuel S. "Sandy"**\* (1830–1868). His mining interests made Bowers a millionaire. Sandy married Eilly Orrum and built a mansion near Carson City, Nevada, but eventually lost everything and died a poor man. He is buried on the hillside behind the Bowers Mansion, which is open to the public. His wife, Eilly Orrum (1816–1903), and their adopted daughter, Persia (1862–1874), are beside him. A wrought iron fence surrounds the three graves.

**118. Bowie, James "Jim"** (1795–March 6, 1836). A native of Tennessee, Bowie left home at an early age and for a number of years engaged in various enterprises. He worked as a lumberjack, took part in the slave trade, developed sugar plantations, and bought and sold land in Louisiana. Later he became well known for his efforts to locate silver in Texas. Bowie joined Texas' fight for independence from Mexico. He took part in several battles and, while suffering from pneumonia, died along with the other defenders of the Alamo in early March 1836. The bodies of those killed were burned by the Mexican soldiers.

**119. Bowlegs, Billy.** See Billy Bowlegs.

**120. Bowman, Thiophilus (Mason T. "Mace")**\* (1847–June 5, 1883). He was a Colfax County, New Mexico, sheriff. Bowman was christened "Thiophilus Bowman." He began to call himself "Mason T. Bowman" when he went to Texas, where he took part in the Lee-Peacock feud. He died of hemorrhage of the lungs or consumption (some think he was poisoned) aggravated by an old bullet wound. He is buried in the Springer Cemetery, Springer, New Mexico. The cemetery is on the north side of US 56 just east of Springer. To locate the grave: from US 56, turn north and drive to the last gate (on right), entering the cemetery. The grave is about fifty feet to the right of the entrance and is next to the street. There is a marker.

**121. Boyce, Reuben H.**\* (January 8, 1853–May 23, 1927). Lawman "Dee" Harkey claimed that as a ten-year-old, he worked for Boyce for a short time. Boyce supposedly killed his brother-in-law, but after his arrest he was not convicted. Wanted in Brown County, Texas, for assault, Boyce made the 1900 Texas Ranger "List of

Fugitives from Justice." He was captured in New Mexico and tried in Austin, Texas, on charges of being a member of the "Pegleg stage robbers." He was found not guilty. Later Boyce ran a restaurant in Coahama, Texas. He died there and is buried in the Coahama Cemetery in a marked grave. To locate the cemetery and grave: go south from Coahama on a blacktop road; when that road bears sharply right, turn left on a narrow, blacktopped road to the cemetery on the left. Enter through the second (main) entrance and drive toward the back of the cemetery, looking to the right for the easily seen Boyce plot.

122. **Bozeman, John\*** (January 1835–April 20, 1867). He and John Jacobs marked the Bozeman Trail from Fort Laramie in Wyoming to the goldfields of Montana. He was killed by Indians on the bank of the Yellowstone River. His body was taken to Bozeman, Montana, where he was buried in Sunset Hills Cemetery in the Nelson Story plot. There is a headstone. To locate the grave: from Bozeman Post Office take US 10 east for 0.6 mile to the entrance to a park. Turn right for 0.2 mile, then right for 0.2 mile. Turn right again for about 150 feet. The Bozeman grave is on the right in the plot. To locate the spot where Bozeman was killed: take US 10 to Livingston (twenty-six miles) on the east side of Bozeman Pass. Continue east 12.8 miles to a highway sign designating the spot.

123. **Brady, Patrick William "Pat"\*** (August 16, 1829–April 1, 1878). He was sheriff of Lincoln County at the start of the Lincoln County War. Pat was shot and killed by Billy the Kid and others on the main street in Lincoln. He was buried on his ranch east of town. The graves of Brady and his deputy, George Hindman, are in a pasture some 100 yards south of US 380 and almost directly opposite the old Fritz house, which can be seen about one-quarter mile north of the highway. There is a United States military marker for Brady, but the marker for Hindman was missing in 1985. Part of Brady's original headstone is in the Lincoln Museum.

124. **Bratton, William E.\*** (July 27, 1778–November 11, 1841). He was a member of the Lewis and Clark Expedition. He is buried in the old cemetery at Waynestown, Indiana. There is a granite obelisk at his grave site.

**125. Breakenridge, William Milton "Billy"*** (December 25, 1846–
January 31, 1931). He was a deputy sheriff under Johnny Behan at
Tombstone, Arizona. He died of a heart attack and is buried in
Evergreen Cemetery in Tucson, Arizona. To locate the grave: enter
the cemetery from Oracle Road through the Oracle entrance. Go
straight ahead to the fifth row of graves. Turn right to the twelfth
grave. This is in the Elks Section (section F). There is a marker.

**126. Brewer, Richard M. "Dick"*** (February 19, 1850–April 4, 1878;
NOTE: Some writers give January 10, 1852, as the year of birth).
Brewer was born in Vermont, but the family moved to Wisconsin in
1860. He became a leader of the McSween-Tunstall faction in the
Lincoln County War in New Mexico and was shot and killed by
Andrew "Buckshot" Roberts in the fight at Blazer's Mill. Roberts
was also killed in the fight. The two men were buried near each other
at Blazer's Mill. The two graves were marked in 1991 with inscribed
wooden crosses. In addition, there is also an inscribed, ground-level
marble stone at Brewer's grave. It was placed there by some of his
descendants.

**127. Briant, Elijah S. "Lige"*** (1861–December 22, 1933; NOTE: His
headstone incorrectly gives the year of his death as 1932). He was
sheriff of Sutton County, Texas. He killed Will Carver as Carver
was attempting to rob Jack Owens' bakery and grocery store at
Sonora, Texas. Lige died in San Angelo, Texas, at age seventy-two
and is buried in Fairmont Cemetery, Block 73, Lot 6. His wife,
Myrtle A. Briant, is beside him. Also in the Briant plot are B.P.
Nolen (1851–1936), Edward A. Ahern (1892–1959), and Myrtle G.
Ahern (1891–1985). To locate the grave: enter the cemetery from
West Avenue N, directly across from the office. Drive around the
gazebo and turn right on the second lane beyond the gazebo. Drive
past the tree in the center of the lane and, just beyond the second
narrow lane, look for the Blank monument on the left. The Briant
plot is next to the Blank plot. A large marble stone marked with the
single work, "Briant," is easily seen. There are individual ground-
level markers for each of those buried in the plot.

**128. Bridger, James "Jim"*** (March 17, 1804–July 17, 1881). He was a mountain man, fur trader, and scout. Bridger had little formal education but possessed a remarkable memory. When he died in 1881, he was buried on his farm near Kansas City. Later General Grenville Dodge had his remains removed to a prominent place in Mount Washington Cemetery in Independence, Missouri. To locate the grave: from Truman Road enter the cemetery just east of a stone arch across the road. Proceed about two blocks straight ahead. Pass over a small bridge; on the right in a small triangular plot of ground is a large stone bearing a likeness of Bridger. This monument was erected by General Dodge on December 10, 1904.

129. **Broadwell, Richard L. "Dick"** (?–October 5, 1892). He was a Dalton Gang member and was killed in the gang's attempt to rob two banks simultaneously in Coffeyville, Kansas. His brother, George Broadwell, and brother-in-law, H.A. Wilcox, claimed the body. He was taken to Hutchinson, Kansas, for burial. The cemeteries in Hutchinson have no record of his burial. Since Wilcox was a prominent citizen of Hutchinson, he is probably buried in the Wilcox plot.

130. **Brown, Charles G.** (December 26, 1832–October 5, 1892). He was born in Schenectady, New York, and served an apprenticeship as a shoemaker at Rochester, New York. In 1847 he went to California where he mined and prospected until 1860. He then spent twenty-two years in Michigan before moving to Coffeyville, Kansas, in 1883. When the Dalton Gang attempted to rob two banks simultaneously on October 5, 1892, Brown, along with three other citizens, was killed. Cemetery records indicate that he was buried in Elmwood Cemetery on the south side of Coffeyville. However, I was told at the Dalton Museum that his wife had his body taken elsewhere for burial.

131. **Brown, Frederick H.\*** (?–December 21, 1866). During the Civil War he rose through the ranks from enlisted man to captain. After the war he served at Fort Phil Kearny. Being a reckless man, he enjoyed engaging in Indian skirmishes. While awaiting transfer to Fort Laramie, he joined his friend William J. Fetterman in pursuit of Indians who had attacked a wood party near the fort. The detach-

ment was ambushed and the entire eighty-one-man group was killed. Brown is buried in the Custer Battlefield National Cemetery in Grave 78, Section B. Captain Fetterman is buried beside him.

**132. Brown, George S.**\* (November 1849–June 22, 1882). He became marshal of Caldwell, Kansas, in 1882 and was killed a short time thereafter on June 22, 1882. He was fatally shot by two brothers, Steve and Jess Green, in the Red Light, a saloon and brothel in Caldwell. The Greens were originally from Canada and had worked as herders south of the Red River. Both were escaped convicts from the Texas state penitentiary. They were later shot and killed by a posse of lawmen. Brown was buried in the Caldwell Cemetery. To locate the cemetery and grave: from Caldwell, go north on Highway 49 to Avenue G (just beyond the water tower). Turn left on Avenue G to the cemetery. From the office-maintenance building, drive to the flagpole, which is in a small circle. Just beyond the flagpole on the right, look for a four-foot obelisk near the Ridings (the author of *The Chisholm Trail*) marker. This is Section 3, Lot 108. Brown's marker says that he was 32 years, 8 months of age.

**133. Brown, Henry Newton** (Fall 1857–April 30, 1884). He took part in the Lincoln County War on the side of the McSween-Tunstall faction. He was a lawman at Tascosa, Texas, and shortly thereafter he became the marshal of Caldwell, Kansas. While he was marshal there, he and his assistant, Ben F. Wheeler, along with William Smith and John Wesley, attempted to rob the bank at Medicine Lodge, Kansas. Brown was shot and killed, and the other three were captured and lynched. They were buried just outside the Medicine Lodge Cemetery. Brown's body may have been returned to his wife at Caldwell and buried there. The exact location of the grave is not known.

**134. Brown, James M. "Jim"** (circa 1838–September 6, 1892). He was sheriff of Lee County, Texas, and the man who hanged "Wild Bill" Longley at Giddings, Texas. Brown was killed in Chicago, Illinois, in a shootout with local police. He is buried in Oakwood Cemetery in Fort Worth, Texas, Block 20, Lot 56, but the grave is not marked. Brown had three sons, Garland, James Edgar, and William, and a daughter, Annie.

135. **Brown, Neal*** (March 21, 1844–March 16, 1926). He was a lawman and a good friend of Bill Tilghman. They were business partners in many enterprises. Brown served eight years as a deputy United States marshal and later was jailer under Tilghman in Lincoln County, Oklahoma. He died in 1926, shortly before his eighty-second birthday. He is buried in Block 16, Lot 22, Space 1, in Oak Park Cemetery at Chandler, Oklahoma. There is no marker for Neal, but there are markers for two of his children who are buried beside him, William S. (1887–1953) and Ethel Brown (1897–1977).

136. **Bruner, Hickman "Heck"** (February 15, 1859–June 21, 1899). He was a lawman for most of his life, the latter part as a deputy United States marshal in Oklahoma Territory. He drowned while trying to swim the Grand River at flood stage. His body was recovered the next day, and he was buried in Pryor Creek (now Pryor), Oklahoma. He was given a Masonic funeral. Bruner was survived by his wife and three children. The exact grave location is not known.

137. **Bryant, Charles "Black Face Charley"** (?–August 23, 1891). He was a member of the Dalton and Doolin gangs. He was killed in 1891, and his body was claimed by relatives from Decatur, Texas. A number of Bryants are buried in the Decatur Cemetery, but there is no marker for Charley.

138. **Bryant, Robert Edward "Ed"*** (March 5, 1866–August 20, 1940). Bryant served more than fifty years as a respected lawman in Texas. He was born in Ysleta, Texas, and enlisted in Captain George W. Baylor's Company A, Texas Rangers, in 1883. He later served under Captain Frank Jones and took part in the battle on Pirate Island near El Paso, in which Jones was killed. He remained in Company D under Captain John R. Hughes until he finally left the service in 1900. He continued in law enforcement as a deputy sheriff and as a deputy United States marshal until his retirement in 1940. He died while on a trip to Los Angeles, California, where he was visiting several of his children. He is buried in Evergreen Cemetery in El Paso, Texas, beside his wife, Louisa, and a son, John Patrick. His grave is in Section X, Lot 23, Space 1. To locate the grave: enter the cemetery from Alameda Avenue through the westernmost entrance

and immediately take the center of three drives. Section X will be on the right. About halfway up this drive look on the right for the Nellie McSorley marker. The Bryant plot is in the same row, about five or six graves from the drive. There are markers for several family members.

**139. Bugler, Henry** (?–June 13, 1866). He was a jailer at Independence, Missouri, and was killed by the Jesse James Gang during an attempted bank robbery. He is buried in Woodlawn Cemetery at Independence. A flat marble stone covers his grave.

**140. Bull, Hiram C.*** (1821–October 12, 1879). He was the founder of Bull City (now Alton), Kansas, in 1870. He was a state representative and first probate judge of Osborne County, Kansas. He was killed by his pet elk and is buried in Sumner Cemetery, which is three-quarters of a mile east of Alton and one-half mile north of Highway 24. To locate the grave: enter the cemetery and go to the second lane on the right. Bull's grave is on the corner, and his monument is topped by a large round ball.

**141. Bullion, Laura*** (1876–December 2, 1961). Best known as the girl friend of Wild Bunch member Ben Kilpatrick, Laura was born in Arkansas. At age five, she and the rest of her family moved to Texas to live with her grandparents. As a young girl she met and fell in love with Will Carver, another Wild Bunch member. When Will was killed by Sheriff Elijah S. Briant while attempting to rob a store in Sonora, Texas, Laura became the girl friend of Kilpatrick. After taking part in a train robbery in Montana, Kilpatrick and Laura were arrested in St. Louis for passing some of the stolen money. Upon their conviction, Ben was given a fifteen-year prison sentence, while Laura received a five-year term. After serving her sentence, Laura moved to Lincoln. When she died in 1961, she was buried in Memorial Park Cemetery in Memphis. Later a marker was placed on her grave, giving her name as Freda Bullion Lincoln. Underneath her name are the words, "Laura Bullion."

**142. Bullis, John Lapham*** (April 17, 1841–May 25, 1911). He was a career army man and reached the rank of brigadier general before his retirement. In 1873 he commanded the Fort Clark (Texas) Seminole-Negro Scouts. He served in many other capacities until his retirement in 1905. He died of a stroke while watching a boxing match and is buried in the San Antonio, Texas, national cemetery. A large monument marks his grave just inside the main entrance to the cemetery.

143. **Bullock, Seth\*** (1847–September 23, 1919). Born in Canada, Bullock went to Montana and was elected sheriff of Lewis and Clark County in 1873. Three years later he moved to Deadwood, South Dakota, where he was appointed sheriff of Lawrence County. He later served as deputy United States marshal and became a good friend of Teddy Roosevelt. Bullock died in Deadwood and is buried on the mountain top above Mount Moriah Cemetery. A path leads from the cemetery to the grave site. A granite stone marks the graves of Seth and his wife, Martha. The graves are surrounded by a wrought iron fence.

144. **Bunch, Eugene F.\*** (February 9, 1843–August 19, 1892). He was a train robber and outlaw. He was killed either by a posse or by "Curnell" Edward S. Hobgood. Bunch is buried just off Highway 10 in the Morris Cemetery, which is behind a large dairy about one mile east of Franklinton, Louisiana. His body was removed from its original, badly eroding burial site about 100 yards east of town in the 1930s. A marble obelisk marks his present grave. To locate the grave: drive east on Main Street in Franklinton, past the hospital on the right. About one-half mile beyond the hospital, turn right on a dirt road to the cemetery. This road is just before the large dairy on the right. The grave is in the extreme south part of the cemetery.

145. **Burnett, Samuel Burk\*** (January 1, 1849–January 26, 1922). He was a Texas cattleman who started the famous 6666 (Four Sixes) Ranch. He became a good friend of Quanah Parker when he ran cattle in Oklahoma. Burnett was the founder of the Texas Cattle Growers Association. He is buried in a large granite vault in Oakwood Cemetery, Fort Worth, Texas.

146. **Burrow, Ruben Houston "Rube"\*** (December 11, 1855–October

8, 1890). He was an outlaw in Texas and Louisiana. Burrow was captured in Marengo, Alabama, and placed in jail at Linden, Alabama. He was killed there while attempting to escape and is buried in Friendship Cemetery northeast of Vernon, Alabama. There is a marker. To locate the cemetery: from Vernon, take Highway 18 east. Turn left on Highway 49 to Fellowship Church on the left. The cemetery is beside the church.

**147. Bussell, Richard "Dick"*** (November 18, 1845–July 12, 1935). A historical marker in Canadian, Texas, credits Bussell as being the first commercial buffalo hunter. He is buried in the Canadian Cemetery. A large marble marker with Studer on one side and Bussell on the other indicates the grave site. There is a concrete curbing around the plot.

**148. Byars, Noah T.*** (May 17, 1808–July 18, 1888). He was a minister and the armorer for Sam Houston at the Battle of San Jacinto. The Texas Declaration of Independence was signed in his blacksmith shop, a replica of which still stands at Washington-on-the-Brazos, Texas. He is buried in Greenleaf Cemetery, Brownwood, Texas. There is a very tall monument at his grave. To locate the grave, see Webb, Charles M.

149. **Cabanne, Jean Pierre, Sr.*** (October 18, 1773–June 27, 1841). He was a fur trader associated with John Jacob Astor and Manuel Lisa. He died at St. Louis, Missouri, and is buried there in Calvary Cemetery. There is a marker. A map of the cemetery showing the location of his grave, along with many others, is available at the office.

150. **Cahill, T. Joe*** (1877–February 12, 1965). He was the deputy sheriff who hanged Tom Horn at Cheyenne, Wyoming. He died of circulatory failure at age eighty-seven and is buried in Mount Olivet Cemetery in Cheyenne in Circle 3, Lot 11, Space B. To locate the grave: enter the cemetery from Pershing Boulevard and drive straight ahead to the circle. Turn right on the circle and drive counterclockwise until opposite the lane by which you entered the cemetery. A few feet across the circle toward the cemetery entrance are a large Cahill plot marker and a small, ground-level stone inscribed "T. Joe."

151. **Calamity Jane.** See Cannary, Martha Jane.

152. **Campbell, George W.** (December 23, 1850–April 14, 1881). At one time he was marshal of El Paso, Texas. He was shot and killed in a gunfight by Dallas Stoudenmire at El Paso. The location of his grave is unknown.

153. **Campbell, Robert*** (February 12, 1804–October 16, 1879). He was a fur trapper and trader. He is buried beside his wife, Virginia J. Campbell (December 5, 1822–January 30, 1879), in Bellefontaine

Cemetery in St. Louis, Missouri. There is a large marble marker at the grave site. A map of the cemetery is available at the office.

**154. Canby, Edward Richard Sprigg\*** (November 9, 1817–April 11, 1873). He was a career army man and had reached the rank of brigadier general some time before his death. During the Modoc Indian War, he was killed by Captain Jack, a Modoc Indian, while unarmed and in conference with the Modoc leaders. The site of his murder is marked in Lava Beds National Monument in northern California. His body was eventually taken to Indianapolis, Indiana, and buried there in Crown Hill Cemetery in Lot 1, Section 9. The grave is directly behind the mausoleum and by the flagpole. His wife, Louisa H. (1818–1889), is buried beside him. There is a very large monument.

**155. Cannary, Martha Jane "Calamity Jane"\*** (May 1, 1852–August 2, 1903). She was a frontier character and self-proclaimed scout. For more than thirty years she roamed throughout most of the West, living near mining camps and army posts. She was once married to a man named "Burke." She claimed that at one time she was married to "Wild Bill" Hickok, but no authentic record for the marriage has ever been found. She died at Deadwood, South Dakota, and is buried there in Mount Moriah Cemetery near Hickok. There are large grave markers for both "Calamity" and "Wild Bill." A map of the cemetery showing the location of these graves and a number of others can be obtained from the office near the entrance.

**156. Canton, Frank\*** (September 15, 1849–September 27, 1927). His true name was Josiah W. "Joe" Horner, but he changed it after trouble in Texas led to a prison sentence followed by an escape in 1879. He took part in the Johnson County War in Wyoming, was a Wyoming lawman, a deputy United States marshal, worked as deputy United States marshal in Alaska, and later was adjutant general of Oklahoma. Canton died in Edmond, Oklahoma, and is buried in Lot 153, Block 19, Section 3, of Fairlawn Cemetery, Oklahoma City, Oklahoma. The grave location is on the eastern side of the cemetery near two cannon. There is a small, ground-level marker.

157. **Captain Jack (Chief Keintpoos)*** (circa 1837–October 3, 1873). He was a Modoc renegade leader who killed General Edward R.S. Canby in California while they were in conference and under a flag of truce. He was captured and hanged along with three others at Fort Klamath, Oregon. The four marked graves, side by side, can be seen near the museum at Fort Klamath.

158. **Carlisle, William "Bill"** (May 4, 1890–June 19, 1964). He was an outlaw and train robber. Bill robbed four Union Pacific trains single-handed. In his later years he operated a tourist court near Laramie, Wyoming. He died of cancer at the home of a niece, Hikda S. Cammie, in Coatsville, Pennsylvania, at the age of seventy-four. He is buried in the family plot in Riverview Cemetery in Wilmington, Delaware. His real name was William L. Cottrell.

159. **Carson, Christopher Houston "Kit"*** (December 24, 1809–May 23, 1868). He was a frontiersman, a fur trapper, and later a colonel in the United States Army. At one time he was commanding officer of Fort Garland, Colorado, and at another time he commanded Fort Stanton in New Mexico. He died of a hemorrhage at Fort Lyon, Colorado, and is buried beside his wife, Josephine (1828–1863), and several descendants in the old pioneer cemetery at Taos, New Mexico. This cemetery, which is now called the Kit Carson Cemetery, is on the north side of town. There is a marker at the grave site.

160. **Carson, Moses Bradley** (September 12, 1792–January 1, 1868). He was a half-brother of Kit Carson. Moses died at Eagle Flat, Texas, an old mining camp southeast of El Paso. He was buried in the Masonic Cemetery, now a part of Concordia Cemetery, in El Paso. The exact location of his grave is unknown.

161. **Carver, William Todd "Will"*** (circa 1866–April 2, 1901). He was an outlaw who rode with Ben Kilpatrick and the Ketchum brothers. He was killed in a petty robbery attempt at Sonora, Texas, by Sheriff Elijah S. Briant and is buried in the Sonora Cemetery. A small headstone giving only the date of his death was placed there by friends.

**162. Catron, Thomas "Tom"**\* (October 6, 1840–May 15, 1921). He was a New Mexico businessman and politician. Along with a number of his influential Republican friends, he controlled the infamous Santa Fe Ring which was involved in the Colfax County War as well as the Lincoln County War of the late 1870s. He was born near Lexington, Missouri, graduated from the University of Missouri, and fought for the Confederacy in a number of important battles. His political career was climaxed by his becoming one of the first United States senators from New Mexico, along with his political foe, Albert B. Fall. After fifty years of dominating New Mexico politics, Catron died in Santa Fe at the age of eighty and was buried in Fairview Cemetery, which is on Cerillos Road in Santa Fe. His large granite vault is near the maintenance building beside the lane which parallels Cerillos Road.

**163. Cerré, Michel Sylvestre** (May 6, 1802–January 5, 1860). He was a trader on the Santa Fe Trail and later a fur trader in the Northwest. He died of pneumonia in St. Louis, Missouri. His grave site is unknown.

**164. Champion, Ben F.**\* (June 1860–circa 1925). Brother of Nate and Dudley Champion, he was a cowboy who took no part in the Johnson County War. He died of a heart attack and is buried beside his brother, Nate, in Willow Grove Cemetery in Buffalo, Wyoming. His grave is in Block 8 and is marked.

**165. Champion, Dudley** (circa 1859–May 23, 1893). He was a younger brother of Nate. Dudley was shot and killed by Mike Shonsey near Horseshoe Bar Ranch which is near Lusk, Wyoming. His grave site is unknown.

**166. Champion, Nathan D. "Nate"**\* (September 29, 1857–April 9, 1892). He was a brother of Dudley Champion. He was killed along with Nick Ray by the Invaders at the KC Ranch south of Buffalo, Wyoming, during the Johnson County War. He and Ray are buried in Block 8 of Willow Grove Cemetery in Buffalo. His brother, Ben, is also buried there. The graves are marked.

*Left: Amos Chapman, Brumfield Cemetery, Seiling, Oklahoma.*
*Right: John Simpson Chisum, Chisum family cemetery, Paris, Texas.*

*Martha Jane "Calamity Jane" Cannary, Mount Moriah Cemetery, Deadwood, South Dakota.*

44

167. **Chapman, Amos\*** (March 15, 1837–July 18, 1925). He was a teamster, buffalo hunter, and army scout. Chapman, Billy Dixon, and four soldiers fought off more than 100 Kiowas at the Battle of Buffalo Wallow in the Texas panhandle. Chapman was wounded in the leg, and it had to be amputated below the knee. All six men received the Congressional Medal of Honor but later Chapman and Dixon were removed from the role of recipients because they were not members of the armed services, only scouts. Both men were restored to the Medal of Honor list in June 1989. He was originally buried in a family cemetery near his home at Seiling, Oklahoma. Amos and his wife, Mary (1847–1931), were moved to the Brumfield Cemetery in Seiling about 1979 or 1980. The cemetery is just north of town a few hundred yards west of US 183. There is a marker at the grave site.

168. **Charbonneau, Jean Baptiste\*** (February 11, 1805–May 16, 1866). He was the son of Sacajawea and Touissaint Charbonneau and was born at Fort Mandan north of present-day Bismarck, North Dakota. He was educated in Europe and spent a great part of his life in California, where he sometimes served as a guide. While on a trip from that state to the goldfields of Montana, he developed pneumonia and died at Inskip's Ranch, where he was buried. His grave is a few miles north of US 95 near Arock in eastern Oregon. It is marked.

169. **"Cherokee Bill."** See Goldsby, Crawford.

170. **Chew, William\*** (April 1, 1826–May 24, 1911). He was a pioneer in Brown's Park in northwestern Colorado and is buried in the old Lodore Cemetery in Brown's Park. The cemetery is on the south side of the paved highway passing through Brown's Park and is near the restored Lodore schoolhouse. There is a marker.

171. **Chihuahua\*** (1822–July 25, 1901). He was a Chiricahua Apache leader. He is buried in the Apache Cemetery on the Fort Sill, Oklahoma, military reservation. A map showing the exact location of the cemetery can be obtained at the entrance gate to Fort Sill. The grave is marked.

172. **Chiles, James J. "Jim Crow"*** (May 1, 1833–September 21, 1873). He was a Missouri badman who once rode with William Quantrill during the Civil War. He was known to have killed several men and had a particular aversion to black people. Forty-seven-year-old James Peacock, assistant city marshal of Independence, Missouri, had no fear of Chiles. When Chiles threatened Peacock's fifteen-year-old son, a fight between the two men took place on the city streets. In the hand-to-hand fight that resulted, Chiles was killed by a bullet fired by Peacock. During the fight, the lawman was shot in the back by Chiles' twelve-year-old son, Elijah, who in turn was shot by Peacock's son, Charles. Elijah died four days later. Peacock recovered from his wound and was later mayor of Independence. Chiles and his son are buried in Woodlawn Cemetery in Independence. A very tall obelisk marks the graves, which are beside a large tree a short distance from the grave of George Todd, a lieutenant of Quantrill's during the Civil War. To locate the grave, see Todd, George.

173. **Chisholm, Jesse*** (1805–March 4, 1868). He laid out the Chisholm Trail in Oklahoma and Kansas. He is said to have died from eating food cooked in bear grease which was poisoned by being cooked in a brass kettle. His death took place at the home of his Indian friend, Left Hand, and he is buried there near Left Hand Spring a few miles from Geary, Oklahoma. To locate the grave: from Geary, drive north on US 281. Where 281 angles left, turn right on a paved road, then left on the next paved road. From this point go four miles and turn right. Go two miles, crossing the river, to the first dirt road beyond the river. Turn left on the dirt road to the grave (about one-half mile) and ruins of Left Hand's house. The grave is to the left between the ruins and Left Hand Spring and is marked.

174. **Chisum, James*** (September 25, 1827–March 17, 1908). The name was originally "Chisholm." He was the brother of the more famous John Chisum. Along with his two sons, Walter and William, and his daughter, Sallie James, he lived at the South Springs Ranch south of Roswell, New Mexico, but was never made a partner in the ranching operation. After John Chisum died in 1884, James and his family, along with his brother, Pitzer, operated the ranch for a few years, but

in 1891 the Jinglebob Land and Cattle Company was dissolved. James Chisum was buried in Woodbine Cemetery in Artesia, New Mexico. There is a marble headstone set on a dark granite base.

**175. Chisum, John Simpson\*** (August 14, 1824–December 22, 1884). The name was originally "Chisholm." He was a leading Texas and New Mexico cattleman. He owned the vast South Springs Ranch south of Roswell, New Mexico, along with other properties. He had some involvement in the Lincoln County War, but his exact role is not clear. He died of cancer and is buried beside his parents in a family cemetery in Paris, Texas. To locate the grave: follow Washington Street west to the railroad tracks and the burial site. This is the 1100 block of West Washington. There is a large monument at his grave.

**176. Chivington, John Milton\*** (January 27, 1821–October 4, 1894). He was an ordained minister in the Episcopal Church. As a colonel in the Colorado Volunteers, he led the infamous Sand Creek Massacre in Colorado. He died of cancer in Denver and is buried there in Fairmont Cemetery. The main entrance of this cemetery is at Quebec Street and Alameda Avenue in southeast Denver. The grave is in Section 1, Lot 143, Block 2. To locate the grave: as you enter the cemetery through the main gate, the Ivy Chapel is directly in front of you. Stand on the steps at the east side of the chapel and look east. You can see the grave from this point. There is a marker.

**177. Chouteau, Auguste\*** (September 26, 1740–February 24, 1829). He was one of the founders of St. Louis, Missouri. He is buried in Calvary Cemetery in St. Louis, Missouri. There is a large stone marker.

**178. Chouteau, August Pierre** (May 9, 1786–December 25, 1838). He was the son of Jean Pierre Chouteau. He was a fur trader and a soldier in the War of 1812. After the war he again resumed the trading business. He is buried in the Fort Gibson post cemetery in Oklahoma. The exact grave location is unknown.

**179. Chouteau, Jean Pierre\*** (October 10, 1758–July 10, 1849). He was the father of Auguste Pierre and Pierre, Jr., and the half-brother of Rene Auguste Chouteau. He founded a trading post at present-day Salina, Oklahoma, and is known as "The Father of Oklahoma." Jean Pierre is buried in the Chouteau plot in Calvary Cemetery in St. Louis, Missouri. There is a large monument at the grave site. A cemetery map is available at the office.

180. **Chouteau, Pierre, Jr.*** (January 19, 1789–September 6, 1865). He was the son of Jean Pierre Chouteau. As a fur trader, he made many trips up the Missouri River. For twenty years he headed the American Fur Company of John Jacob Astor, the world's largest fur company. He is buried in the Chouteau plot in Calvary Cemetery in St. Louis, Missouri. There is a large marker.

181. **Christian, William T., Jr. "Black Jack"** (1871–April 28, 1897). He was a New Mexico and Arizona outlaw. He was shot and killed by lawmen near Clifton, Arizona, and was buried at Clifton, but the location of his grave has been lost. Black Jack Cave, where he had a hideout, is a short distance south of Highway 78, a few miles east of Clifton. A poor trail leads from the highway to the cave.

182. **Christie, Ned*** (December 14, 1852–November 3, 1892). He was a Cherokee Indian renegade wanted for the murder of a deputy United States marshal. He was a blacksmith by trade and was killed when a large posse of lawmen led by Paden Tolbert surrounded his heavily fortified cabin and used dynamite to flush him outside. He was riddled by bullets. His father had him buried in the old Christie Cemetery in what is now the community of Wauhillaw, a few miles east of Stilwell, Oklahoma. Only the lower half of his tombstone remained in 1984. The upper half is in the possession of a relative. The inscription reads, "Ned Christie, Born Dec. 14, 1852, Died Nov. 3, 1892. He was one time a member of the Executive Council of the C.N. He was a blacksmith by trade, and a brave man."

183. **Claiborne, William Floyd "Billy"*** (October 21, 1860–November 14, 1882). He was at one time a cowboy for rancher John Slaughter. He became friends with the Clantons and Frank McLaury of Tombstone, Arizona, where he was killed in a gunfight with "Buckskin Frank" Leslie. He is buried in Boothill Cemetery at Tombstone.

**184. Clanton, Joseph Isaac "Ike"** (1847–June 1, 1887). He was one of the Clanton Brothers who were members of the cowboy gang of Cochise County, Arizona. Ike became the leader of the band of cattle thieves when his father, N.H. "Old Man" Clanton, was killed. Ike was present when the shootout at the O.K. Corral started but fled without taking part in the fight. He was finally killed by a detective named Brighton. His death occurred at Wilson's Ranch near Globe, Arizona. He was buried there in an unmarked grave.

**185. Clanton, Newman Haynes "Old Man"**\* (1816–August 13, 1881). He was the father of Ike, William, and Phin Clanton. Until his death he led a gang of cattle thieves. He was killed in Guadalupe Canyon in southeastern Arizona by Mexicans. Clanton was originally buried there, but his sons had the body removed to Tombstone's Boothill Cemetery. There is a marker, but no one knows whether it is at the right grave.

**186. Clanton, Phineas "Phin"**\* (circa 1843–January 5, 1906). He was one of the Clanton brothers of Tombstone, Arizona, but did not take part in the shootout at the O.K. Corral. He died of pneumonia brought on by injuries suffered when his wagon team ran away near Black Warrior, Arizona, which is near Globe. Phin is buried in the Globe Cemetery. His grave is about one-quarter of the way up the steep hillside and is a short distance to the left (east) of the right-hand paved drive. It is enclosed by a rusty, wrought iron fence. The headstone is of tan sandstone, is square, and about two and one-half feet tall.

**187. Clanton, William Harrison "Billy"**\* (1862–October 26, 1881). He was the youngest of the Clanton brothers and was killed by the Earps and "Doc" Holliday at the O.K. Corral battle. He is buried in Boothill Cemetery at Tombstone, Arizona. There is a grave marker which may or may not be at the actual grave site.

**188. Clark, Benjamin "Ben"**\* (February 2, 1841–September 24, 1914). He was a celebrated army scout. He took part in the Civil War and scouted under Captain William Tough, Federal chief of scouts on the frontier. He later led several wagon trains on trading expeditions.

He was Custer's chief of scouts, and General Phil Sheridan called him the greatest scout he had ever known. After his wife, Moka, died, Ben's health started to fail and he placed a pistol to his head and committed suicide. He, his wife, and six of their eleven children are buried in the post cemetery at El Reno, Oklahoma. Ben's grave is just inside the entrance and to the right. All of the graves are marked.

189. **Clark, John Rufus\*** (May 24, 1849–January 10, 1878). He was sheriff of Mason County, Texas, during the Mason County (or "Hoodoo") War and was a leader of the German faction. During the latter part of the conflict, Clark resigned and left Mason County for Llano County, where he died a short time later. He is buried in Board Creek Cemetery, which is about three-quarters of a mile north of Lone Grove, a small community some eight miles northeast of Llano, Texas. His parents, Isaiah Clark (December 29, 1823–May 25, 1897) and Sarah E. Clark (July 25, 1824–February 17, 1890), are buried beside him. The three graves are marked by flat, upright headstones and are in the right center, about two-thirds of the way to the back of the cemetery.

190. **Clark, William\*** (August 1, 1770–September 1, 1838). He was an explorer and later, an Indian agent. He was co-leader of the Lewis and Clark Expedition. Clark died in St. Louis, Missouri, and is buried in the Clark plot in Bellefontaine Cemetery in St. Louis. Many of his relatives are buried in the plot, which is easily identified by the very tall monument which is in the center of the circular plot.

191. **Clarke, James "Jim"\*** (1841–August 7, 1895; NOTE: The name is misspelled "Clark" on his headstone). He was an outlaw and later marshal of Telluride, Colorado, and had ridden with William Clarke Quantrill in Missouri. He was ambushed and killed on the streets of Telluride and is buried there in Lone Tree Cemetery. His grave is in the Grand Army of the Republic section, although he fought in the Confederate Army. A marble slab set in concrete marks his grave.

192. **Clements, Archibald "Arch"** (?–December 13, 1866). He was a Confederate soldier and a member of William Quantrill's command. He was killed in battle at Lexington, Missouri. Descendants

believe that he is buried in Mount Olive Church Cemetery south of Napoleon, Lafayette County, Missouri. There is no marker.

**193. Clements, James "Jim"** (May 30, 1843–circa May 22, 1897). He was the brother of Mannen, Gip, and Joe Clements. Jim took part in a trail drive to Kansas in 1871. In May 1897, he disappeared and his fate is not known. Many feel that he was killed by his brother-in-law, Tom Tennille.

**194. Clements, John Gipson "Gip"*** (May 14, 1854–November 4, 1929). He was a first cousin of John Wesley Hardin and was the youngest of the four Clements brothers. He supposedly died in Runnels County, Texas, and is supposedly buried in the Miles Cemetery in Miles, Texas, Block C, Lot 59. There is no marker. Runnels County records in Ballinger, Texas, show that Gip's wife, Lizzie Lelia Clements (May 13, 1860–March 21, 1918), is buried in this plot and that J.G. Clements was the owner of the plot, but there is no record that he died in Runnels County. The Clements plot is near the center of Block C which is in the southeast corner of the Miles Cemetery. The plot is between the Alexander and White plots. A small piece of broken granite at ground-level is the only marker in the Clements plot. Robert N. Mullin incorrectly gives the date of Gip's death as October 17, 1928.

**195. Clements, Joseph Hardin "Joe"*** (December 1, 1849–March 16, 1927). He was a brother of Mannen, Gip, and Jim Clements. He took part in a trail drive to Kansas. He later moved to New Mexico and became the wealthy owner of sheep ranches in both Chaves and Eddy counties. Joe died in Roswell and is buried there in South Park Cemetery, Lot 59, Block 21. The grave is marked. Other Clements family members are also buried there.

**196. Clements, Mannen (Emanuel)*** (February 26, 1845–March 27, 1887). He was one of four Clements brothers and was the father of "Mannie" Clements. The Clements brothers were first cousins of John Wesley Hardin. Mannen was killed in a shootout in Ballinger, Texas, by City Marshal Joe Townsend. Mannen was running for city marshal when trouble occurred between the two men. He is buried in the well-kept Cox Cemetery near Milburn, Texas, in McCulloch County. He was given an International Order of Odd Fellows burial. His grave is in the southeast part of the cemetery and is marked by a small, hand-carved, brown fieldstone.

**197. Clements, Emanuel "Mannie"** (circa 1868–December 29, 1908). He was the son of Mannen Clements, and was a lawman, soldier, and cattleman. He served as a deputy marshal in El Paso, Texas, and also at Pecos City, Texas. Mannie was shot and killed in the Coney Island Saloon in El Paso, possibly by Joe Brown, but no one was ever formally charged with the shooting. He is buried in an unmarked grave in Concordia Cemetery in El Paso.

**198. Clements, Mary Ann\*** (March 8, 1850–June 21, 1917). She was the wife of Mannen Clements. She is buried in Oakwood Cemetery, Fort Worth, Texas, Block 101, Lot 14, beside James "Killing Jim" Miller, her son-in-law. There is a marker.

**199. Clements, May Myrtle\*** (September 14, 1890–November 24, 1907). She was the daughter of "Slick" Clements and Amanda Clements and the granddaughter of Joseph Hardin Clements. She is buried beside her mother, Amanda Clements Adamson, in South Park Cemetery, Roswell, New Mexico. The grave is in Block 5, Lot 122, not far from the office. There is a marker.

**200. Clifton, Charles Daniel "Dynamite Dick"** (?–December 4, 1896). He was an outlaw and a member of the Doolin Gang. He took part in several bank and train robberies and was killed by law officers sixteen miles west of Newkirk, Oklahoma. Some writers say he was buried in Guthrie, Oklahoma, while others say Muskogee, Oklahoma.

**201. Coble, John C.\*** (June 4, 1858–December 4, 1914). He was a Wyoming cattleman. When Tom Horn was hired by the Wyoming Stock Growers Association to eliminate competition believed to be stealing stock, Coble was thought to be the "payoff" man. From his Iron Mountain Ranch near Cheyenne, he moved to Pinedale, Wyoming, and then to Nevada. Despondent, he shot and killed himself in Elko, Nevada. He was brought back to Cheyenne and buried in Lakeview Cemetery, Lot 1230. To locate the grave: follow directions to Ed Smalley's grave. Go past Smalley's grave to the second lane and turn right. The Coble grave is beside the lane on the right as you come to the next cross-lane. A large granite marker with the single word "Coble" marks the plot. There is a ground-level marker for John C. and his wife, Elise V. Coble (1874–1949). His son, John Coble, Jr. (1912–1917), is also buried in the Coble plot.

**202. Cody, William Frederick "Buffalo Bill"*** (February 26, 1846–January 10, 1917). He was a plainsman, scout, and showman. He received the Medal of Honor, had it taken away, and finally restored in June 1989. The Buffalo Bill Museum and grave are located on Lookout Mountain Road five miles west of Golden, Colorado. To locate the grave: from Denver take I-70 west to Exit 256 and follow Lookout Mountain Road.

**203. Coe, Frank*** (October 1, 1851–September 16, 1931). He was a New Mexico rancher and a cousin of George Coe. He took part in the Lincoln County War and was at the gunfight at Blazer's Mill. He died of natural causes and is buried in the Brendle-Coe Cemetery, which is about 100 yards south of US 70 on the east side of Glencoe, New Mexico. There is a marker.

**204. Coe, George*** (July 13, 1856–November 12, 1941). He was a New Mexico rancher and a friend of Billy the Kid. He was at the gunfight at Blazer's Mill, where an errant bullet took off part of one of his fingers. He died at his ranch and is buried in the Perry Cemetery at Glencoe, New Mexico. The cemetery is on private property and access is difficult. In 1986, a granddaughter of George Coe who lives in Glencoe, unlocked gates and guided me to the cemetery. There is an inscribed headstone, and other family members are also buried there.

**205. Coe, Phillip H. "Phil"*** (July 17, 1839–October 9, 1871). He was a partner with Ben Thompson in the Bull's Head Saloon in Abilene, Kansas. He was killed by Wild Bill Hickok in a gunfight at Abilene, and his body was taken to Brenham, Texas, for burial in Prairie Lea

Cemetery, Range 2, Section 2. His grave is marked with an upright, thin stone which is inscribed. Two tall obelisks and some large trees are nearby.

**206.    Coffee, Gideon H. "Gib"** * (February 16, 1862–March 2, 1899). He was a constable at Elgin, Kansas, and was killed in a gunfight by Bob Register, who in turn, was killed by Henry Powell. Coffee is buried in the Elgin Cemetery. There is a marker. To locate the cemetery: from Sedan in southeast Kansas, take Highway 99 south for seven miles. Turn west on a poor blacktopped road and go six or seven miles to Elgin. Turn right in Elgin on a brick-paved street for a couple of blocks and then turn right on a dirt road for a short distance to the cemetery. There is a marker.

**207.    Colcord, Charles "Chuck"** * (August 8, 1859–December 10, 1934). He was a cattlemen and, after becoming wealthy, built several buildings which became the heart of Oklahoma City, Oklahoma. He was a deputy United States marshal and died at his ranch just east of Colcord, Oklahoma. Chuck is buried in Fairlawn Cemetery in Oklahoma City, Block 7, Lot 18. There is a large marble headstone at the grave site.

**208.    Coldwell, Neal*** (May 2, 1844–November 7, 1925). He was a captain in the Texas Rangers and led the cleanup of outlaws in Kimble County. He died at Center Point in Kerr County, Texas, and is buried there in the Center Point Cemetery, just south of the little town of Center Point, on the right hand side of the road to Camp Verde. There is an inscribed headstone. To locate the cemetery and grave: from the middle of Center Point, go south on the Camp Verde Road a short distance to a big curve. The cemetery is on the right. His grave is in the center right of the first third of the long cemetery. More than twenty former rangers are buried there. Coldwell's wife, Carrie (1851–1936), is buried beside him.

**209.    Colgate, George*** (1841–November 1893). As a cook, he was a member of a five-man hunting party along the Lochsa River in Idaho. When he became ill and a storm caught the party, the other four, thinking that Colgate was dying, left him behind. Under the leadership of William Carlin, those four finally made their way down the Lochsa River, first on a raft and then by foot to safety. When Colgate's body was found, it was several miles from where he had been left. His remains were buried beside the Lochsa River. The grave is marked and is beside US 12 at Mile Marker 148. A mound of rocks and a small white cross indicate the grave.

210. **Collins, Caspar Wever\*** (September 30, 1844–July 26, 1865). Lieutenant Collins was killed by Indians at the Battle of the Platte River Bridge near present-day Casper, Wyoming. He was originally buried in the post cemetery, but a year later his body was escorted east by members of his company and reinterred in the family plot in the cemetery at Hillsboro, Ohio. There is a massive granite marker.

211. **Colter, John\*** (circa 1774–May 7, 1812). He was a member of the Lewis and Clark Expedition and later trapped throughout the Northwest. He was probably the first white man to see the Yellowstone geysers. He settled down in Missouri near Daniel Boone's home and died there. His exact grave site is not known with certainty; however, two of his great-great-great-granddaughters, Mrs. Ruth C. Frick and Mrs. Shirley A. Winkelhoch, are convinced that he is buried in a small cemetery on a bluff above the Missouri River about two miles east of New Haven, Missouri. His son, Hiram, is there in a marked grave; beside him is another grave believed to be John Colter's. It is known that Colter once owned this property. A large granite marker with inscriptions on both sides was placed at the site in 1987. The cemetery is on private property and permission to visit the site must be obtained.

212. **Comstock, Henry Thomas Paige\*** (1820–September 27, 1870). He was a trapper, guide, soldier, and miner and was associated with the fabulous Comstock Lode in Nevada. He sold his interest in this mine for a very small amount of money. After repeated failures in the mining business, he committed suicide in 1870 and is buried in Sunset Hills Cemetery in Bozeman, Montana, in the Nelson Story plot. Nelson Story placed a marker at his grave. To locate the cemetery and grave: see Bozeman, John.

213. **Comstock, William Averill "Billy"** (January 17, 1842–August 16, 1868). He was a well known frontiersman and was chief of scouts under George Custer, Phil Sheridan, and Winfield Scott Hancock. He was killed when he went to the camp of Cheyenne Chief Turkey Leg to question him about Indian raids in the vicinity. Sharp Grover, who was with him at the time, escaped. Comstock is buried in the little post cemetery about two miles southeast of Old Fort Wallace, Kansas. There is no marker and the official army position is that the body was never recovered. This cemetery was cleaned up and some markers restored in 1984.

214. **Connell, Edward Fulton "Ed"*** (May 17, 1863–June 19, 1940). He was a Texas Ranger and for four years served under Captain Bill McDonald. After leaving the Rangers, he served on two different occasions as sheriff of Deaf Smith County, Texas. He was six feet, two inches tall and weighed more than 300 pounds. He died of pneumonia at Corpus Christi, Texas, and is buried beside his wife, Sophia Stockton Connell (October 23, 1871–September 4, 1944), in the Stockton Cemetery not far from Bartlett, Texas. Both graves have headstones.

215. **Connelly, Charles T.*** (November 25, 1845–October 5, 1892). He was the city marshal of Coffeyville, Kansas, and was killed by the Dalton Gang in their attempt to rob two banks simultaneously at Coffeyville. He is buried in Section F, Lot 141, in the Independence Cemetery in Independence, Kansas. The grave is in the southwest part of the cemetery and is only a few feet from the grave of deputy United States marshal Lafe Shadley who was killed at Ingalls, Oklahoma, by the Doolin Gang. There is a large marker at Connelly's grave.

216. **Connor, Patrick Edward*** (March 27, 1820–December 17, 1891). He was an army man who rose to the rank of brevet major general. After his retirement, he settled down at Salt Lake City, Utah, where he died. He was buried with military honors in the Fort Douglas post cemetery at Salt Lake City. There is a large, bronze plaque on his headstone.

**217. Cook, David J. "Dave"\*** (August 12, 1840–April 2, 1907). He was
a Colorado lawman and detective. After serving in the Colorado
Cavalry during the Civil War, he was a United States marshal and a
private detective. His most outstanding accomplishment was the
destruction of the notorious Musgrove-Franklin Gang. He died of
natural causes in Denver and is buried there in Block 15, Lot 70, of
Riverside Cemetery beside his first and second wives, Mary E.
(1848–1870) and Nancy (1851–1878). The wives' graves are
marked by a single obelisk, inscribed on two sides. Dave's grave is
unmarked. The Cook plot is in the extreme northern corner of Block
15 and adjacent to the drive. A map of the cemetery is available from
the cemetery office.

**218. Cooley, Scott\*** (1852–late June 1876). He was a Texas Ranger who
later became an outlaw. He took part in the Mason County War
during which he killed lawman John Wohrle. According to the
*Galveston News* of June 27, 1876, Cooley "died this morning about
one o'clock at the house of Esquire D. Maddox, nine miles north of
Blanco, of brain fever." He is buried in Miller Creek Cemetery, a
few miles southeast of Johnson City, Texas. To locate the cemetery:
from Johnson City, drive a little less than six miles south on US 290–
281. Turn left on US 290 where the two routes part. Drive 2.7 miles
from the fork. The cemetery is 0.1 mile to the left (north). A large
slab covering the grave bears the inscription: "Scott Cooley, 1852–
1876, Texas Ranger." The cemetery is in Blanco County.

**219. Cooney, James C.\*** (circa 1840–April 29, 1880). He was a
frontiersman, soldier, and miner and was killed by Indians. His
brother carved a vault in a huge boulder, and Cooney's remains were
sealed inside. The site is not far from Alma, New Mexico, and can
be reached by a poor dirt road. To locate the grave: turn east off US
180 onto Highway 78, which is 1.3 miles south of Alma. About 1.5
miles on this road, a dirt road angles off to the left (north). Follow
this dirt road about 3.5 miles to a huge inscribed boulder on the right.

**220. Cooper, Andy.** See Blevins, Andy.

**221. Cormack, Charles H. "Charley"\*** (May 7, 1846–March 30, 1944).

He was a frontiersman and scout. He took part in the Battle of Beecher Island in Colorado as a scout under Brevet Colonel George A. "Sandy" Forsyth. He had previously enlisted in Company I, Fourteenth Missouri Volunteer Cavalry under the name "A.J. Entler." He was discharged in May 1865. Cormack died in the Benkel, Nebraska, hospital and was buried in the Bird City Cemetery, Bird City, Kansas. To locate the cemetery and grave: go north from Bird City for one mile and turn right (east) for 0.7 mile. Enter the cemetery at the first drive and then turn left at the next lane. About halfway to the white maintenance building, look left to two white marble United States Army markers. One of these is that of Charley Cormack.

**222. Cottrell, William L.** See Carlisle, William.

**223. Courtright, Timothy Isaiah "Long Haired Jim"\*** (1845–February 8, 1887). He was a lawman, army scout, and detective. He was shot and killed by Luke Short at Fort Worth, Texas. Most writers say that he was trying to extort "protection money" from Short, who had a gambling concession in a local saloon. Courtright is buried in Oakwood Cemetery, Fort Worth. The grave is in Block 27, Lot 11½, Space 1. There is a marker. This grave is about 200 feet from Luke Short's.

**224. Cowdery, Oliver\*** (October 3, 1806–March 3, 1850). He was Joseph Smith's scribe and one of the "Three Witnesses" to the Book of Mormon. He is buried in the Richmond Pioneer Cemetery (often called the Mormon Cemetery) in Richmond, Missouri. There is a large monument to the Three Witnesses, but only Cowdery is buried in this cemetery.

**225. Cox, William Webb\*** (November 12, 1854–December 23, 1923). He was a wealthy businessman and lawyer in New Mexico. Many believe that he hired Jim Miller to kill Pat Garrett. He was born in DeWitt County, Texas, and his reputation in Texas was poor. He died in Las Cruces, New Mexico, and is buried in the Masonic Cemetery in Las Cruces, Section 2, Block 2, Lot 16. His large marble marker with the single word, "Cox," is in the south part of the cemetery. It can be seen to the left (west) from Compress Road, which passes by the cemetery.

**226. Craig, William*** (1807–October 16, 1869). He was a mountain man and fur trapper and was a friend of Kit Carson, Jim Bridger, and Joe Meek, among others. Craig was at the Battle of Pierre's Hole. He is buried beside his wife, Isabel Craig, who died May 8, 1886, in a small cemetery a few yards south of the junction at Jacques Corner, which is a few miles west of Culdesac, Idaho. The cemetery is just off US 95 (seventy-five yards south and up a steep little hill on the left-hand side of the road). The cemetery is enclosed by a fence. There is a marker for Craig and his wife.

**227. Craigie, James** (August 11, 1813–September 29, 1895). He was a fur trader for the Hudson's Bay Company and was born in the Orkney Islands. He died at Newport, Oregon, at age eighty-two and is buried there in the Newport Cemetery.

**228. Crawford, Emmett T.** (September 6, 1844–January 18, 1886). He was a major in the army and was one of the greatest of the Indian fighters. He led a detachment of Apache scouts into Mexico in pursuit of a band led by Geronimo and was fatally shot by a Mexican soldier during a truce. He was buried nearby. Later his body was returned to Kearney, Nebraska, and buried in the Kearney Cemetery beside his wife and child. Later he and his wife were reinterred in Arlington National Cemetery in Arlington, Virginia. Only the marker for his child remains in the Kearney Cemetery. It reads, "Lewis W.—Son of E.T. and C.M. Crawford—Died June 3, 1881—Aged 7 months."

**229. Crawford, William Foster "Bill"*** (?–February 27, 1896). In an attempt to rob the City National Bank at Wichita Falls, Texas, Crawford and Elmer "The Mysterious Kid" Lewis killed bank employee Frank Dorsey. Texas Rangers led by Bill McDonald captured them shortly thereafter. They were taken from the jail by vigilantes and lynched and were buried side by side in Riverview Cemetery at Wichita Falls. To locate the graves: from the office, drive directly to the north side of the cemetery. The graves are marked by a single, small marble stone about one foot tall. It is on the right-hand side of the drive with no other graves nearby.

**230. Crazy Horse** (circa 1840–September 5, 1877). He was a famous Oglala Sioux chief. While imprisoned at Fort Robinson, Nebraska, he was stabbed with a bayonet by a soldier named William Gentles when he pulled a knife in an attempt to escape. His body was given to his parents, who buried it in a secret place. The location remains unknown.

**231. Crittenden, E.C. "Zeke"*** (October 15, 1866–October 24, 1895). He was a sometime lawman in Oklahoma. Both he and his brother, Dick, were killed in a gunfight with Eddie Reed, Belle Starr's son. The two brothers are buried in the International Order of Odd Fellows Cemetery about two miles west of Hulbert, Oklahoma, on the "old highway." To locate the cemetery: from Hulbert, go west on Highway 51. Where 51 takes a slight right turn, "old 51" goes straight. Take this old paved road about 1.5 miles to the cemetery on the right. To locate the grave: turn right into the cemetery and go straight ahead to a picnic table. The Crittenden graves are about forty feet ahead and to the right. A single marker, inscribed on two sides, marks the brothers' graves. Dick's wife, Martha (September 4, 1862–September 4, 1896), is also buried there. A cedar tree separates the two headstones. The two inscribed markers are marble obelisks about 3¹/₂ feet tall.

**232. Crittenden, John Jordan*** (June 7, 1854–June 25, 1876). Second Lieutenant Crittenden was a member of the Twentieth Infantry, attached to Calhoun's Company L, Seventh Cavalry, during Custer's 1876 campaign against the Sioux. He was killed along with Custer and all of his immediate command at the Battle of the Little Bighorn. At his father's request, he was first buried where he fell, but in 1931, his remains were moved to the national cemetery nearby. His grave is number 601 in Section A.

**233. Crittenden, Richard "Dick"*** (January 10, 1861–October 24, 1895). Like his brother, Zeke, he sometimes served as a lawman in Oklahoma. Both brothers were killed in a gunfight with Belle Starr's son, Eddie Reed. Dick and Zeke are buried in the International Order of Odd Fellows Cemetery about two miles west of Hulbert, Oklahoma. To locate the cemetery and grave: see Crittenden, E.C. "Zeke."

**234.  Crockett, David "Davy"** (August 17, 1786–March 6, 1836). He was a frontiersman, scout, and soldier. He spent the early part of his life in Tennessee, where he served in both the state legislature and in Congress. He moved to Texas to aid the Texans in their fight for independence from Mexico and was killed at the Alamo. The bodies of all those killed were burned by the Mexicans, but his identified remains, along with those of Jim Bowie and Colonel William Barret Travis, were placed in a stone, coffin-like tomb which is now in the back of the San Antonio, Texas, Catholic cathedral.

**235.  Crockett, Davy, II** (February 4, 1853–September 30, 1876). Born in Tennessee, he was the son of Robert P. and Matilda Porter Crockett and the grandson of David (of Alamo fame) and Elizabeth Crockett. He grew up near Granby, Texas. In 1870, he left Texas and settled in Cimarron, New Mexico. He was a friend of Clay Allison and was known to have killed several men. Crockett was shot and killed by lawmen Joe Holbrook and J.B. McCullough, who were attempting to arrest him. He is buried in Mountain View Cemetery, a short distance south of Cimarron. A wooden marker which stood for years has disappeared, and the exact location of his grave is in doubt but is known to be very near that of the Reverend T.J. Tolby.

**236.  Crockett, Elizabeth*** (May 22, 1788–January 31, 1869). She was the second wife of Davy Crockett. She died in Texas and is buried at Acton State Park, about four miles from Acton, Texas. There is a large marble monument at her grave site. The little family plot constitutes the smallest state park in the nation.

**237.  Crockett, Pauline "Polly"*** (1788–1815). She was the first wife of Davy Crockett. She was born in Hamblen County, Tennessee, and married Davy on August 12, 1806. Polly died in Tennessee and was buried in what is now an abandoned cemetery in a pasture near

Maxwell, Tennessee. She was the mother of John Wesley Crockett (1807), William Crockett (1809), and Margaret Finlay Crockett (1812). A large, inscribed stone about four feet tall marks her grave.

**238. Crockett, Rebecca Hawkins\*** (circa 1756–1834). She was the mother of Davy Crockett and was born in Maryland. She lived with her son, David, at several locations in Tennessee before taking up residence with a daughter five miles west of Rutherford, Tennessee. At her death, she was buried in the Tyson family cemetery. Her remains are now in a memorial plot about one-half mile from the Davy Crockett cabin near Rutherford. The grave is marked.

**239. Crouse, Charles "Charlie"** (November 9, 1851–1906). He was a pioneer in Brown's Park in northeastern Utah. He died while riding in his buggy in Rock Springs, Wyoming, and is buried in the Rock Springs Cemetery. Later his wife, Mary, was removed from her former burial place and reinterred beside Charlie. Crouse was said to have killed several men.

**240. Cruse, Thomas "Tommy"\*** (March 1836–December 20, 1914). He was an Irishman who discovered the famous Drum Lummond Mine at Marysville, Montana, and later became a millionaire. He was born in County Craven, Ireland, and immigrated to America in 1856. He worked for seven years in New York City before going to California. He prospected and mined in that state as well as in Nevada and Idaho. In 1866, he went to Alder Gulch, Montana. Some ten years later, while prospecting the area north of Helena, he struck the fabulous Drum Lummond Mine, a discovery that made him a wealthy man. His many interests included banking and sheep and cattle raising. In 1886, he married Margaret Carter, sister to United States Senator Thomas H. Carter. She died in the same year, leaving an infant daughter, Mary (called "Mamie"). Mary died in 1912 at the age of twenty-six after having lived a rather scandalous life. Tommy gave a large amount of money toward the construction of St. Helena Cathedral in Helena before his death in 1914. He is buried in Resurrection Cemetery in Helena, along with his wife and daughter. The cemetery is about one mile north of Helena on the east side of Montana Boulevard. The huge Cruse mausoleum is the largest in the cemetery.

**241. Cubine, George B.*** (August 25, 1856–October 5, 1892). He was killed by the Dalton Gang in their attempt to rob two banks simultaneously in Coffeyville, Kansas. Cubine was born in Mechanicsburg, Virginia, and went to Coffeyville, Kansas, in 1875. During the attempted bank robbery, several citizens tried to prevent the robbery, and Cubine was one of four citizens killed by the gang. He is buried in Elmwood Cemetery at Coffeyville. To locate the grave: after entering the north end of the cemetery, drive south past the Frank Dalton grave (on the left and indicated by a sign on a metal post) to the end of the drive. Turn right; a few feet ahead on the left is Cubine's large grave marker. Two of his daughters are buried in the Cubine plot: Jennie (October 20, 1882–December 31, 1882) and Ethel (September 17, 1890–August 27, 1892).

**242. Culbertson, Alexander*** (May 20, 1809–October 27, 1879). He took part in the Florida Indian campaign and later became a noted fur trader in the Northwest. He died in Orleans, Nebraska, at the home of his daughter, Mrs. Julia Roberts, and is buried near the back of the Orleans Cemetery close to an elevated mound. A gray marble, upright stone gives an abbreviated history of Culbertson's life.

**243. Cummings, Mary K. "Big Nose Kate Elder"*** (November 7, 1850–November 2, 1940). She was the girlfriend, or common-law wife, of Doc Holliday in Kansas and Arizona. She was born in Hungary and her maiden name was Haroney. She died at the Arizona Pioneers Home in Prescott, Arizona, and is buried in the Pioneer Cemetery on the northwest side of Prescott. There is a ground-level marker. The grave is not far from the fence on the lower side of the hillside cemetery. To locate the cemetery: from downtown Prescott, go west on Gurley to Green Avenue. Turn right on Green for about three blocks and then bear left on Miller Valley Road. At the wye, take the Iron Springs Road to the left. The cemetery is a short distance on the right, just beyond the large shopping center. There is a parking space at the top of the hill.

**244. Cummins, James Robert "Jim"*** (January 31, 1847–July 9, 1929). Jim was the last survivor of the James Gang. He died of natural causes in the Missouri Confederate Home near Higginsville, Mis-

*Mary K. "Big Nose Kate" Cummings, Pioneer Cemetery, Prescott, Arizona.*

*Bob Dalton, Grat Dalton, and Bill Power, Elmwood Cemetery, Coffeyville, Kansas.*

souri, and is buried in the Confederate Home Cemetery there. There is a grave marker which reads: "James R. Cummins, 1847–1929, One of Shelby's Men."

**245. Cunningham, James\*** (April 8, 1816–July 8, 1894). He was a Texas Ranger and attained the rank of captain. He is buried in the Newberg Cemetery south of Comanche, Texas. To locate the cemetery: from Comanche, drive south on Highway 16 about ten miles and turn left on County Road 1476 for 0.3 mile. The cemetery is on the left. There is an inscribed headstone and a historic marker. Many Cunninghams are buried there.

**246. Curly\*** (circa 1857–May 22, 1923). He was a Crow Indian who was born in Montana Territory. He became a scout in the Seventh Cavalry and, after witnessing George Custer's demise at the Little Bighorn, carried the news of the battle to the steamer, *Far West.* Curly contracted pneumonia and died near Crow Agency, Montana. He is buried in the Custer Battlefield National Cemetery, Grave 1446, Section A.

**247. Currie, George Sutherland "Flat Nose George"\*** (March 20, 1871–April 17, 1900; NOTE: Although many writers spell the last name "Curry," all of the gravestones in the family plot use the spelling "Currie"). He was an outlaw and a member of the Wild Bunch. He was killed in Utah by a sheriff's posse, and his body was removed to Chadron, Nebraska, by his family who lived there. He is buried in the Chadron Cemetery in Lot 21, Block 4, Space 7. There is a marble headstone. His father, John (1849–1922); mother, Annie (1848–1915); and brother, Donald (1880–1901), are buried beside him. All of the graves are marked.

**248. Curry, John.** See Logan, John.

**249. Curry, "Kid."** See Logan, Harvey.

**250. Curry, Lonny.** See Logan, Lonny.

**251. Cushman, Pauline** (June 30, 1833–December 2, 1893). She was a

Federal spy during the Civil War and later appeared on the stage. She died penniless in her tiny apartment at 1118 Market Street in San Francisco. The Grand Army of the Republic took charge of her funeral and erected a plaque over her grave. It reads: "Pauline Cushman Tyler—Federal Spy and Scout of the Cumberland." Her grave is in the GAR plot in the national military cemetery in San Francisco, California, overlooking the Golden Gate.

252. **Custer, George Armstrong** (December 5, 1839–June 25, 1876). He was breveted major general in the Civil War. After the war he commanded the Seventh Cavalry with the permanent rank of lieutenant colonel. He took part in the Battle of the Washita and led an expedition of 1,200 men through the Black Hills of South Dakota. He was killed, along with more than 260 of his men, by Sioux and Cheyenne Indians at the Battle of the Little Bighorn. Custer's body was taken to New York and buried on the grounds of the United States Military Academy at West Point, New York. There is a large marker.

253. **Custer, Thomas "Tom"**\* (March 15, 1845–June 25, 1876). He was the younger brother of George A. Custer and was awarded two Congressional Medals of Honor during the Civil War. He was killed along with George and more than 260 members of the Seventh Cavalry at the Battle of the Little Bighorn. He is buried in the Fort Leavenworth National Cemetery at Fort Leavenworth, Kansas. His grave is marked with the gold-lettered Medal of Honor headstone.

# D

**254. Dalton, Emmett** (May 3, 1871–July 13, 1937). He was a member of the Dalton Gang and was seriously wounded and captured in the attempted robbery of two banks simultaneously in Coffeyville, Kansas. After serving a prison sentence, Emmett married and became a successful real estate businessman. He died in Los Angeles, California, and his body was cremated. Years later his wife buried the ashes in the Dalton family plot in the cemetery at Kingfisher, Oklahoma. Several other members of the Dalton family are buried there.

**255. Dalton, Franklin "Frank"*** (June 8, 1860–November 27, 1887). He was a deputy United States marshal in Oklahoma and was the brother of Grat, Bob, and Emmett Dalton. He was killed in the line of duty while trying to arrest a horse thief and whiskey peddler. He is buried in Elmwood Cemetery in Coffeyville, Kansas. A square marble headstone marks his grave. It is not far from the graves of his two outlaw brothers, Bob and Grat. A sign on a metal post placed beside the driveway indicates the grave.

**256. Dalton, Gratton Hanley "Grat"*** (March 30, 1861–October 5, 1892). Grat was a member of the Dalton Gang of train and bank robbers. He served as a deputy United States marshal for a time before turning to crime. He was killed in the gang's attempt to rob two banks simultaneously in Coffeyville, Kansas, and is buried beside his brother, Bob, and another gang member, Bill Power, in Elmwood Cemetery in Coffeyville. To locate the graves: upon entering the cemetery from Elmwood Street, the graves are a short distance to the right in the first row of graves and next to the railroad tracks. There is a single marker for those buried here. For many years the graves were marked only by a curved piece of metal, the hitching rail to which they had tied their horses during the attempted bank robbery. When Emmett returned to Coffeyville many years later, he had the present simple stone placed at the graves.

257. **Dalton, James Lewis** (February 16, 1826–July 16, 1890). He was the father of the Dalton boys. He and his wife, Adeline Younger Dalton (1835–1925), had fifteen children, eleven of whom reached adulthood. He died suddenly while on a trip with his family from Missouri to Indian Territory. According to Dalton authority Phillip W. Steele, he was buried in an unmarked grave in the Robbins Cemetery at Dearing, Kansas.

258. **Dalton, Julia Johnson Gilstrap Lewis\*** (March 5, 1870–May 20, 1943). She was the wife of Emmett Dalton. Emmett was wounded and captured at Coffeyville, Kansas, in 1892, when the Dalton Gang tried to rob two banks simultaneously. He was tried, convicted, and served fourteen years in the penitentiary before being pardoned. Julia Johnson and Emmett married after he was released from prison. When he died in California in 1937, Julia had the body cremated. Later the ashes were taken to Kingfisher, Oklahoma, and buried in the Dalton family plot. Julia died in Fresno, California, was cremated, and her ashes were taken to Dewey, Oklahoma, and buried in the Johnson plot. There is a small, ground-level marker in the Dewey Cemetery, which is on the east side of US 75 a short distance north of Dewey.

259. **Dalton, Littleton\*** (October 2, 1857–January 2, 1942). He was a brother of Bob, Grat, Emmett, and Bill Dalton but took no part in their outlaw activities. He never married and spent most of his life ranching in California. He died of bronchopneumonia near Sacramento, California, and was buried in Woodland Cemetery in Woodland, California, Lot 7, Block 6, Grave 15. There is a marker.

260. **Dalton, Robert Rennick "Bob"\*** (May 13, 1869–October 5, 1892). He was a member of the Dalton Gang of train and bank robbers and was killed, along with his brother, Grat, in the gang's attempt to rob

two banks simultaneously in Coffeyville, Kansas. Prior to becoming an outlaw, he had served as a deputy United States marshal. He is buried in Elmwood Cemetery in Coffeyville beside his brother, Grat, and gang member Bill Power. To locate the grave: see Dalton, Gratton.

261. **Dalton, William Marion "Bill"**\* (1865–June 8, 1894). He sometimes used the name "Mason Frakes Dalton." He was a brother of Grat, Bob, and Emmett Dalton. He lived in California until the Coffeyville, Kansas, bank raid in 1892. After his brothers, Grat and Bob, were killed and Emmett was sent to prison, Bill became an outlaw in the Bill Doolin Gang. He was killed by Loss Hart, a lawman, and was first buried at Atwater, California. Later his body was transferred to the Bliven family plot in Turlock Memorial Park in Turlock, California. This was his wife's family plot. He is in one of the two unmarked graves in the plot. To locate the grave: enter the cemetery, turn right at the first intersection, and go to the dead end. Turn left and go as far as you can. Then walk to the front fence and go five rows to the right. Note: Harrell McCullough, in his book, *Selden Lindsey: US Deputy Marshal,* says that Lindsey fired the shot that killed Bill Dalton.

262. **Daniels, Benjamin F. "Ben"**\* (November 4, 1852–April 20, 1923). He served in many capacities as a lawman, including United States marshal for Arizona. He served in the Spanish-American War at age forty-six and was sheriff of Pima County, Arizona, in 1920. He died of a heart attack and is buried in Evergreen Cemetery in Tucson, Arizona. To locate the grave: enter the cemetery from US 89 through the Fort Lowell entrance. Daniels is buried in the eleventh row from the entrance and the eighteenth grave to the right of the drive. There is a large headstone.

263. **Dart, Isom** (1855–October 1900). He was a black cowboy who came to Brown's Park, Colorado, from Texas. After being accused of cattle rustling, he was killed by Tom Horn at his cabin on Cold Springs Mountain. He is buried in what was later a cattle lot near the site of his cabin. There is a small, inscribed headstone. A four-wheel-drive vehicle and a topographic map are recommended for

those attempting to locate the grave site, which is now in a little grove of aspens.

264. **D'Autremont Brothers,\* Ray** (March 31, 1900–December 21, 1984), **Roy** (March 31, 1900–June 17, 1983), and **Hugh** (1904–March 29, 1959). On October 11, 1923, the three brothers held up a train at Tunnel 13 near the Oregon-California state line south of Ashland, Oregon. They killed four members of the train crew but got nothing for their efforts. All three were eventually captured, Hugh in the Philippine Islands and the other two in Ohio. They were tried at Jacksonville, Oregon, and sentenced to life imprisonment. After many years in prison, Hugh and Ray were released. Hugh died of cancer within a few months. Roy, while still in prison, became hopelessly insane and died in the Oregon State insane asylum. Ray worked for a while as a janitor at the University of Oregon. All three brothers are buried beside their mother, Belle (?–February 2, 1945), in Belcrest Cemetery in Salem, Oregon. The marked graves are numbers 3, 4, 5, and 6 in Block 16, Section 14. To locate the cemetery: take Commercial to Liberty Road. Take Liberty to Browning Avenue and turn right. Belcrest is on the right, about one-half mile from Liberty. Directions for locating the graves can be obtained at the office.

265. **Daugherty, Roy "Arkansas Tom Jones"\*** (1870–August 16, 1924; NOTE: Some writers give his year of birth as 1868). He was a member of the Bill Doolin Gang of bank robbers and served two prison sentences before he was shot and killed by Detective Len H. Van Deventer. He is buried in Fairview Cemetery in Joplin, Missouri, in the Northeast-West Division, Grave 10, Tier 2. There is no grave marker. According to cemetery records, he was buried on August 22, 1924.

266. **Davis, Jackson Lee "Diamond Field Jack"** (August 12, 1863–January 2, 1949). He was hired by cattlemen in southern Idaho to keep sheep off the range. When two sheepmen were killed, Davis was tried, convicted, and sentenced to hang. His sentence was later commuted to life imprisonment. He was finally released from prison and went to Nevada, where he struck gold and became

wealthy. When the mines played out, he went broke. On December 28, 1948, he stepped off a curb in Las Vegas, Nevada, and was struck by a taxi cab. He died a few days later and was buried there in an unmarked grave.

**267. Day, Barney B.**\* (October 10, 1832–July 4, 1883). He was one of the men killed in the Fourth of July shootout in Grant County, Colorado, involving the sheriff, three county commissioners, and a county judge. One commissioner, J.G. Mills, moved all county records from Hot Sulphur Springs to Grand Lake while the other commissioners were in Denver on business. Upon their return, two commissioners, E.P. Weber and Barney Day, and Judge "Cap" Dean, went to Grand Lake to recover the records. Mills, Sheriff Charles Royer, and the three Redman brothers, put on masks and ambushed the three men. In the fight that followed, Mills shot Weber and in turn was killed by Day. The sheriff killed Day, and other shots mortally wounded Cap Dean. The sheriff rode to Georgetown and a short time later committed suicide. Day and Dean are buried in the Hot Sulphur Springs Cemetery, which is on a hill about three-quarters of a mile east of town. To locate the cemetery and grave: take Byers Avenue (gravel) at the east end of town and go about three-quarters of a mile to the cemetery on the left. The graves of both Day and Dean are at the top of the hill on the west side of the cemetery. Day's wife, Sophronia N. Day (January 2, 1839–April 22, 1907), is buried beside him.

**268. Dean, Thomas J. "Cap"**\* (May 22, 1826–July 17, 1883). He was one of several men killed in the Fourth of July shootout at Grand Lake, Colorado. Dean (called "Cap" from his former army rank) is buried at Hot Sulphur Springs. His wife, Nancy E.M. Dean (December 9, 1826–August 19, 1881), is buried beside him, and both graves are marked. Dean served as captain of Company D of the Fifth Michigan Cavalry. See Day, Barney B., for cemetery location and details of the fight.

**269. Decre, Phillipe**\* (?–September 27, 1852). His name is sometimes given as Phillipe Dejie. He was a member of the Lewis and Clark Expedition and is buried at St. Paul Parish in the Willamette Valley in Oregon. There is a marker on Oregon Highway 219 about 0.1 mile from the St. Paul Catholic church. The marker is beside the road and on the opposite side of the church from the St. Paul Cemetery. He was not one of the group which finally reached the Pacific Ocean.

**270. Deno, Lottie.** See Thurmond, Charlotte.

**271. De Smet, Pierre Jean (Peter John)*** (January 30, 1801–May 23, 1873). Born in Belgium, he became a Jesuit missionary to the Indians of the West. Father De Smet founded the St. Mary's Mission in Montana's Bitterroot Valley and was greatly loved by the Indians. He crossed the Atlantic nineteen times seeking help to enable him to carry on his missionary work. He died at St. Louis University of Bright's disease and was buried at St. Stanislaus Seminary in Florissant, Missouri, near St. Louis. To locate the cemetery: from Florissant, take Charbonier Road to Howdershell Road. Turn left here for 0.7 mile to the seminary. De Smet's grave in the small cemetery is marked. The cemetery is south of the quadrangle at the seminary.

**272. Dilts, Jefferson*** (?–September 1, 1864). He was a corporal in the First Minnesota Cavalry when he and seven other soldiers were killed by Indians in the Battle of Fort Dilts in southwestern North Dakota. All eight of the soldiers were buried on the battlefield, which is about twenty miles west of Bowman, North Dakota, and two miles north of US 12 by way of a dirt road. The graves are marked.

**273. Dixon, William "Billy"*** (September 25, 1850–March 9, 1913). He was a buffalo hunter and noted scout for the army. He took part in the Battle of Adobe Walls in the Texas panhandle as well as the Battle of Buffalo Wallow. He was awarded the Congressional Medal of Honor. His name was removed from the Medal of Honor list because he was not a member of the armed services; however, he was restored to the Medal of Honor list in June 1989. He died at Texline, on the Texas-New Mexico state line and is now buried on the site of the Battle of Adobe Walls near the Canadian River in Hutchinson County, Texas. There is a large marker. Dixon had a ranch about a mile south of the battlefield, and his old ranch house was still occupied in 1984.

**274. Dolan, James Joseph\*** (May 2, 1848–February 26, 1898). He was a New Mexico pioneer and businessman who had been born in Ireland. After coming to America at a young age, he spent a total of five years in military service. The Murphy-Dolan forces opposed the Tunstall-McSween forces in the Lincoln County War in New Mexico. In 1879, Dolan married Caroline Fritz, daughter of Charles Fritz, a wealthy rancher. When she died, he married Maria Eva Whitlock. At one time he served in the New Mexico territorial senate. He is buried in the Fritz Cemetery just east of the Rio Bonito, which is a few miles east of Lincoln, New Mexico. The cemetery is on the north side of Highway 280. There is a large, elaborate marker.

**275. Doniphan, Alexander William\*** (July 9, 1808–August 8, 1887). He was an army officer who rose to the rank of brigadier general before his retirement to enter politics. He once refused an order to execute Joseph Smith, president of the Mormon Church. He died at Richmond, Missouri, and is buried beside his wife and two sons in Fairview Cemetery in Liberty, Missouri. A twenty-four-foot monument was erected over his grave.

**276. Doolin, William "Bill"\*** (1858–August 25, 1896). He was an outlaw with the Dalton Gang. After the Daltons were annihilated at Coffeyville, Kansas (Bill was not present), he formed his own gang. He was arrested by Bill Tilghman but escaped from the Guthrie, Oklahoma, jail. Doolin was later killed by a shotgun blast fired by Heck Thomas. He is buried in the Summit View Cemetery in Guthrie, Oklahoma. There is a headstone. The grave is about 200 feet to the left of a tool shed in an area that was at one time a trash dump. Several other outlaws are buried nearby.

**277. Doran, Thomas M.\*** (1859–1944). He was a member of the posse that captured the bank robbers at Medicine Lodge, Kansas. The robbers, who were led by Henry Brown, marshal of Caldwell, Kansas, were taken from the jail and lynched. Doran is buried in the Medicine Lodge Cemetery. There is a marker.

**278. Dorsey, Frank\*** (January 5, 1862–February 25, 1896). He was the cashier of the City National Bank of Wichita Falls, Texas, and was killed by Bill Crawford and "Kid" Lewis in an attempted bank robbery. Dorsey is buried in Riverside Cemetery in Wichita Falls. A four-foot, brown stone marks his grave, which is about 150 feet from that of Crawford and Lewis, who were buried in a single grave.

**279. Douglas, Percy\*** (January 30, 1861–January 29, 1897). He was a California badman who was born in Sunderland, England. After serving two prison sentences, he was killed by a shotgun blast fired by Deputy Marshal Edwin L. Willow at Bakersfield, California. He is buried there in Union Cemetery, Block 460, Lot 5. There is a large marker. Buried beside Percy is his brother, John Stobart Douglas (1855–1919). To locate the grave: enter the cemetery and drive past the office to the back of the cemetery. Turn left and drive to the third lane. The grave is on the farther corner beside the lane.

**280. Dripps, Andrew\*** (December 1789–September 1, 1860). He fought in the War of 1812 and then became a fur trader. Later he joined the Missouri Fur Company and was in charge of several trading posts in the Northwest. Dripps died at the home of his sister, Mrs. Mulkey, in Kansas City, Missouri, and is buried in the St. Mary's Cemetery there beside his wife, Mary (circa 1800–June 1, 1846).

**281. Duck, Bluford "Blue"\*** (June 17, 1859–May 7, 1895). He was a Cherokee Indian and friend of Belle Starr (many say her lover). In 1886 he was tried, convicted, and sentenced to death for the murder of a boy named Wyrick. Later his sentence was commuted to life imprisonment. After he developed tuberculosis, he was pardoned by President Grover Cleveland on March 20, 1895. He died at the home of his father less than two months later. He is buried in the Dick Duck Cemetery at Catoosa, Oklahoma, about six miles east of Tulsa. To locate the cemetery and grave: from I-44 east of Tulsa, turn north on Highway 167 for 0.9 mile. Turn right on Pine Street to the cemetery entrance on the right. The grave is in the southeastern part of the cemetery. An inscribed, vertical slab of marble, rounded on the top, marks the grave. His father, Richard "Dick" Duck (September 1, 1835–July 28, 1903), is buried beside him.

*Left: William "Bill" Doolin, Summit View Cemetery, Guthrie, Oklahoma.*
*Right: Christopher "Chris" Evans, Mount Calvary Cemetery, Portland, Oregon.*

*Wyatt Berry Stapp Earp and Josephine Marcus Earp, Hills of Eternity*
*Memorial Park, Colma, California.*

**282. Duggan, Martin "Mart"\*** (November 10, 1848–April 19, 1888). He was a lawman in Leadville, Colorado. He was killed by an unknown gunman and his body was taken to Denver, Colorado, for burial in Riverside Cemetery. The headstone once present in Block 2 is now gone. To locate the cemetery: go west on I-70 to Brighton Boulevard. Exit and go north on Brighton to the cemetery which is a short distance on the left.

**283. Dull Knife\*** (circa 1810–1883). He was a Northern Cheyenne chief who led his warriors in many battles along the Bozeman Trail. He is most famous, along with Little Wolf, for leading some 300 of their people out of Oklahoma in an attempt to return to their homeland in the north. When the group split into two bands, Dull Knife led his band to Fort Robinson in Nebraska, where they surrendered. In a later escape attempt, many of his band were killed. He died in what is now Montana and was buried in the Indian cemetery just north of Highway 212 on the east side of Lame Deer, Montana. His friend, Little Wolf, lies beside him. Both graves are marked with brass plaques on concrete bases and are in the southeastern part of the cemetery.

**284. Dunn, Bee\*** (February 8, 1868–November 6, 1896). He was a petty thief in Oklahoma Territory. He and his brother, John, killed "Bitter Creek" Newcomb and Charlie Pierce for the reward. Bee was killed by Frank Canton and is buried near the center of the Ingalls Cemetery, just north of what was at one time the little town of Ingalls, Oklahoma. There is a marker.

**285. Dunn, John Boggs** (February 2, 1862–January 24, 1933). He was a lawman and rancher in Montana. While sheriff of Carbon County, Montana, he hanged the only man executed in that county. He died at Red Lodge, Montana, and is buried there in the Red Lodge Cemetery.

**286. Durfey, Jefferson "Jeff"\*** (June 17, 1846–January 30, 1931). He was born in Ohio, served in the Civil War, and then moved to Kansas, where he built the first house in Osborne County. The house still stands, and an outline of the log structure is engraved on his headstone. Durfey was one of the most noted buffalo hunters in the West and later became a very successful wheat farmer. He died at age eighty-four and is buried in the Osborne Cemetery beside his wife, Mary Burke Durfey (1850–1933). To locate the cemetery and grave: from the junction of US 281 and US 24, go west on US 24 for one mile to the cemetery on the left. Turn left and go south on the dirt road on the east side of the cemetery. Drive to the second entrance from US 24, enter the cemetery, and drive to the fifth lane. Turn right, and a short distance from the last turn, watch on the left for a large, gray marble stone with an engraved cabin.

287. **Duval, John Crittenden*** (March 1816–January 15, 1897). He escaped the massacre at Goliad, Texas, and was the last survivor of Fannin's army when he died in Fort Worth, Texas. He is buried in Oakwood Cemetery in Austin, Texas. A three-foot, gray granite monument marks his grave.

288. **Dynamite Dick.** See Clifton, Charles Daniel.

**E**

289.  **Earp, Adelia Douglas.**  See Edwards, Adelia Douglas Earp.

290.  **Earp, James Cooksey "Jim"**\* (June 28, 1841–January 25, 1926). He was a brother of Wyatt, Morgan, Virgil, and Warren Earp. He died of natural causes and is buried in Mountain View Cemetery in San Bernardino, California, in Block "Bubah," Grave 5. Also buried there are his sister, Adelia; her husband, William T. Edwards; and their son, Raymond T. Edwards. The graves are all together, directly in front of the mausoleum, and have small, marble, ground-level markers.

291.  **Earp, Morgan S.**\* (April 24, 1851–March 18, 1882). He was one of the numerous Earp brothers. Morgan was shot while playing billiards in R.S. Hatch's Bank Exchange Saloon in Tombstone, Arizona. He was buried in Colton, California, in a cemetery west of town. The eight bodies from this cemetery were later removed to Hermosa Cemetery on the west side of Colton. The plot in which these bodies are buried is known but the exact location within that plot is not. In 1991, a large marker for Morgan was placed at the approximate location of the grave.

292.  **Earp, Newton Jasper** (October 7, 1837–December 18, 1928). He was a half-brother of Wyatt, Virgil, Morgan, Warren, and Jim Earp. His parents were Nicholas and Abigail Storm Earp. He died near Sacramento, California.

293.  **Earp, Nicholas Porter** (September 6, 1813–November 12, 1907). He was the father of the famous Earp brothers. He died in California

at the Soldiers' Home in Sawtelle. ("Sawtelle" is the old name for a section of Los Angeles adjoining Santa Monica.) He is buried in the national cemetery there. There is a standard United States military headstone.

**294. Earp, Virgil Walter*** (July 18, 1843–October 19, 1905). He was one of the famous Earp brothers and a one-time marshal of Tombstone, Arizona. He took part in the so-called "O.K. Corral Gunfight" and later was shot by an unknown gunman, resulting in loss of the use of one of his arms. After leaving Arizona, he became marshal of Colton, California. Virgil died at Goldfield, Nevada, and his body was taken to Portland, Oregon, where he is buried in River View Cemetery. The grave is in the old part of the cemetery in the Bertrand Lot (Lot 18, Section 15, Grave 1) and is marked by a low cylindrical, marble stone. The grave is near the southern boundary of Section 15, and is twelve rows west of the drive which forms the eastern boundary of Section 15. It is shaded by a thick English holly.

**295. Earp, Virginia Ann Cooksey** (February 2, 1821–January 14, 1893). She was the mother of Wyatt, Virgil, Morgan, Jim, and Warren Earp. She died in San Bernardino, California. I have been unable to locate her grave either in the old Pioneer Cemetery or Mountain View Cemetery in San Bernardino.

**296. Earp, Warren*** (March 9, 1855–July 7, 1900). He was another of the famous Earp brothers. Warren was shot and killed at the Headquarters Saloon in Willcox, Arizona, by John Boyette. He is buried in the old unused cemetery on the southeast side of Willcox. In 1990 an inscribed wooden marker was erected a short distance from the cemetery entrance. It may or may not be at the actual grave location. To locate the cemetery: from Business 10 in downtown Willcox, take Stewart Street southeast across the railroad tracks to Third Avenue (dirt). Turn left on Third for a few blocks to the cemetery on the right. The grave marker can be seen from the entrance.

**297. Earp, Wyatt Berry Stapp*** (March 19, 1848–January 13, 1929). He was the most famous of all the Earp brothers and served as a lawman in Kansas and Arizona. After leaving Arizona following the so-called "Gunfight at the O.K. Corral," he engaged in mining in Idaho, Alaska, and California. Wyatt died at his home in California and his body was cremated. His ashes are buried in the Hills of Eternity Memorial Park. His wife, Josephine Sarah Marcus Earp (1861–1944) was later buried beside him. The cemetery is at Colma, California, on the south side of San Francisco. There is a marker.

298. **East, James Henry "Jim"**\* (August 30, 1853–June 30, 1930). He was sheriff of Oldham County, Texas, and both lawman and judge in Douglas, Arizona. He shot and killed a man by the name of Clark in Tascosa, Texas, and was a member of Pat Garrett's posse that killed Tom O'Folliard and Charlie Bowdre and captured Billy the Kid at Stinking Springs, New Mexico. He is buried beside his wife, Nettie Bouldin East (1866–1931), in the Douglas Cemetery, location F-162-7. There is a headstone.

299. **Edwards, Adelia Douglas Earp**\* (January 16, 1861–January 16, 1941). She was the sister of the Earp brothers. She is buried in Mountain View Cemetery in San Bernardino, California, in Block "Bubah," Grave 8. This is directly in front of the mausoleum. Also here are her husband, William T. Edwards (1856–1921); her brother, Jim (1842–1926); and her son, Raymond T. (1898–1917).

300. **Edwards, John Newman**\* (January 4, 1839–May 4, 1889). Born in Virginia, Edwards went to Missouri at the age of twelve. During the Civil War he advanced to the rank of major in the Confederate Army and served under General Jo Shelby. When the war was over he went to Mexico but later returned to Missouri, where he helped found the *Kansas City Times.* He continued as a newspaperman for over twenty years. He is most noted for defending Jesse and Frank James during their outlaw years. He died at Jefferson City, Missouri, and was buried in the Dover Cemetery at Dover, Missouri. To locate the cemetery and grave: from US 24 in Dover, go south on Highway F about 0.3 mile to the cemetery on the left. Enter the cemetery and turn right at the flagpole. Directly south of the flagpole and just beyond a lane, is an engraved marble stone with the top slanted at a forty-five-degree angle. It is directly behind (west of) the Neer marker on the right of the drive.

**301.  Elder, Big Nose Kate.** See Cummings, Mary K.

**302.  Elliot, Joel*** (October 27, 1840–November 27, 1868).  During the Civil War he served as an officer in the First, Second, and Seventh Indiana Cavalry units.  After the war he was commissioned a major in the Seventh Cavalry under George A. Custer.  During the year that Custer was suspended from his command, Elliot commanded the Seventh Cavalry.  At the Battle of the Washita, Elliot and more than a dozen of his men became separated from the main body of Custer's men; all were killed by the Kiowa and Cheyenne warriors.  Custer was greatly criticized for not going to Elliot's aid.  The major was first buried at Fort Arbuckle, Oklahoma, but later his remains were taken to the Fort Gibson, Oklahoma, national cemetery and placed on Officer's Row in Grave 2233.

**303.  Ellis, Abraham "Bullet Hole Ellis"*** (April 24, 1815–March 14, 1885).  He was born in Green County, Ohio, son of Henry and Charity Ellis.  He married Elizabeth Haughy in 1843 and taught school and farmed until he and his wife moved to what is now Miami County, Kansas, in 1857.  As school superintendent in 1860, he met William C. Quantrill who was teaching in Stanton, Kansas.  Ellis served in both the territorial and state legislatures (1859–1861).  He joined General James H. Lane's irregulars in September 1861, and served under James Montgomery, his immediate commander.  On March 7, 1862, Ellis stopped over at Aubry (now Stillwell) in Johnson County, Kansas.  During Quantrill's raid on Aubry, Ellis, while looking out of the second story window of the house in which he had spent the night, was struck in the forehead by a .38 caliber bullet fired by Quantrill.  When he saw whom he had hit, Quantrill apologized for having shot the wrong man.  After several months Ellis recovered and lived until 1885.  Some eight months before his death, the courts had ruled him insane.  He is buried in Oak Hill Cemetery at Elk City, Kansas, beside his wife, Elizabeth (1820–1875).  To locate the cemetery and grave: turn east off US160 onto State Road 39 and go 0.3 mile to the cemetery on the right.  The Ellis plot is in the northeast quadrant, about thirty feet southeast of the massive Bryant monument.  Ellis' marker is a three-foot obelisk with "Ellis" at the bottom.

**304. Emge, Joe.** See Sheepmen's Mass Grave.

**305. Esse-too-yah-tay.** See Striding-along-in-the-dark.

**306. Evans, Christopher "Chris"*** (March 2, 1846–February 9, 1917).
He was a member of the Evans-Sontag Gang of train robbers. In one
of his many encounters with lawmen, one of his eyes was shot out.
He was eventually captured and served a long prison sentence in
California. After his release from prison he lived in Portland,
Oregon, until his death of cancer. He is buried in Portland in Mount
Calvary Cemetery, 333 Southwest Skyline Boulevard, in Grave 8,
Block 6, Section F-1. There is a ground-level marker.

**307. Ewing, Jesse** (?–?). He was a Brown's Park pioneer. At one time
he ran a station on the Overland Trail, and later he mined in the
western (Utah) part of the park. He was shot and killed by a man
named Duncan and is buried in Brown's Park, across the Green
River from the John Jarvie store, which is now a historic site owned
and operated by the Bureau of Land Management.

**F**

**308. Faber, Charlie** (?–December 21, 1876). He was deputy sheriff of Bent County, Colorado. He was shot and killed by Clay Allison in Las Animas, Colorado. I have been unable to locate his grave.

**309. Fairchild, Olive Ann Oatman*** (1837–March 20, 1903). She was captured by Indians in Arizona and spent many years with them. All of her family except a brother, Lorenzo, and a sister, Mary Ann, were killed in the Indian attack. She finally was released and some years later she married John B. Fairchild. She died in Sherman, Texas, and is buried in West Hill Cemetery. The grave is in the northeast quadrant of the cemetery and is about 150–200 feet west of the mausoleum and about 20 feet from the very tall, pink marble, four-columned, Dillard monument which is topped by a large urn. The family plot has a large, gray marble stone with the single word, "Fairchild." There are small markers about two and one-half feet high for Olive and her husband. There is also a low, metal, historical marker.

**310. Fairweather, William H. "Bill"*** (June 14, 1836–August 25, 1875). He captained the party that discovered gold at Alder Gulch, Montana, in May 1863. He was born in Canada in Woodstock Parish, Carlton County, New Brunswick, and died at Daly's Ranch (now called "Robbers Roost"), Madison County, Montana. He is buried in the Virginia City, Montana, Cemetery on a hill overlooking the stream where he discovered gold. The grave is surrounded by an iron fence with an inscribed plate.

**311. Fall, Albert Bacon*** (November 21, 1861–November 30, 1944).

As secretary of the interior, he was associated with the Teapot Dome scandal. Fall was born in Frankfort, Kentucky, but went west at an early age. He engaged in teaching, the cattle industry, and mining before being admitted to the bar. By 1905 he had begun putting together one of the largest ranches in New Mexico at Las Cruces. He became active in politics and in 1920 was appointed secretary of the interior by President Warren G. Harding. Later he was accused of taking large bribes in exchange for illegal oil leases on government lands. After serving a prison sentence, he died in poverty in El Paso, Texas. He is buried there in Evergreen Cemetery, Section K, Lot 212, Space 2. His wife, Emma Morgan Fall (1865–1943), and daughter, Jouette Fall Elliot (1894–1956), are buried beside him. The Fall plot is on the corner of Section K nearest the office.

**312. Fannin, James Walker "Jim"\*** (January 1, 1804–March 27, 1836). He was a frontiersman and soldier. He was killed at Goliad, Texas, by Mexican soldiers during the Texas Revolution. He was buried along with many of his command in a common grave near Goliad. A large monument bearing the names of those killed marks the mass grave.

**313. Farnham, Ethan Allen\*** (October 5, 1859–June 5, 1908). He was deputy sheriff of Routt County, Colorado, under Sheriff Charlie Neiman and took part in the capture of Harry Tracy and David Lant. Later he was elected sheriff. He died of cancer at Grand Junction, Colorado, and was buried in the Craig Cemetery at Craig, Colorado. Many of his family members are buried at Grand Junction. To locate the Craig Cemetery and the grave: from downtown Craig, take any street north to Seventh Street. Turn right (east) on Seventh until it ends in a T at the cemetery. Turn right and then left into the cemetery. Then bear right to the south end of the cemetery. Farnham's grave is on the south side of the third lane from the extreme south end. Across the lane from the grave is the very large Chapman marker. Farnham's grave is marked by a six-inch high, pink marble stone on a concrete foundation and is inscribed.

**314. Farr, Edward J. "Ed"\*** (November 22, 1867–July 18, 1899). He was the sheriff of Huerfano County, Colorado, and was killed in

Turkey Canyon near Cimarron, New Mexico, by the Ketchum Gang. He is buried in the Masonic Cemetery north of Walsenburg, Colorado. There is a marble headstone on a concrete base. The cemetery is on Elm Street, about one mile north of the courthouse and about one block west of the business route. To locate the grave: from the very large Kimbrel vault, stand with your back to the door of the mausoleum and look forty-five degrees left and across the gravel drive to a large, square, pink marble stone about fifty feet away. This stone marks Farr's grave. Other members of the Farr family are also buried there.

315. **Fetterman, William Judd*** (circa 1833–December 21, 1866). During the Civil War he was breveted major and then lieutenant colonel for bravery. After the war he was given the permanent rank of captain in the Twenty-seventh Infantry stationed at Fort Phil Kearny in what is now Wyoming. When a wood detail was attacked near the fort, Fetterman took eighty men and went to their aid. He disregarded the orders of the commanding officer, Colonel H.B. Carrington, and chased the Indians out of sight of the fort and into an ambush. All eighty-one men were killed. Fetterman is buried in the Custer Battlefield National Cemetery in Grave 77 of Section B, beside his friend, Captain Frederick H. Brown.

316. **Fisher, John King*** (1854–March 11, 1884). He was a Texas gunman and outlaw during his younger days. Later he became deputy sheriff of Uvalde County, Texas. He was killed, along with his friend, Ben Thompson, as a result of Thompson's having killed Jack Harris a short time before. Their murders took place at the Turner Hall opera house in San Antonio, Texas. Fisher was buried in Uvalde, Texas. His body was later exhumed from the original burial site and reburied in the Frontier (or Pioneer) Cemetery in Uvalde. A wrought iron fence encloses the grave, which is marked with a headstone and a historical marker.

317. **Fitzpatrick Thomas "Broken Hand"** (1799–February 7, 1854). He was a mountain man, fur trapper, and later, Indian agent. He died of pneumonia at Washington, D.C., and is buried in the Congressional Cemetery there. A small, upright stone is inscribed "Thomas Fitzpatrick, Major, U.S. Indian Agent, February 7, 1854."

**318. Flatt, George W.*** (1853–June 19, 1880). He was originally from Tennessee. On July 7, 1879, Flatt, while serving as a posse member in Caldwell, Kansas, shot and killed George Wood when Wood resisted arrest and fired at Flatt. After Caldwell was incorporated on July 22, 1879, Flatt was appointed the first city marshal. Shortly after becoming marshal, he married a woman of eighteen named Fannie Lamb. Three months after his appointment as marshal, Flatt was shot and killed on Main Street of Caldwell. The fatal shotgun blast was fired from ambush. The murderer was never identified, but many believed that Mike Meagher, mayor of Caldwell, was involved. Four days after Flatt's death, his wife, Fannie, gave birth to a boy. Flatt is buried in the Caldwell Cemetery. To locate the grave: follow the directions for locating the grave of George S. Brown. Then look south and a little to the east to the Seaman marker. Flatt is just beyond and a little to the left from this marker. A very small stone, about fourteen inches high, inscribed "Georgia Flatt" marks the grave of his child who died April 2, 1883. George is beside the child, but his grave has no marker.

**319. Floyd, Charles*** (circa 1782–August 20, 1804). He was the only member of the Lewis and Clark Expedition to die during the journey. He probably died of a ruptured appendix. Floyd was buried on what is now known as "Floyd's Bluff" near Sioux City, Iowa. When the Missouri River cut into the banks and exposed some of Floyd's bones, his remains were moved to a new grave nearby. Later, in 1895, his bones were placed in urns and on August 20, 1895, the ninety-first anniversary of his death, the urns were reburied and covered by a concrete slab. A 100-foot-high monument was erected over the grave.

**320. Fly, Camillus S.*** (1850–October 12, 1901). He was a photographer at Tombstone, Arizona, and took the famous pictures of General George Crook's meeting with Geronimo. In 1895 he was elected sheriff of Cochise County, Arizona, and served two years. He died in Bisbee, Arizona, but his body was taken to Tombstone for burial in the Tombstone Cemetery (not Boothill). To locate the grave: follow Allen Street west to the cemetery on the left. A pink marble headstone on the right of the central drive marks his grave.

**321. Fontenelle, Logan** (May 6, 1825–July 17, 1855). He was a noted leader of the Omaha Indian tribe and was the son of Lucien Fontenelle, a famous fur trader of the West. He was killed in battle by the Sioux, and his body was returned to Bellevue, Nebraska, where he is buried. A large monument marks his grave.

**322. Ford, Charles Wilson "Charley"*** (July 9, 1857–May 6, 1884). He was the brother of Bob Ford, the man who killed Jesse James, and was in the room when the killing took place. He committed suicide by shooting himself in the heart with a pistol at Richmond, Missouri, and is buried in the Richmond city cemetery near the top of the hill, some say in the same grave with his brother, Bob. There is no marker for Charley, but there is a bronze, ground-level marker for Bob. To locate the grave: see Ford, Robert Newton "Bob."

**323. Ford, John Salmon "Rip"*** (May 26, 1815–November 3, 1897). At various times he was a soldier, a Texas Ranger, a doctor, a newspaperman, and a politician. He was commander of the Rio Grande District during the Civil War. After an illustrious career he died at San Antonio, Texas, at the age of eighty-two. He is buried there in the Confederate Cemetery. There is a large, pink marble official Texas state marker.

**324. Ford, Robert Newton "Bob"*** (January 31, 1862–June 8, 1892). He killed Jesse James while James was living in St. Joseph, Missouri, under the name of Thomas Howard. Ford was killed in Creede, Colorado, by Ed O'Kelley (sometimes called Ed O. Kelley). He was originally buried in the cemetery on the mountainside above Creede; a marker still indicates the original grave site. His body was later returned to Richmond, Missouri, and reinterred in the Richmond city cemetery on the west side of the city. The grave is near the top of the hill and is indicated by a ground-level, bronze marker. To locate the grave: enter the cemetery through the very narrow, easternmost entrance and go straight ahead until the drive starts to curve left. Ford's grave is on the right, not far from the curve.

**325. Fornoff, Frederick "Fred"*** (February 6, 1859–November 26, 1935). At various times he was a miner, a brick maker, and a lawman. He was a member of the Rough Riders in the Spanish-American War and later commanded the New Mexico Mounted Police. He died in Sheridan, Wyoming, but his body was shipped to Santa Fe, New Mexico, for burial in the national cemetery, Section T, Grave 8. There is a regulation United States military marker.

326. **Fountain, Albert Jennings\*** (October 23, 1838–circa April 1, 1896). A controversial figure, Fountain engaged in the practice of law, was a newspaperman, and at one time president of the Texas senate. He made many enemies, among them political boss Albert B. Fall and cattleman and politician Oliver Lee. In 1896, Fountain and his eight-year-old son, Henry, were returning to Mesilla, New Mexico, from a court session in Lincoln, New Mexico, when they disappeared without a trace. Oliver Lee; his foreman, Jim Gililland; and Bill McNew were tried for the murders but were acquitted. Many, however, still believed they were guilty. Although neither body was ever found, there is a memorial United States military headstone in Section A, Block 12, Lot 18–19 in the Masonic Cemetery at Las Cruces, New Mexico.

327. **Fraker, Charles L.\*** (1841–1922). He drove wagons on the Santa Fe Trail (1855–1868). He is buried in a little cemetery at the foot of Wagon Mound, just east of the little town of Wagon Mound, New Mexico. A large stone with a metal plaque marks his grave.

328. **Fransal, August\*** (August 9, 1843–July 30, 1927). He was a stagecoach driver on the Ben Ficklin Overland Mail Line from San Antonio to El Paso, Texas, and served as a Texas Ranger (1881–1882) under Captain George Baylor. He is buried at Sierra Blanca, Texas. A rectangular marble stone about one foot high and a Texas historical marker are at his grave.

329. **Frazer, George A. "Bud"\*** (April 18, 1864–September 14, 1896). He was a Texas Ranger and, later, sheriff of Reeves County, Texas, from 1891 to 1895. "Killing Jim" Miller used a shotgun to kill Frazer in a Toyah, Texas, saloon. He was first buried at Toyah, but later his sister, Ella, had the body removed to East Hill Cemetery in Fort Stockton, Texas. His sisters, Ella (1871–1953) and Emma (1869–

1912), are also buried in the same plot. Another sister, Annie Riggs (November 24, 1858–May 17, 1931; her husband was the Texas gunman, Barney Riggs), is buried in a nearby plot. There is a small headstone for Frazer. To locate the grave: from US 285 south of Fort Stockton, follow Cemetery Drive to the cemetery. Enter through the gate in the stone wall and drive to the back (south) side of the cemetery. Frazer's marker is on the left and is beside the eighth cross-lane from the entrance. Annie Riggs (his sister) is buried on the right of the main drive near the sixth cross-lane. Many relatives of both are buried in this cemetery.

330. **Free, Mickey** (October 1851–December 31, 1913). He was a famous scout for the United States Army during the Southwest Indian Wars. He was originally buried at the Fort Apache military cemetery in Arizona. When the bodies of all military personnel were removed to the national cemetery at Santa Fe, New Mexico, Free's body was reinterred on a high point of land overlooking his home-land. His United States military headstone has been stolen. An Indian guide from Fort Apache is necessary when attempting to locate the grave.

331. **French, John William "Peter"*** (April 30, 1849–December 26, 1897). He was a famous Oregon cattleman and ran the P Ranch near present-day Frenchglen, Oregon. It was the largest ranch in the eastern part of the state. He was shot and killed in the Sodbusters War by Ed Oliver. Oliver was tried and acquitted. French is buried in Oak Hills Cemetery in Red Bluff, California. The grave is marked and is near the office.

332. **Fryer, Pauline Cushman.** See Cushman, Pauline.

**G**

**333. Gabriel, J.P. "Pete"** (circa 1842–July 30, 1898). He was born in Germany but was brought to America as a child. He served as a lawman in California and Arizona for more than twenty years. Pete was elected sheriff of Pinal County, Arizona, three times and was also a deputy United States marshal. Enmity developed between Gabriel and Joe Phy, a friend who had also served as his deputy. This resulted in a gunfight at the Tunnel Saloon in Florence, Arizona. Phy received fatal wounds and Gabriel was seriously injured but finally recovered. Pete owned mining property in his later years. He died, probably from drinking poisoned water, and was buried by friends near his mine at Dripping Springs, northeast of Florence. A bronze plaque marks his grave.

**334. Gall "Pizi"\*** (circa 1832–December 5, 1894). He was a Hunkpapa Sioux war chief and led one band of Indians at the Battle of the Little Bighorn. He is buried near the center of the St. Elizabeth Mission Cemetery, which is just north of the little town of Wakpala, South Dakota. The cemetery is on the top of a hill and is not the one beside the Catholic church. There is a marker.

**335. Gallagher, Jack\*** (?–January 14, 1864). He was a member of Henry Plummer's gang of outlaws known as "The Innocents." He was hanged by vigilantes in Virginia City, Montana, and is buried there in Boot Hill Cemetery. Four other gang members were hanged with him. They were Asa Hayes Lyons, George Lane, Frank Parrish, and Boone Helm. All five graves are marked.

**336. Galusha, Jandon R.\*** (May 24, 1880–December 31, 1961; NOTE:

his headstone gives 1878 as the year of his birth but his death certificate gives 1880). Born at Palmyra, Missouri, he lived for a time in Mitchell County, Texas, before settling in Guadalupe County, New Mexico. He became a railroad policeman and a special duty New Mexico Mounted Police officer. He captured train robber "Broncho Bill" Walters after Walters had escaped from the territorial prison at Santa Fe. After New Mexico gained statehood, Galusha joined the reorganized New Mexico Mounted Police and also held a commission as a deputy United States marshal. In 1916 he became marshal of Albuquerque, New Mexico, and held that job for ten years. He is credited with solving the murder of Clyde Armour, heir to the Armour meat packing fortune. Elbert W. Blancett was later hanged for the murder after having been arrested by Galusha. Jandon died at Albuquerque and was buried in Fairview Park Cemetery. To locate the grave: from Central Avenue, go south on Yale Boulevard. After about five blocks on Yale, turn left into the cemetery and drive straight ahead to the flag pole. Park. Count four rows of graves on the left after passing a lane on the right. Walk left down this row some twenty graves to the ground-level marker. Galusha's wife, Effie B. (1880–1962), is buried beside him.

337. **Garnier, Baptiste "Little Bat"**\* (1854–December 16, 1900). He was a scout for the United States Army and was shot and killed by Jim Haguewood, a bartender, at Fort Robinson, Nebraska. He was originally buried at Fort Robinson military cemetery near Crawford, Nebraska, but was later reinterred at Fort McPherson national cemetery, about twelve miles southeast of North Platte, Nebraska. There is a standard United States military marker.

338. **Garrett, Buck**\* (May 24, 1871–May 6, 1929). He was an Oklahoma lawman who took part in Wyoming's Johnson County War as a member of the Invaders. He died of paralysis and is buried in Rose Hill Cemetery in Ardmore, Oklahoma. To locate the grave: enter the cemetery from C Street and go straight ahead to Lane 15. Turn right and go to a small brick mausoleum. Turn right at the first lane beyond the mausoleum and go past the first cross-lane. About forty or fifty feet beyond the intersection, the grave will be found on the right, next to the drive. This is Block 153, Lot 19, NW$^{1}/_{4}$. A large

marker inscribed "Garrett" marks the family plot. To locate the cemetery, which is on the south side of Ardmore: from downtown, go east on Main Street and turn right on Washington, which curves left at the underpass and becomes Lake Murray Drive. Turn right from Lake Murray Drive onto C Street, which leads to the cemetery.

**339. Garrett, Patrick Floyd Jarvis "Pat"*** (June 5, 1850–February 29, 1908). At one time he was a Texas Ranger and was later sheriff of Lincoln County, New Mexico. He killed Billy the Kid at Fort Sumner, New Mexico. At other times, Garrett was a buffalo hunter and a rancher. He was shot and killed a few miles east of Las Cruces, New Mexico, probably by either Wayne Brazel or "Killing Jim" Miller. He is buried in the Masonic Cemetery at Las Cruces, New Mexico. His grave is on the west side of Compress Road in a plot with his wife, Apolinaria G. Garrett (1861–1936); two sons, Patrick Floyd, Jr. (1896–1927) and Dudley Poe (1882–1932); and a daughter, Ida Garrett (1881–1896). To locate the cemetery: going west on I-10, exit to US 85 north on the west side of Las Cruces. Go a few blocks north on US 85 to Amador Road. Turn right on Amador for a short distance to Compress Road. Go left on Compress Road to the cemetery.

**340. Gass, Patrick*** (June 12, 1771–April 2, 1870). He was a sergeant on the Lewis and Clark Expedition and wrote a book relating his experiences. He served in the War of 1812 and lost an eye in the Battle of Lundy's Lane. Gass was the last living member of the expedition until his death in 1870. He died in Brooke County, West Virginia, at the age of ninety-eight. He was first buried on the Bauer Farm (later the Shrimplin Farm) in the Buffalo District of Brooke County. On March 15, 1921, his remains were taken up and reinterred on a prominent knoll in Brooke County Cemetery in Wellsburg, West Virginia, beside his wife, Maria Hamilton Gass (1812–1849). Patrick was sixty years old when he married Maria, and they had a total of seven children. He was forty-one years older than his wife. A beautiful, gray marble stone on a hillside in the southeast part of the cemetery marks the graves of Patrick and his wife.

**341. Gentles, William\*** (September 1828–March 20, 1878). Born in Ireland, Gentles enlisted in the United States Army in 1856 and served more than twenty years. He was the soldier who killed Sioux chief Crazy Horse at Fort Robinson, Nebraska, on September 5, 1877. The chief had resisted when he was about to be placed in the guardhouse and grabbed a knife. He slashed Little Big Man who was with him, and Gentles then thrust his bayonet almost through Crazy Horse. Crazy Horse died within a few hours. Gentles died of asthma at Fort Douglas, Utah, some eight months later and was buried in the national cemetery at Fort Douglas, which is on the east side of Salt Lake City. He is interred in Section 4, Grave 16. To locate the grave: enter the cemetery and look ahead and to the left for the large brown obelisk of James Duane Doty. From that monument, go up the hill to the next row of graves and then to the right for three or four graves. Gentles' regulation United States military headstone incorrectly gives his date of death as May 20 instead of the correct date of March 20.

**342. George, Hiram J. "Hi"\*** (April 7, 1834–October 22, 1911). "Hi" George was a member of William Clarke Quantrill's command briefly in 1862 before joining the regular Confederate Army that August. He later rejoined Quantrill and took part in the sacking of Lawrence, Kansas. Hiram also took part in the Battle of Baxter Springs. He died of a stroke in 1911 on his farm near Oak Grove, Missouri, and is buried in the George (or Owings) Cemetery. To locate the cemetery: see George, John Hicks.

**343. George, John Hicks\*** (March 24, 1836–July 29, 1926). As a young civilian, he was repeatedly hanged for several minutes at a time by Union soldiers trying to force him to tell the whereabouts of William Clarke Quantrill and his men. He refused to tell. He soon joined Quantrill's command during the early part of the Civil War, as did his brother, Hiram J. In 1862, he joined General Jo Shelby's brigade. After being wounded, he was captured and sent to prison in Illinois. Following a prisoner exchange, he moved through the South until he finally surrendered in Louisiana. After the war he became a carpenter and then a farmer in Missouri. He died of natural causes and was buried in the George (or Owings) Cemetery southwest of

Oak Grove, Missouri. There is a large, inscribed headstone. His brother, Hiram, and several other family members are buried there. To locate the cemetery: from Oak Grove go south on Highway F 1.2 miles to a gravel road to the right (west). Turn right for one mile and then left a short distance to the small cemetery on the right.

344. **Gerard, Frederic Francis*** (November 14, 1829–January 29, 1913). A Missourian, Gerard traded throughout the Dakotas and became fluent in several Indian languages. Shortly after he married an Arikara woman, he became an interpreter and was assigned to Reno's command in Custer's expedition against the Sioux. His later years were spent in Minnesota where he died at St. Cloud in 1913. Gerard is buried in the St. Joseph Cemetery in St. Joseph, Minnesota. To locate the cemetery and grave: from County Road 75 in St. Joseph, go south on College Avenue. The cemetery is on the right, immediately past the St. Joseph Catholic Church and the St. Benedict's Convent. Enter the cemetery and walk to the back (west) side. Turn right and go five rows of graves to Gerard's twenty-four-by-twenty-inch, inscribed, granite headstone.

345. **Geronimo "Goyahkla"*** (June 1829–February 17, 1909). He was a Chiricahua Apache and led raids against Mexicans and Americans in southern Arizona and New Mexico as well as Mexico. Geronimo surrendered in 1886 and his band was sent to Florida, then Alabama, and finally in 1894, to Fort Sill, Oklahoma. He died of pneumonia at Fort Sill and is buried in the Apache cemetery a few miles from the Fort Still post cemetery. A map showing the location of the cemetery can be obtained at the entrance to the Fort Sill Military Reservation, or instructions can be obtained at any of the museums at Fort Sill. A stone pyramid marks Geronimo's grave.

346. **Gildea, Augustine Montague "Gus"*** (April 23, 1854–August 10, 1935). He was the son of James E. and Mary Adele Lorraine Gildea. He married Virginia Rubinson Boehmer (May 6, 1862–December 11, 1956) at San Antonio, Texas, on July 22, 1885. They became the parents of four children, Helen Cecilia "Nellie," Grazella, Ethyl Gertrude, and Mary. Gus and Virginia were later divorced. She died in Del Rio, Texas, and is buried there in Westlawn Cemetery. Gus

was a Texas Ranger for a short time and was a deputy sheriff of Kinney County, Texas. He was later one of John Selman's "scouts" and was on Territorial Governor Lew Wallace's list of wanted men in New Mexico for a time. He owned a small gold mine in the Dragoon Mountains of Arizona in his later life. When he became ill, friends took him to Douglas, Arizona, where he died. He was taken to Bisbee, Arizona, for burial in Evergreen Cemetery in Section 20. His grave is in the extreme northeast corner of the cemetery and is covered by a concrete slab. There is a small, inscribed marble headstone. Gus's mother was the daughter of Edward Louis Lorraine and Suzanne LaFitte. Suzanne is believed by descendants to have been the sister of Jean LaFitte, the famous pirate.

347. **Gillett, James Buchanan "Jim"**\* (November 4, 1856–June 11, 1937). He was a Texas Ranger and later city marshal of El Paso, Texas. After his lawman days he became a cattleman and had a ranch near Marfa, Texas, where he died. He is buried in the Marfa Cemetery. To locate the grave: from Highway 90, turn north on the street bordering the cemetery. Drive to the third entrance and turn left. The Gillett grave is on the left in the sixth block from the entrance. The entrance lane is bordered on the left by a row of cedars. There is a marker.

348. **Gillett, James S.**\* (April 1, 1810–May 17, 1874). He was the father of Texas Ranger Jim Gillett and was famous in his own right. A major in the army (1846–49), Gillett served in the Mexican War, was adjutant general of Texas (1851–56), served in the Texas Rangers (1859–60), and in the Confederate Army (1861–65). He died in Lampasas, Texas, and is buried there in Oak Hill Cemetery, Block 1. His wife, Elizabeth Harper Gillett, is buried beside him. To locate the cemetery and grave: from Key Street (US 281) in downtown Lampasas, turn north on North Avenue and drive ten blocks to Porter Street. Turn right on Porter for a few blocks to the cemetery. Enter and drive to the extreme rear of the cemetery. This is Block 1. Look for the official Texas historical marker at the grave.

349. **Glaspie, Robert M. "Bob"**\* (1861–June 29, 1946). When Mort Blevins disappeared at the beginning of the Pleasant Valley War in

Arizona, Glaspie and some of his friends quit their jobs with the Hashknife Outfit to enter the valley and search for Blevins. When they approached a cabin occupied by members of the Tewksbury faction, a fight erupted. Hamp Blevins and John Paine were killed; Glaspie and Tom Tucker were seriously injured. Bob was shot through the leg and crawled for three days and two nights without food until he reached the Blevins Ranch where his wounds were treated. He took no further part in the conflict and later worked as a cowboy in New Mexico and Arizona. He died in Coolidge, Arizona, at age eighty-six and was buried in the Valley Memorial Cemetery, which is on the north side of Highway 287 between Florence and Coolidge. He is in Section Y, Block 20, Lot 3, Grave 6. His wife, Nana E. (1874–1958), is buried beside him. A ground-level double stone marks their graves in the second row of burials from the center north-south lane, about two-thirds of the way down the lane on the right.

350.  **Glispin, James "Jim"**\* (1844–November 23, 1890). He was the Minnesota sheriff who led the posse that killed Charlie Pitts and captured the Younger brothers near Medelia, Minnesota, after their attempt to rob a bank in Northfield, Minnesota. Glispin was later marshal of Spokane (1885) and sheriff (1887–1888) of Spokane County in Washington State. He died after a short illness at Spokane and is buried there in Fairmount Memorial Park beside his mother, Anastasia Glispin (1810–1894). The graves are marked.

351.  **Godey, Alexis**\* (1818–January 19, 1889). He was a fur trapper and a friend of Jim Bridger and Kit Carson. He later became a famous scout and explorer and was with John C. Frémont on one expedition. He died of blood poisoning after being accidentally scratched by a lion at a circus. He is buried beside his son, Alexis, Jr., in Block 272, Lot 1, in Union Cemetery in Bakersfield, California. There is a four-foot-high, white marble headstone which is weathered yellow. His son, Alexis, Jr., died April 8, 1887, at the age of twenty.

352.  **Goff, Thomas Jefferson "Tom"**\* (March 11, 1871–September 13, 1905). Goff was born in Keytesville, Missouri, but his family moved to Texas when he was a baby and ranched at Throckmorton. He

*Geronimo, Apache cemetery, Fort Sill, Oklahoma.*

*James Butler "Wild Bill" Hickok, Mount Moriah Cemetery, Deadwood, South Dakota.*

worked as a cowboy on the Reynolds Ranch on the Clear Fork of the Brazos, helped drive a herd of cattle to North Dakota in 1887, and took part in several other drives. He joined the Texas Rangers in 1893. He married a girl named "Ruby" and they had one son called "Little Tom." Goff was killed by Augustin Garcia as Garcia was being taken to jail at Terlingua, Texas. Tom's horse slipped and fell on a steep rocky trail, pinning Goff underneath. Garcia grabbed Goff's rifle and shot him. He died a few hours later. Garcia was never captured. Goff was buried at Throckmorton, Texas, beside his grandmother. To locate the Throckmorton Cemetery and grave: turn off Highway 183, go east on Fifth Street and then turn right and then left to the cemetery. Enter the stone gate entrance and go straight ahead to the large, black Navarro monument. About fifty feet beyond is Tom's small, gray sandstone marker which is about 1½ feet tall. A small, three-foot obelisk is beside Tom's grave.

353. **Goldsby, Crawford "Cherokee Bill"**\* (February 8, 1876–March 17, 1896). He was an Oklahoma renegade of mixed ancestry. Goldsby killed several men and was hanged at Fort Smith, Arkansas, for the murder of prison guard Lawrence Keating. He is buried in the Cherokee national cemetery at Fort Gibson, Oklahoma. There is a ground-level marker bearing several names, including that of Crawford Goldsby. The marker is near the large Ross marker.

354. **Goodnight, Charles**\* (March 5, 1836–December 12, 1929). He was a Texas and New Mexico cattleman and was at one time owner of the famous JA Ranch in the Texas Panhandle. Goodnight is generally credited with having developed the chuckwagon. He died in Tucson, Arizona, but was buried beside his wife, Mary Ann "Mollie," in the little Goodnight Cemetery at Goodnight, Texas. The graves are enclosed by a fence. The cemetery is a short distance north of US 287 at Goodnight. The Goodnight home still stands on the south side of US 287 in the little town.

355. **Goodyear, Miles Morris**\* (February 24, 1817–November 12, 1849). Born in Connecticut, he became a mountain man and gold miner. He accompanied the Marcus Whitman party to Fort Hall in 1836 and then spent some time in the Northwest in the fur trading

business. Later he guided the Mormons to Salt Lake City, Utah. Goodyear discovered gold in California but died a short time thereafter of pneumonia. He is buried in the cemetery at Benicia, California. There is a headstone which reads, "The Mountaineer's Grave, Here Sleeps Near the Western Ocean Wave, Miles M. Goodyear." The Goodyear plot is at the top of the hill; many of the stones are broken and some of the inscriptions cannot be read.

**356. Gotebo "Kau-Tau-Bone"*** (1847–1927). He was a Kiowa Indian leader and was the first Kiowa to be baptized at the Rainy Mountain Church. He is buried in the Rainy Mountain Cemetery in Oklahoma. There is an inscribed headstone of pink marble, about four feet tall. To locate the cemetery: from the intersection of Highway 9 and Highway 115 in Mountain View, Oklahoma, go west on Highway 9 for almost two miles. Turn left (south) on a paved road for 2.2 miles. Turn right (west) on another paved road for about 0.5 mile; then jog left and then right again to the cemetery. The Rainy Mountain Baptist Church is nearby.

**357. Goyahkla.** See Geronimo.

**358. Graham, John*** (?–September 21, 1887). He was killed by a posse led by Sheriff William Mulvenon during the Pleasant Valley War in Arizona. Earlier he, along with Tom Graham and others, had killed John Tewksbury and William Jacobs. He is buried in the Young Cemetery just north of Young, Arizona, on the west side of the road leading to Heber, Arizona. There is a ground-level marker among the weeds.

**359. Graham, Thomas "Tom"*** (July 26, 1853–August 2, 1892). He was the leader of the Graham faction in the Pleasant Valley War in Arizona (the Tewksbury-Graham Feud). He was killed by Ed Tewksbury, who shot him from his wagon near present-day Tempe, Arizona. Some historians say that it was John Rhodes who killed Graham. Many years later, Ed Tewksbury's widow told how her husband had committed the murder. Graham is buried in the Old Pioneer Cemetery in Phoenix, Arizona. This cemetery is bounded on the south by West Harrison Street between South Fifteenth and

South Thirteenth avenues. Graham's grave is just inside the Harrison Street entrance on the right. The grave of his child is beside him. In 1986, his headstone (a marble obelisk with an anchor and Ancient Order of United Workers symbol) was overturned and broken. It has since been repaired (1990). It is in Block 20, Lot 1, Grave 7.

360. **Graham, William\*** (circa 1869–October 17, 1887). He was killed in a gunfight by Deputy Sheriff James D. Houck during the Pleasant Valley War in Arizona. He is buried in the Young Cemetery which is just north of Young, Arizona, and on the west side of the road leading to Heber, Arizona. There is a small, ground-level marker among the weeds.

361. **Gressett, Susan I.\*** (1834–September 19, 1870). She was the daughter of William Barret Travis. She is buried in the Old Masonic Cemetery at Chapel Hill, Texas, which is east of Brenham, Texas. Her brother, Charles Edward Travis, is also buried here. There is a marker.

362. **Gridley, Ruel\*** (January 23, 1829–November 24, 1870). On his monument are the words, "The Soldiers Friend." He helped raise $275,000 during the Civil War by auctioning a sack of flour, starting in Austin, Nevada, and continuing in many other cities. The money was turned over to the Sanitary Commission, forerunner of the Red Cross. He is buried in the Stockton Rural Cemetery, Stockton, California, beside his wife, Susan, who died March 11, 1910. He is in the veterans' section. To locate the grave: on entering the cemetery from Cemetery Lane, keep to the right until reaching the veterans' section beside the circular drive. His monument is very large and is California Landmark 801.

363. **Griego, Juan Francisco "Pancho"** (1837–November 1, 1875). He was a New Mexico gunman who killed many men. He was shot and killed by Clay Allison in Cimarron, New Mexico, at age thirty-eight. Griego was originally buried at Cimarron, but his body was removed by his wealthy mother in 1877 and reinterred March 4 of that year in Rosario Cemetery in Santa Fe, New Mexico, in Section Z. Rosario Cemetery adjoins the Santa Fe national cemetery on the east

side. Cemetery records confirm the reburial, but I was unable to locate the headstone in June 1988.

**364. Griffin, B.G.*** (April 24, 1794–May 23, 1867). He was the jailer in Richmond, Missouri, who was shot and killed by the James-Younger Gang when they robbed the Richmond bank in 1867. His son, G.F.S. Griffin, was also killed during the robbery. B.G. Griffin is buried in the Old Pioneer Cemetery (Mormon) in Richmond. His wife, Lucy Asbury Griffin (June 30, 1803–March 26, 1876), is buried beside him, as is his son. Flat marble stones cover the graves.

**365. Grimes, Ahijah W. "Hi"*** (July 5, 1850–July 19, 1878). Born in Bastrop, Texas, he was at one time a Texas Ranger. While he was deputy sheriff of Williamson County, Texas, he was killed in a gunfight with the Sam Bass Gang at Round Rock, Texas. He is buried in the extreme northeast corner of the Round Rock Cemetery, about sixty feet from the east fence and about twenty-five feet from the north fence. Both the original headstone and a new marble stone (1991) mark the grave.

**366. Grover, Abner T. "Sharp"*** (circa 1822–February 16, 1869; NOTE: His middle initial is variously given as "T," "L," or "S," and his death is sometimes given as June 16, 1869; his grave marker gives February 16, 1869). He was said by some to be the greatest scout in the United States Army. He and scout William Comstock were detailed to visit Chief Turkey Leg's camp to obtain information on recent Indian uprisings. They were driven from the camp and both men were shot. Comstock died instantly. Grover escaped and finally made his way back to Fort Wallace in western Kansas. He later took part in the Battle of Beecher Island in eastern Colorado. Grover was killed in a fight at Pond Creek, Kansas, a small settlement near Fort Wallace. He is buried in the old Fort Wallace Cemetery a mile east and a mile south of the old fort. There is an inscribed wooden marker which says that he was killed by John Mooney. Other sources say that the man's name was John Morrissey.

**367. Guerrier, Edmund "Ed"*** (January 26, 1840–February 22, 1921). He was a half-blood army scout. His mother was a full-blood

Cheyenne and his father a French fur trader. He scouted for General Winfield Scott Hancock and General George Armstrong Custer. The latter part of his life was spent in Oklahoma, where he became a successful rancher. An Oklahoma town was named for him although the name has since been anglicized to "Geary." He died at his ranch and is buried in the Geary Cemetery. His wife, Julia Bent Guerrier, and a son survived him. There is a large, inscribed headstone, which probably is not at the site of the actual grave.

**368. Gunnison, John William*** (November 11, 1812–October 26, 1853). Gunnison was a topographical engineer and a graduate of the United States Military Academy. He took part in the Seminole War as well as the removal of the Cherokees from Georgia, Tennessee, and North Carolina to Indian Territory. He worked on surveys throughout the United States. In 1853, Pahvant Utes led by Mosnoquas killed him and seven other members of his surveying party near Sevier Lake in western Utah. Although struck by several arrows, Gunnison died from a gunshot wound to the head. A few days later his remains were taken to Fillmore, Utah, and buried in the south-central part of Fillmore Cemetery, Block 54, Lot 4. Many years later, Dr. Nolie Mumey placed a small granite headstone bearing a bronze plaque at the grave site. The cemetery is south and east of town and is just beyond the Mormon Church.

**369. Hadji Ali "Hi Jolly"*** (circa 1828–December 14, 1902).  He was a Syrian camel driver.  When camels were brought to the United States in 1856 and 1857 for experimental desert use, Hi Jolly came with them.  When the camel experiment was disbanded, Hi Jolly stayed in Arizona and did some mining.  Upon his death in 1902, he was buried in the Quartzite Cemetery in Quartzite, Arizona.  The cemetery is about 200 yards east of the highway.  The grave is marked by a pyramid of native stone topped by a copper camel.

**370. Haines, Wiley Green*** (October 7, 1860–September 24, 1928).  He was an Oklahoma lawman and a deputy United States marshal.  He died of a heart attack on the courthouse steps at Pawhuska, Oklahoma, and is buried in the first grave on the right on entering the Hominy Cemetery in Hominy, Oklahoma.  There is a marker.  The cemetery is just north of town beside Highway 99.

**371. Hall, Leigh "Lee"*** (October 9, 1849–March 17, 1911).  He was a Texas Ranger and later served in other capacities as a lawman.  Hall became an alcoholic and died in San Antonio, Texas, at age sixty-one.  He is buried in the San Antonio national cemetery a short distance from the entrance.  There is a large marble monument and an official Texas historical marker.  The San Antonio national cemetery is at 517 Paso Hondo Street.

**372. Hall, Maggie "Molly B'Dam"*** (November 26, 1853–January 17, 1888).  She was a gold camp pleasure queen.  After many stops throughout the West, she arrived at Murray, Idaho, in 1884.  Maggie died in Murray after a lingering illness and is buried in the Murray

103

Cemetery. There is a marker at her grave.

373. **Hamblin, Jacob\*** (April 12, 1819–August 31, 1886). Known as the "Colonizer," he was a famous Mormon who became friends with the Navajo Indians. He died at age sixty-seven and was first buried at Pleasanton, New Mexico. Later his body was removed to the Alpine Cemetery at Alpine, Arizona. To locate the cemetery: from Alpine, drive east on US 180 about 1 1/2 miles. A little dirt road goes north about 100 yards to the cemetery. More than thirty relatives of Jacob are also buried here. Hamblin died when he fell off a load of lumber and was crushed by a wheel. There is a large headstone.

374. **Hanks, Camillo (Camilla) "Deaf Charlie"** (1863–April 16, 1902). He also used the name "Charley Jones." He was at one time a member of Butch Cassidy's Wild Bunch. He was killed by officer Pink Taylor while resisting arrest in San Antonio, Texas, and is buried in Cemetery Number 3 in San Antonio.

375. **Hanks, Charles R. "Charley"\*** (November 6, 1881–February 19, 1970). As a fourteen-year-old, he tended horses for Butch Cassidy. He died in Green River, Utah, and is buried there in the Green River Cemetery, about one mile east of town and north of US 50. There is an inscribed marker. NOTE: There are several Gillies buried here. They were relatives of Butch Cassidy, whose mother was a Gillies.

376. **Hanks, Romulus "Rome"\*** (February 14, 1822–December 30, 1876). He was a pioneer at Elgin, Kansas. He died there and is buried in the Elgin Cemetery northwest of town. There is an inscribed headstone. To locate the cemetery: see Coffee, Gideon H.

377. **Hardesty, R.J.\*** (1833–1910). He was a Dodge City, Kansas, pioneer and businessman. He is buried in Maple Grove Cemetery in Dodge City in Block 8, Lot 57, Grave 3. There is a marker. The old Hardesty home is part of the Dodge City museum complex.

378. **Hardin, John Wesley\*** (May 26, 1853–August 19, 1895). He was a Texas gunman and later a lawyer. He killed possibly as many as forty men. After serving a long prison sentence for killing lawman

Charley Webb, he moved to El Paso, Texas, to practice law. He was shot from behind and killed by John Selman. Hardin is buried in Concordia Cemetery in El Paso. There is a ground-level marker near the northwest corner of the cemetery. It was placed there in September 1965 by a committee led by C.L. Sonnichsen after years of feuding with cemetery officials who did not want the grave marked. The grave of John Selman, his killer, is nearby but unmarked.

379. **Hardin, Joseph G. "Joe"**\* (January 5, 1850–May 31, 1874). He was a lawyer and the brother of John Wesley Hardin. After John Wesley killed Deputy Sheriff Charley Webb, a mob hanged Joe and two of the Dixon brothers, William and Tom, at Comanche, Texas. The three were originally buried on a hillside near the Hardin home, but were later removed to the Comanche Cemetery and placed in a common grave. Small, white, inscribed stones, placed there around 1990, mark the graves, which are in the northwest quadrant of the cemetery beside one of the drives.

380. **Harkey, Daniel R. "Dee"**\* (March 27, 1866–June 17, 1958). He was a New Mexico lawman and wrote a book, *Mean as Hell,* about his experiences. He died in Carlsbad, New Mexico, and is buried in the Carlsbad Cemetery. His grave is in the International Order of Odd Fellows Section, Block 24, Lot 1, Space 4. His wife, Sophie N. (January 7, 1869–April 17, 1935), is buried beside him. The two graves are marked by a single headstone of marble. Their daughter, Myrtle D. Harkey (September 3, 1899–January 13, 1960), is buried beside them.

381. **Harmonson, G. Frank.**\* (August 28, 1856–January 19, 1889; Note: This name is usually incorrectly spelled "Harmison"). He was a lawman and was killed by outlaw George Marlow in a gunfight near Graham, Texas. He is buried in Oak Grove Cemetery in Graham. His grave is about fifty feet southwest of that of Sheriff M.D. Wallace. Also in the Harmonson plot are his wife, Cornelia Ann Harmonson (1864–1937), and their son, William J. Harmonson (February 3, 1883–December 22, 1908).

**382. Harris, Martin\*** (May 18, 1783–July 10, 1875). He was one of the Three Witnesses to the Book of Mormon. He is buried in the Clarkson Cemetery in Clarkson, Utah. There is a very tall monument of dark gray marble and a historical marker. Clarkson can be reached by driving twelve miles north from Logan, Utah, on US 91 to Richmond, Utah. At Richmond, turn left (west) on Utah 142 for eleven miles.

**383. Harris, William H.\*** (July 11, 1845–February 6, 1895). He was part owner of the Long Branch Saloon in Dodge City, Kansas, and a member of the Dodge City Peace Commission. After becoming influential in politics in the East, he went to Kansas City, Missouri. He suffered financial difficulties, and in 1895, he committed suicide by taking an overdose of morphine. His funeral was held in the Calvary Baptist Church, and he was buried in Union Cemetery in Kansas City, Missouri. His grave is in Section 3.1, Lot 4R, which is in the southeast section of the cemetery. There is a ground-level marker of marble.

**384. Hart, Caleb Lawson "Loss"\*** (1862–January 31, 1934). He was a deputy United States marshal in Oklahoma Territory. As a member of a posse, he shot and killed outlaw Bill Dalton on June 8, 1894. He died of natural causes and is buried in the McGee Cemetery about two miles north of Stratford, Oklahoma. A large marble monument marks the grave site. NOTE: A recent book says that Selden Lindsey killed Bill Dalton.

**385. Hays, John Coffee "Jack"\*** (January 28, 1817–April 21, 1883). He was a commander of the Texas Rangers and later founder of Oakland, California. He died near Piedmont and is buried in Mountain View Cemetery in Oakland, California, in Plot 2, Lot 15. There is a very large, impressive monument and a historical marker.

**386. Hazen, Joseph "Joe"\*** (1854–June 6, 1899). He served two terms as sheriff of Converse County, Wyoming. On June 5, 1899, Hazen was shot by outlaws about forty miles north of Casper, Wyoming, and died the next day. He is buried in the Douglas Cemetery, Douglas, Wyoming, Sections 18 and 19, Block 7, Lot 1, Grave 3. There is a headstone.

**387. Heddon, Cyrus*** (March 4, 1821–March 29, 1911). He took part in the famous Indian fight at Battle Rock on the Oregon coast. He later ran a store at Scottsburg, Oregon, for more than sixty years. He died at age ninety-one and is buried in the Scottsburg Cemetery about one mile east of town on the north side of Highway 38. To locate the cemetery and grave: from Highway 38, about a mile from town turn north on Golden Avenue and then left on a gravel road to the cemetery. The Heddon plot is to the left of the entrance gate in the southeast corner of the cemetery. There are many Heddons in the plot, and all of the graves are marked.

**388. Helm, Boone*** (January 28, 1827–January 14, 1864). Born in Kentucky, he spent his early years in Missouri. He later became a member of Sheriff Henry Plummer's outlaw band in Virginia City, Montana, and at one time supposedly was guilty of cannibalism. He was hanged along with four others by vigilantes. All five are buried in Boot Hill Cemetery at Virginia City in marked graves.

**389. Henderson, Howard*** (1842–November 18, 1908). He went to Texas in 1857 and served in the Union Army during the Civil War. He survived the Battle of the Nueces in 1862 and later served as a Texas Ranger. He married Narcissa Turknett in 1866, and they settled six miles west of Kerrville, Texas. He is buried in the Henderson Cemetery two miles north of State Road 27 near Kerrville. A dirt road leads to the nicely maintained cemetery. There is a historical marker where the road to the cemetery leaves State Road 27.

**390. Hendricks, A.R.*** (?–December 27, 1875). He was a friend of Jim Taylor and was killed, along with Jim and Mace Arnold, during the Taylor-Sutton Feud in DeWitt County, Texas. He is buried in the Taylor-Bennett Cemetery a few miles south of Cuero, Texas. Hendricks' wife was Elizabeth Day Bennett Rivers Kelly Hendricks (1836–1887). To locate the cemetery: see Taylor, James "Jim."

**391. Hennessey, Patrick "Pat"*** (?–July 4, 1874). He was a freighter who was killed when his wagon train, which was on its way to the Kiowa Agency on the Chisholm Trail, was attacked by Indians. Pat was tied to a wagon wheel and burned. Three of his drivers were also killed. A large, gray granite stone marks his grave in the little town of Hennessey, Oklahoma.

392. **Henry, Andrew** (circa 1775–January 19, 1832). He was a fur trapper and trader in the Northwest and was a major in the United States Army during the War of 1812. He lived his last years in Washington County, Missouri, where he died. His grave site is unknown.

393. **Herron, Alice I.*** (September 25, 1869–January 19, 1893). She was the first wife of James "Jim" Herron. She is buried in the Beaver Cemetery in Beaver, Oklahoma. The cemetery is about three miles south of town and about 0.6 mile west of US 270. To locate the grave: after turning west off US 270, drive up a lane lined with trees for about 0.6 mile and turn left on the first lane entering the cemetery. Go to the far end of the cemetery (pass a white water tank) and turn right to the third poorly defined lane. Turn right again, and go to the top of the hill (about 100 feet). The grave is on the left beside the pink marble Loufbourrow marker. Alice's headstone is of white marble and is about six feet tall. Buried beside her are her parents, Ansel and Eliza J. Groves, and her brother, Gene Groves (1872–1924).

394. **Herron, Anna May*** (February 27, 1876–November 17, 1904). She was the second wife of Jim Herron and is buried in the Tombstone Cemetery in Tombstone, Arizona. To locate the cemetery and grave: follow Allen Street west to the cemetery on the left. The grave is to the right of the central drive and is marked by a gray metal obelisk. A daughter of Jim and Anna May, Rita Herron McGrew (1897–1985), is buried beside her mother.

395. **Herron, James "Jim"*** (1866–September 4, 1949). He was the first sheriff of Beaver County, Oklahoma, and later was on the Owl Hoot Trail for fifty years as the result of some trouble in Meade, Kansas. The appropriately titled book, *Fifty Years on the Owl Hoot Trail,* recounts his experiences. He died in California and is buried in the Hills Ferry Cemetery in Newman, California, in the Tony and Millie Borba plot (Block 77, Lot 10). Millie was Jim's daughter. A son, James, Jr., is buried in Superior, Arizona.

**396. Hesse, Fred George S.\*** (April 3, 1853–March 3, 1929). Hesse was
an Englishman who came to the United States in the early 1860s. He
learned ranching in Texas and later drove a herd of cattle to
Wyoming for the Frewen brothers. He started the 28 Ranch near
Buffalo, Wyoming, around 1891 and was one of the leaders of the
big stockmen prior to and during the Johnson County War. He and
Frank Canton may have been the killers of Orley "Ranger" Jones.
Hesse left Wyoming but returned in 1892 with a band of hired
gunmen, mostly Texans, to invade Johnson County in an attempt to
drive out or kill the small ranchers and homesteaders. He was
arrested along with other invaders but was never tried, and the
charges were eventually dropped. He became wealthy dealing in
cattle and oil. He died at his ranch and is buried in Willow Grove
Cemetery in Buffalo. A large, gray marble stone marks his grave.
Buried beside him are his wife, Isabella R. Sutherland Hesse (1860–
1952), and several children: Vivienne S. Hesse (1888–1975), Marion
Windsor Hesse (April 30, 1896–May 9, 1900), Horace Kemp Hesse
(October 14, 1890–May 9, 1900), and Ethelberta Plunkett Hesse
(May 9, 1885–May 20, 1900). All of the graves are in a long narrow
section to the right immediately after entering the cemetery.

**397. Heywood, Joseph Lee\*** (August 12, 1837–September 7, 1876). He
was the acting cashier of the First National Bank of Northfield,
Minnesota, who was killed by the James-Younger Gang in an
attempted bank robbery. He is buried in the Northfield Cemetery.
There is a grave marker. Heywood's portrait and a memorial tablet
hang in the Carleton College library. He had been the treasurer of
Carleton College at Northfield.

**398. Hickman, William Adams "Wild Bill"\*** (April 15, 1815–August
21, 1883). Born in Kentucky, Hickman became a member of the
Church of Jesus Christ of Latter Day Saints (Mormon) and had ten
wives. He fathered thirty-five children. At one time or another he
was a lawman, a trader, and an outlaw. He became known as
"Brigham's Destroying Angel," which became the title of his
autobiography. After being excommunicated from the church, he
moved to Wyoming, where he lived for some time about six miles
west of Lander. When his health failed, he was taken to Lander,

where he died at the Lander Hotel. He was first buried in the Lander Cemetery, but according to a 1988 book by a descendant, his body was later taken to an area near his home west of Lander and reburied. The author claims that a sandstone and rock structure on the Diamond H Ranch (private property) is Hickman's burial place. Many local residents express doubt, as do I after visiting the site in 1991. Only an exhumation could determine the truth.

**399. Hickok, James Butler "Wild Bill"*** (May 27, 1837–August 2, 1876). He was a famous lawman in Kansas. He was shot and killed by Jack McCall in a saloon in Deadwood, South Dakota. Hickok was first buried at Ingleside, near Deadwood, but in 1879, he was reinterred in Mount Moriah Cemetery in Deadwood. There is a large marker at the grave site. Calamity Jane is buried nearby.

**400. Higgins, John Calhoun Pinckney "Pink"*** (March 28, 1851–December 18, 1913). He was a Texas gunman and rancher who took part in the Higgins-Horrell Feud in Lampasas County. He later established a ranch in the Texas panhandle where he killed Billy Standifer in a classic gunfight. He died at his ranch near Spur, Texas, of a heart attack and is buried in the Spur Cemetery, Block 24, Lot 1. To locate the cemetery and grave: from Highway 70, take Cemetery Road one-half mile east and turn left at the second entrance. Go to the fourth cross-drive. The grave is here, on the northeast corner. His second wife, Lena Rivers Sweet Higgins (February 9, 1868–December 28, 1937), is buried beside him. Higgins' headstone gives December 21, 1913, as the date of his death; cemetery records show that is actually the date of his burial.

**401. Higley, Brewster, III*** (1822–May 11, 1911). He is credited with composing the song, "Home On the Range." His cabin, now a small museum, still stands north of Smith Center, Kansas, just off Highway 8. Higley is buried in Fairview Cemetery at Harrison and Grant streets in Shawnee, Oklahoma. His wife, Sarah Ellen Higley (1844–1911); son, Everett (1880–1914); and son's wife, Viola (1879–1962), are buried in the same plot. A large, gray granite stone marks the family plot.

**402. Hildebrand, Samuel "Sam"**\* (January 6, 1836–March 21, 1872). He served under William Quantrill during the Civil War. He was killed while resisting arrest by officer John L. Ragland in Pinckneyville, Perry County, Illinois. He was using the name "John Smith" at the time. He wounded Ragland with a knife before being shot through the head. His body was taken to Elvins, Missouri, and buried in the Hampton Cemetery. There is a small grave marker.

**403. Hindman, George**\* (?–April 1, 1878). He was a Lincoln County, New Mexico, deputy under Sheriff Pat Brady. Both Brady and Hindman were shot and killed on the streets of Lincoln, New Mexico, by Billy the Kid and members of his gang. He was buried beside Sheriff Brady on the Brady Ranch east of Lincoln. For exact location of the grave, see Brady, Patrick William. Hindman's headstone was missing in 1985 although Brady's was still in place.

**404. Hite, Clarence B.**\* (September 26, 1861–March 12, 1883). He was a cousin of Jesse and Frank James and lived in Adairsville, Kentucky. When the James boys were living in Tennessee, they often visited the Hites. Clarence is buried beside his wife, N. Cornelia Hite (November 25, 1854–July 29, 1886), in Greenwood Cemetery in Adairsville. To locate the cemetery and grave: from the square in Adairsville, follow Gallatin Street east about one-quarter mile to the cemetery on the left. Enter the cemetery at the first drive and go straight ahead about 110 feet. The grave is on the left beside the drive. It is directly in front of the pink marble Scruggs marker. There is a double headstone for Clarence and his wife.

**405. Hobek, "Ole"**\* (?–March 13, 1912; NOTE: His name is often spelled "Beck"). He was shot and killed, along with Ben Kilpatrick, by railroad express guard D.A. Trousdale when the two attempted to rob the Galveston, Harrisburg, and San Antonio Train No. 9, eleven miles east of Sanderson, Texas. The two were buried in the Cedar Grove Cemetery on the east side of Sanderson. The graves are in the extreme southwest corner of the cemetery and are marked by a large, inscribed, gray marble monument placed there in 1985 by the Terrell County Historical Society. It is believed that Hobek and Kilpatrick met in prison.

**406. Hobgood, Edward S. "Curnell"** (?–October 1921). He may have been the man who killed train robber Eugene F. Bunch. Hobgood was stabbed to death by an unknown person in Madison Parish, Louisiana. He is buried in the small Hobgood plot in a cemetery near Tylertown, Mississippi, beside his brother, Rob, who died in 1915. Only Rob's grave is marked.

**407. Hockensmith, Clarke L.*** (February 21, 1843–May 10, 1865). One of Quantrill's Raiders, he followed Quantrill to Kentucky in 1865. When Quantrill's horse was shot in an engagement, he called for help from his retreating forces. Hockensmith turned back and attempted to help, but both he and Quantrill received fatal wounds. Clarke was buried in the Bloomfield Cemetery in Bloomfield, Kentucky. To locate the cemetery: from US 62 in Bloomfield, go north on Main Street for 0.2 mile to the cemetery on the right. The grave is in the south-central part of the cemetery and is marked by a small, inscribed, Confederate military headstone which is difficult to read. NOTE: Read the two-sided Kentucky historical marker at the cemetery entrance.

**408. Hodges, Benjamin "Ben"*** (June 3, 1857–1929). He was a small-time badman around Dodge City, Kansas. He was born in Chihuahua, Mexico, of a black father and a Mexican mother. He is buried in Maple Grove Cemetery on the west side of Dodge City. His grave is next to the fence adjacent to the Mexican section. In 1965 the Ford County Historical Society placed a large marker at his grave.

**409. Hoerster, Daniel*** (September 5, 1843–September 29, 1875). He was brand inspector for Mason County, Texas, and was shot from his horse and killed in the town of Mason during the Mason County, or "Hoodoo," War. He is buried in the tiny Hoerster Cemetery (only two or three graves) about one-half mile north of Art, Texas. Art is about nine miles east of Mason on Highway 29. To locate the cemetery: turn north from Highway 29 at a small country store. The cemetery is on the right, beside the dirt road and has a wrought iron fence around it. There is a marker.

**410. Holladay, Benjamin "Ben"*** (October 14, 1819–July 8, 1887). He

*John Henry "Doc" Holliday, Glenwood Cemetery, Glenwood Springs, Colorado.*

*Left: Thomas "Tom" Horn, Columbia Cemetery, Boulder, Colorado. Above: John Calhoun Pinckney "Pink" Higgins, Spur Cemetery, Spur, Texas.*

founded the Holladay Mail and Express Company. He died in Portland, Oregon, and is buried on the south side of Mount Calvary Cemetery. There is a large monument at his grave, which is on the top of a hill and beside the drive. His wife is buried beside him.

**411. Holliday, John Henry "Doc"**\* (August 14, 1851–November 8, 1887). Doc was born in Griffin, Georgia, but the family moved to Valdosta, Georgia, when he was a small boy. He graduated from the Pennsylvania College of Dental Surgery in Philadelphia in 1872. He went west and became a gambler and gunman. He was a friend of Wyatt Earp and took part in the so-called "Gunfight at the O.K. Corral" in Tombstone, Arizona. He died of tuberculosis in Glenwood Springs, Colorado, and is buried in the Glenwood Cemetery (or Old Hill Cemetery) in Glenwood Springs. There is an elaborate tombstone with some erroneous information misidentifying the dental school that he attended.

**412. Hollister, Cassius M. "Cash"**\* (December 7, 1845–October 23, 1884). He was marshal and then mayor of Caldwell, Kansas. Later he held a deputy United States marshal's commission while at the same time holding the position of deputy sheriff of Sumner County, Kansas. Hollister was shot and killed while attempting to arrest Bob Cross at Cross's home. He is buried in the Caldwell Cemetery in Block 2, Lot 394, a few feet from the flagpole. A small obelisk marks the grave.

**413. Hollow Horn Bear (Daniel)**\* (March 1850–March 15, 1913). Born in northern Nebraska, Hollow Horn Bear was the son of Chief Iron Shell. He fought in the Wagon Box Fight, served as a scout for the army, and later became a member of the Sioux Indian Police. Hollow Horn Bear became chief of his Sioux band upon the death of Iron Shell. After Sitting Bull was killed, Hollow Horn Bear worked for peace and presented a list of Indian problems to President Benjamin Harrison in Washington, D.C. Hollow Horn Bear also represented the Sioux at Theodore Roosevelt's 1905 presidential inauguration. Twenty-nine chiefs representing all tribes in the United States chose him to officiate at the dedication of a statue on Staten Island, New York, honoring all Indians. While visiting in Washington, D.C., in 1913, he developed pneumonia and died. He was buried there, but later his remains were taken back to the Rosebud reservation in South Dakota and reinterred in the cemetery at St. Francis. An inscribed marker stands at his grave near the parking area on the north side of the cemetery.

**414. Hoover, George M.*** (1847–1914). He was one of the pillars of Dodge City society. At one time or another he was mayor of Dodge, the owner of the Alamo Saloon, a wholesale liquor dealer, a banker, and a representative in the Kansas legislature. When he was elected mayor in April 1884, he recommended Bill Tilghman for city marshal. The city council confirmed the choice, with Thomas C. Nixon as assistant marshal. Hoover died in Dodge of natural causes in 1914 and was buried in Maple Grove Cemetery. There is a large marker at the grave, which is near the office.

**415. Horn, Thomas "Tom"*** (November 21, 1860–November 20, 1903). He was a scout and a range detective and was hired by Wyoming ranchers to rid the area of cattle thieves. He was hanged at Cheyenne, Wyoming, for the murder of a young boy, Willie Nickell, and is buried beside his brother, Charles, in Columbia Cemetery in Boulder, Colorado. His headstone incorrectly gives his year of birth as 1861.

**416. Horner, Josiah W. "Joe".** See Canton, Frank.

**417. Horsely, Albert E.** See Orchard, Harry.

**418. Houston, Sequoyah** (1854–1894). He was a Cherokee lawman and was killed by Cherokee Bill Goldsby. He and his father, Tla-sto-ma Houston, are the only ones whose graves remain in the Old Blue Springs Cemetery near Gideon, Oklahoma, a few miles north of Tahlequah, Oklahoma. An iron pipe fence surrounds the large marble headstone which is supported on each side by two columns. This old cemetery is not easily found and a guide and permission to visit the grave should be obtained. It is located in Section 26, R21E, T18N.

**419. Houston, Samuel "Sam"*** (March 2, 1793–July 26, 1863). He was a soldier and later president of the Republic of Texas. He died on his farm near Huntsville, Texas, and is buried in the Oakwood Cemetery there. A large monument and Texas historical marker are at the grave site, which is near the entrance.

420. **Houston, Samuel, Jr., "Sam"*** (May 25, 1843–May 3, 1894). He was the son of Sam Houston. He is buried in the Independence Cemetery at Independence, Texas. There is an inscribed headstone and a Confederate States Army marker at his grave.

421. **Houston, Temple Lea*** (August 12, 1860–August 15, 1905). A son of Sam Houston, he was a noted gunman and lawyer. On October 8, 1895, he shot and killed Ed Jennings in a saloon fight at Woodward, Oklahoma. Houston died of a brain hemorrhage at Woodward and is buried in the Woodward Cemetery in Section 1. This is in the northwest part of the cemetery. There is a simple, rectangular, ground-level marker at the grave site. He was buried in Oklahoma at his own request.

422. **Howell, Amazon C.*** (January 19, 1817–August 30, 1890). He was the father-in-law of John Slaughter and is buried in the Tombstone Cemetery in Tombstone, Arizona. His wife, Mary Ann Howell (July 29, 1836–April 9, 1920), is buried beside him. To locate the grave: go west on Allen Street to the cemetery on the left. The grave is to the right of the central drive. A large, gray marble stone marks the grave.

423. **Hoy, Harold "Harry"*** (August 1855–April 1906). He was a pioneer cattleman in Brown's Park, Colorado, and was a brother of Valentine Hoy, whom Harry Tracy killed. He is buried in the Lodore Cemetery in Brown's Park near the restored old Lodore school-house. The grave is marked.

424. **Hoy, Valentine*** (1849–March 2, 1898). He was a pioneer cattle-man in Brown's Park, Colorado. While acting as a posse member, he was shot and killed by outlaw Harry Tracy. His body was taken to Fremont, Nebraska, and on March 9, 1898, he was buried in the Stark Cemetery in Fremont, Lot 4, Block 143, beside two of his infant children, one of whom died October 30, 1884, and the other

on January 13, 1885. On the other side of the children is Hoy's sister, Winnie Chamberlain. There are no markers. The Hoy plot is directly in front of the marker for C.R. and Henrietta Anderson. To locate the cemetery and grave: follow Military west to Stark. Turn right (north) on Stark to the cemetery on the left. Enter the cemetery through the main entrance and turn right on McPherson Avenue to Calvary Avenue. Turn left on Calvary and watch for the Block 143 marker on a low metal sign on the left. Walk left from the 143 marker about two-thirds of the distance to the next lane. The burial site, which is not marked, is in front of the Anderson marker.

425. **Hueston, Thomas J. "Tom"*** (August 4, 1855–September 2, 1893). He was a deputy United States marshal and was killed by the Doolin Gang in the battle at Ingalls, Oklahoma. He is buried in Fairlawn Cemetery in Stillwater, Oklahoma. To locate the grave: from US 51 (Sixth Street), enter the cemetery through the westernmost entrance. Go past the first paved drive. About fifty feet beyond this drive is the Hueston grave on the left and adjacent to the entrance road. The grave is marked by a four-foot-tall obelisk. His wife, Amelia S. Hueston (April 29, 1860–December 15, 1893), is buried beside him.

426. **Hughes, Bella Metcalf*** (April 6, 1817–October 3, 1902). He is best known for his contributions to western transportation. He was a partner in Russell, Majors and Waddell, which operated the Central, Overland, California and Pike's Peak Express Stage Line as well as the short-lived Pony Express. When the company merged with Wells, Fargo & Co., Hughes became the company attorney. Later he became a member of the last Colorado territorial legislature. He died in 1902 and was buried in Lot 55, Block 24 of Fairmont Cemetery in Denver, Colorado. There is a large marble monument at his grave.

427. **Hughes, John Reynolds*** (February 11, 1855–June 3, 1947). He was a Texas Ranger and attained the rank of captain. After retiring from the Rangers, he became a successful businessman. At the age of ninety-two and in ill health, he shot and killed himself at Austin, Texas. He is buried near the top of the hill in the state cemetery in Austin.

**428. Hulse, Alfred*** (1856–October 14, 1906). He was a California outlaw who killed lawman William Tibbet in the Joss House Battle at Bakersfield, California. He had sided with his friend, outlaw Jim McKinney, whom lawmen were trying to arrest or kill. He was tried and convicted of second-degree murder and sentenced to life imprisonment. While still in jail in Bakersfield, he used a razor to cut his throat. He died almost instantly. He was buried in an unmarked grave in Union Cemetery in Bakersfield, Block 350, Lot 16.

**429. Hunt, Wilson Price*** (March 20, 1783–April 13, 1842). He was a mountain man and fur trader and led the Astorians on their epic march to the Pacific Ocean. He died in St. Louis, Missouri, and is buried there in Bellefontaine Cemetery in a very large, temple-like tomb.

**430. Hurley, Thomas J. "Tommy"*** (May 3, 1856–August 17, 1886). He was a member of the "Molly Maguires," a labor organization, in Pennsylvania. After many of this gang were hanged or imprisoned, he moved to Colorado. He was arrested for killing Luke Curran with a knife in 1886. While in jail in Gunnison, Colorado, awaiting trial, he committed suicide by cutting his throat with a razor left in the cell by Alferd (Alfred) Packer, the "Colorado Cannibal," who had left the cell earlier in the day. Hurley was from Pottsville, Pennsylvania. He is buried in the Gunnison Cemetery, and there is an inscribed headstone. The grave is in Block 6 in the southeast quadrant of the cemetery next to a wire fence.

**431. Hutchinson, William H.*** (June 7, 1845–January 14, 1911). He was the Escambia County, Florida, sheriff who helped Texas Ranger John Armstrong capture John Wesley Hardin in Florida. He is buried in St. Johns Cemetery in Pensacola, Florida, in Section 11, which is just beyond the office on the right near the first intersection. His wife, Alice; his parents, Ann and Thomas Hutchinson; and several brothers and sisters are also buried here. All of the graves are marked. Do not confuse this cemetery with the St. Johns Catholic Cemetery.

# I

**432. Ikard, Bose*** (July 1843–January 4, 1929). Ikard was born a slave in Mississippi and came to Texas with the family of his owner, Dr. Milton L. Ikard. After he was emancipated, he remained with Dr. Ikard, but joined a cattle drive to Colorado led by Charles Goodnight and Oliver Loving in 1866. Bose became one of Goodnight's best cowhands and a trusted friend. He settled in Weatherford, Texas, and he and his wife, Angelina, had a total of six children. Bose died at Weatherford at the age of eighty-five and is buried in the Weatherford Cemetery. The granite marker at his grave was placed there by Goodnight. There is also an official Texas state historical marker at the grave, which is beside the westernmost drive in the cemetery.

**433. Irvine, William C. "Billy"*** (March 3, 1852–July 27, 1924). He worked as foreman on a cattle ranch in Nebraska before driving his own herd of cattle from Texas to Wyoming. He became a leader in the Wyoming Stock Growers Association and was also one of the leaders in the invasion of Johnson County by a group of gunmen hired by the big ranchers in Wyoming to drive out or kill the small ranchers and homesteaders who were thought to be rustling stock. Irvine died in California but his body was returned to Cheyenne, Wyoming, for burial in Lakeview Cemetery. A three-foot marble stone marks the Irvine plot.

**434. Ivers, Alice "Poker Alice"*** (February 17, 1851–February 27, 1930). She was a famous gambler and proprietress of a house of pleasure. She died at Rapid City, South Dakota, but her body was taken to Sturgis, South Dakota, for burial in the Sturgis Cemetery.

There is a large marble marker at her grave. The name given on her headstone is Alice Tubbs. The Poker Alice Tubbs House in Sturgis is believed to be the only brothel on the National Register of Historic Places.

# J

**435. Jackson, David E.\*** (circa 1790–December 24, 1837). He was a famous mountain man. Jackson Hole, Jackson Lake, and Jackson, Wyoming, are named for him. After engaging in the fur business for some time, he did some trading on the Santa Fe Trail. He died at Paris, Tennessee, of typhoid fever and is buried there in the Jackson family cemetery. There is no marker for David but there are markers for his son and several other family members. The cemetery is six miles east of Jackson.

**436. James, Alexander Franklin "Frank"\*** (January 10, 1843–February 18, 1915). He was the brother of Jesse James. He rode with William Quantrill and later engaged in bank and train robberies as a member of the James-Younger Gang. Frank died at his home near Kearney, Missouri, and his body was cremated. The ashes were later buried in a family plot in Hill Park Cemetery in Independence, Missouri. His wife, Ann Ralston "Annie" James (1853–1944), is buried beside him. The cemetery is located at Twentieth Street and Willow Avenue. A low stone wall surrounds Frank's and Annie's graves, which are marked with a single, ground-level stone.

**437. James, Jesse Woodson\*** (September 5, 1847–April 3, 1882). Jesse, along with his brother, Frank, and several others, including the Youngers, comprised a gang of bank and train robbers for many years. Prior to that, he had ridden with William Quantrill. He was shot and killed at his home in St. Joseph, Missouri, by Bob Ford, who, along with his brother, Charlie, was living in the James home. At the time of his death, Jesse was using the name "Tom Howard." He was originally buried in the yard of the old Samuel home near

Kearney, Missouri. Years later his body was removed to the Mount Olivet Cemetery at Kearney. Jesse's wife, Zerelda Amanda (July 21, 1845–November 13, 1900); his mother, Zerelda; her husband, Dr. Reuben Samuel; and Jesse's half-brother, Archie P. Samuel (July 26, 1866–January 26, 1875), are all buried in the Samuel-James plot. All of the graves are marked, as is Jesse's original grave site at the old James Farm. A marker indicating his Confederate Army service was placed at his grave in 1990.

**438. Jarrette, John\*** (?–?). Many local historians believe that a man buried in Mount Olivet Cemetery at Kearney, Missouri, under the name of "James Jannett, Captain" is in reality the Captain John Jarrette who was with William Quantrill's Raiders during the Civil War. Others are doubtful. A regular headstone and an official Confederate States of America marker are at the grave site, which is about seventy-five feet up the hill from the grave of Jesse James.

**439. Jarvie, John\*** (1844–July 6, 1909) He was a pioneer in the Brown's Park, Colorado-Utah, area, and ran a store in the western (Utah) part of Brown's Park. He was killed by two men who robbed the store and then tied his body to an old boat and pushed it out into the Green River. The body was found twenty miles downstream, some eight days later. He was buried in the old Lodore Cemetery near the restored Lodore school. There is a marker.

**440. Jeffords, Thomas Jonathan "Tom"\*** (January 1, 1832–February 19, 1914). He was a frontiersman who led a varied life. Tom was a sailor on the Great Lakes, drove a stagecoach, and acted as a scout and messenger during the Civil War. He later became a friend of the Apache chief, Cochise. Tom was appointed Indian agent for the Chiricahuas and later engaged in mining. He died at Owls Head, about thirty-five miles north of Tucson, Arizona, and is buried in Evergreen Cemetery in Tucson. The inscribed marker at his grave was placed there in 1964 by the Daughters of the American Colonies. The grave is at 25-B-16, which is in the southeast corner of the block fronting on Oracle Road and next to the big ditch which runs east-west through the cemetery. To locate the grave: enter the cemetery through the Fort Lowell entrance and immediately turn left

*James-Samuel family plot, Mount Olivet Cemetery, Kearney, Missouri.*

*Alexander Franklin James and Ann Ralston James, Hill Park Cemetery, Independence, Missouri.*

and walk to the ditch. The grave is on the corner just as you reach the ditch.

**441. Johnson, Liver-Eating.** See Johnston, John.

**442. Johnson, William Harrison\*** (1842–August 17, 1878). He married the sister of Bob and John Beckwith during the hostilities in Lincoln County, New Mexico. Johnson told his father-in-law, Hugh Beckwith, that he had been a captain in the Civil War. Later when Beckwith, an ardent Southerner, found out that Johnson had been a captain in the Union Army, he took a shotgun and killed him. Johnson was buried in the Seven Rivers Cemetery. When a dam was built in 1989 to form a lake on the Pecos River, all of the bodies from the Seven Rivers, New Mexico, Cemetery were taken to Artesia, New Mexico, and reburied in the Twin Oaks Cemetery just north of town. Johnson's crypt of brown stone is the largest in the Seven Rivers section, which is to the west of the main part of Twin Oaks in a treeless area. There is a large marker. To locate the cemetery: from Artesia, follow US 285 north until Highway 2 branches right. Take Highway 2 a short distance to the cemetery on the left.

**443. Johnston, Albert Sidney\*** (February 2, 1803–April 6, 1862). He was an army officer and a West Point graduate. He attained the rank of brigadier general and commanded the United States forces in Utah during the Mormon War. At the outbreak of the Civil War, he resigned from the United States Army and was appointed general in the Confederate forces. He was killed in the Battle of Shiloh and was first buried in New Orleans, Louisiana. In 1867, his body was removed to Austin, Texas. He is now buried near the center of the state cemetery. A very impressive tomb holds his remains.

**444. Johnston, John "Liver Eating Johnson"\*** (circa 1823–January 21, 1900). He was a frontiersman and later a lawman in Montana. He died at the National Soldiers Home in Santa Monica, California, and was buried there. Later his remains were reinterred at Old Trail Town just west of Cody, Wyoming. There is a marker. Supposedly he once ate the liver of an Indian he had killed.

**445. Jolly, Hi.** See Hadji Ali.

**446. "Jones, Arkansas Tom."** See Daugherty, Roy.

**447. Jones, Charles Jesse "Buffalo Jones"*** (January 1844–October 2, 1919). Born in Illinois, he went to Kansas at the age of twenty-one. He became a successful buffalo hunter, but when the buffalo faced extinction, he exerted a great effort to conserve those that remained. He established a herd in northern Arizona which was the beginning of the herd maintained today in Rock House Valley. Later Jones roped and captured wild animals in Africa for sale to zoos. A fever contracted on one of his trips to Africa led to his death some five years later at Topeka, Kansas. He was buried in the Valley View Cemetery in Garden City, Kansas, a town that he had founded in 1878. To locate the cemetery and grave: from downtown Garden City, take Third Street north about a dozen blocks to the cemetery on the left. Enter the cemetery at the second drive. Go to the first cross-drive and turn right. Jones's grave, marked by a large marble stone with the inscription on top, will be on the right, adjacent to the drive, about halfway to the next cross-drive. Shrubbery is at either end of the headstone.

**448. Jones, Frank*** (June 12, 1856–June 30, 1893). He was a Texas Ranger who attained the rank of captain. He was killed in Mexico by Mexican bandits and was buried on Ranger Captain George W. Baylor's property on the American side of the Rio Grande. In 1936, his remains were taken to Ysleta, Texas, and reinterred beside Zaragosa Avenue, about one mile west of the Tigua Indian reservation and Ysleta Mission. The grave is in a small plot in the fork formed by Zaragosa and a side street which branches right.

**449. Jones, Gerry*** (May 24, 1852–November 5, 1937). He was a brother of Texas Ranger Captain Frank Jones. He enlisted in the Ranger service in 1875 and left the service in 1877. In 1886 he enlisted in his brother's Company D. He served until September 1888, and shortly thereafter married Elizabeth Rebecca Putnam. In his later years, he was a farmer, a rancher, and practiced law for some time. He died at Legion near Kerrville, Texas, and is buried in the

Kerrville national cemetery, which is south of Kerrville on Spur Road 100 just south of the United States Veterans' hospital, which is on State Road 27. Jones's grave is in the second row and is the sixth grave from the left (western) boundary of the cemetery. It is marked by a standard United States military headstone.

**450. Jones, John B.*** (December 22, 1834–July 19, 1881). He was the commander of the Frontier Battalion of Texas Rangers and later adjutant general of the state of Texas. Jones died in Austin, Texas, and is buried in that city in Oakwood Cemetery in Section 1, Plot 337 (moved from Plot 332). To locate the grave: enter the cemetery from Navasota and drive to the second narrow lane beyond the office. Turn right and drive to the fence at the back of the cemetery. A very tall monument (approximately fifteen feet), topped with an angel, marks Jones's grave. It is on the corner and to the left.

**451. Jones, John Stykes*** (February 20, 1811–July 11, 1876). Born in Kentucky, Jones came to Missouri and started in the freight business before the Civil War. He later operated a freighting company with William H. Russell as his partner. They were successful in obtaining several government contracts. At one time they operated 500 wagons. Jones died in Boulder, Colorado, and was buried in Denver, Block 6, Lot 69, of Riverside Cemetery. There is a large, gray marble headstone for John and his wife, Sophia S. Neff Jones (1824–1903).

**452. Jones, Orley E. "Ranger"*** (October 7, 1864–November 28, 1891). He was one of the small ranchers who fought against the big cattlemen in the Johnson County War in Wyoming. He was shot and killed from ambush. Either Fred Hesse or Frank Canton was believed to have been the killer. Jones is buried in Willow Grove Cemetery in Buffalo, Wyoming. A small granite stone marks his grave, which is to the left immediately beyond the entrance to the cemetery (Block 20, Lot 3, Space 10). Other Jones family members in the plot are John H. Jones (1856–1948) and Orley H. Jones (August 10, 1894–August 6, 1930).

**453. Joseph, "Old Chief Joseph"*** (1790–1873). He was the father of

Young Chief Joseph of the Nez Percé. He is buried in the Indian cemetery at the north end of Wallowa Lake, just south of the town of Joseph, Oregon. There is a large headstone at his grave.

**454.** **Joseph "Young Chief Joseph"**\* (circa 1840–September 21, 1904). He was the chief of the Nez Percé tribe and led his people in the famous retreat from Oregon to final surrender at Bear Paw in Montana. He was placed on the Colville reservation in the state of Washington, where he died. He is buried in the Colville Indian cemetery. There is a grave marker. The cemetery is just north of the little town of Nespelem, Washington. His grave faces the entrance in the southeast corner of the little Catholic cemetery. The grave of Yellow Wolf (circa 1855–August 21, 1935) is nearby.

**455.** **Julian, J.E. "Ed"**\* (?–April 15, 1886). He operated a restaurant in Dodge City, Kansas. Before going to Dodge, he had served in Company D, Seventh Indiana Cavalry. Ed was shot and killed near his restaurant by former assistant city marshal Ben Daniels. They had not been on good terms for some time. Although armed, Ed did not fire a shot. He is buried in Maple Grove Cemetery in Dodge City, Block 1, Lot 2, in the west Grand Army of the Republic section. There is a United States military headstone. The grave is the second from the northeast corner of the section and adjacent to the drive.

**456. Kau-tau-Bone.** See Gotebo.

**457. Kearny, Stephen Watts\*** (August 30, 1794–October 31, 1848). He was a United States Army officer who rose to the rank of major general. He was commander of the Army of the West during the Mexican War and led his army of 1,600 men on a march to Santa Fe, New Mexico, which he took over without opposition. He died in St. Louis, Missouri, of a tropical disease he had contracted while serving in Vera Cruz, Mexico. He is buried in St. Louis' Bellefontaine Cemetery. There is a large marker. A map showing the location of many interesting graves can be obtained at the office.

**458. Keintpoos, Chief.** See Captain Jack.

**459. Kelley, James H. "Dog"\*** (February 19, 1834–September 9, 1912). He was a saloon keeper and mayor of Dodge City, Kansas. He died at the Kansas State Soldier's Home at Fort Dodge, Kansas, and is buried in the Old Post Cemetery, which is on the north side of Highway 154 a few miles east of Dodge City. During the Civil War, Kelley served in Company I, First Iowa Cavalry. He has two headstones, located in different parts of the cemetery.

**460. Kelly, Luther Sage "Yellowstone Kelly"\*** (July 27, 1849–December 17, 1928). He was a scout under General Nelson A. Miles, served in the Philippines, and later was Indian agent for the San Carlos Indian reservation in Arizona. He died at Paradise, California, but his wife had his body taken to Montana. He is buried on the high bluff above the Yellowstone River just north of Billings, Montana. There is a large marker at his grave, which is enclosed by a fence.

**461. Kempton, Martin R.**\* (September 1, 1878–February 10, 1918). He was a deputy sheriff under Sheriff Robert F. McBride of Graham County, Arizona. He was killed along with Sheriff McBride and Kane Wootan by the Power boys, John and Tom, at the Power home in the Galiuro Mountains near Klondyke, Arizona. Kempton is buried in the Safford Cemetery at Safford, Arizona. A short lane leads to the cemetery from US 666, just south of Safford. His wife, Sena P. Kempton (1881–1973), is buried beside him. A gray granite headstone marks their graves.

**462. Keokuk**\* (circa 1780–April 1848). He was a Sauk Indian leader. He died in Kansas, but his remains were reinterred in a city park at Keokuk, Iowa. There is a large monument at his grave. A beautiful, curving drive beside the Mississippi River passes the monument.

**463. Ketchum, Ami "Whit"**\* (1855–December 11, 1878). He was a homesteader who, along with Luther Mitchell, was killed near Callaway, Nebraska, by I.P. "Print" Olive and some of his men. They were hanged, shot, and then partially burned. Ketchum's body was taken to Kearney, Nebraska, by his brothers and buried in the Kearney Cemetery. He was originally buried at the edge of the cemetery, but in 1893 his body was reinterred at its present location. The grave is marked by a two-foot-high, pink marble stone inscribed, "Pioneer Ami Ketchum, 1855–1878, A Victim of the Homesteaders and Cattlemen Conflict of Custer County, Nebraska." To locate the grave: from US 30 (Twenty-fifth Street) in Kearney, turn north on Avenue I, which ends at the cemetery. Enter the cemetery and take the center of three drives. Go to the first lane to the left (Sixteenth Avenue). Turn left on Sixteenth and almost immediately look to the left about ten feet from the drive and almost behind the larger of two cedar trees for the marker. The inscription on the stone faces away from the drive.

**464. Ketchum, Samuel "Sam"** (1854–July 24, 1899). He was an outlaw who, along with his brother, Tom, Will Carver, and others, operated as the "Black Jack Gang" in New Mexico and Arizona. They robbed post offices, banks, and trains. After being wounded in a battle with lawmen, he was captured and imprisoned at Santa Fe, New Mexico.

He died there of his wounds and was buried in Santa Fe by the Odd Fellows. According to some historians, when I-25 was built across the corner of the cemetery, his body was not removed and is now covered by pavement.

**465. Ketchum, Thomas E. "Black Jack"\*** (October 31, 1863–April 29, 1901). He was the leader of the "Black Jack Gang," which included his brother, Sam, and Will Carver. When he left the gang and attempted to rob a Colorado Southern train by himself, he was wounded by Conductor Frank E. Harrington. The next day he was captured beside the railroad tracks. He was taken to Clayton, New Mexico, tried, and sentenced to death. He was completely decapitated when he was hanged at Clayton. He was buried near Clayton. On September 10, 1935, his remains were reinterred in the new Clayton Cemetery. The grave was marked in 1991, and is easily located. It is near the main entrance in the narrow median separating the two lanes of traffic. Flowers grow on the grave, which is outlined by a cement curbing.

**466. Kicking Bird\*** (1835–May 4, 1875). He was a Kiowa chief and was known as the "Peace Chief." When a contingent of Kiowa Indians were sent to Fort Marion, Florida, as prisoners, he was chosen to select the seventy who were to go. A few days after the prisoners left, Kicking Bird was taken ill and died in a few hours. The post surgeon gave the cause of death as poisoning by strychnine. He was buried on Chief's Knoll in the post cemetery at Fort Sill, Oklahoma. There is a marker.

**467. Kidder, Jefferson P. "Jeff"\*** (November 15, 1875–April 5, 1908). Born near Vermillion, South Dakota, he became an Arizona Ranger and was killed by Mexican police in a shootout at Naco, Sonora, Mexico. He was taken to Inglewood, California, for burial in Inglewood Park Cemetery. The grave's location is 396 Sequoia. The small, ground-level marker may be obscured by cut dried grass. The marker incorrectly gives 1910 as the year of his death. His mother, Ada Kidder (January 28, 1855–December 23, 1943), is buried in the San Jacinto Valley Cemetery at San Jacinto, California. Also at San Jacinto is a nephew, Marion Kidder Goff (1886–1931).

**468. Kilpatrick, Ben "The Tall Texan"\*** (circa 1870–March 13, 1912).
Born in Texas, Ben was associated with the "Black Jack" Ketchum
Gang and later with Butch Cassidy's Wild Bunch. After taking part
in a train robbery in Montana in 1901, he was captured in St. Louis,
along with his girlfriend, Laura Bullion, tried and sentenced to
fifteen years in prison. Laura received a lesser sentence. After
serving ten and a half years, Ben was released. He later was killed
along with a former prison mate, "Ole" Hobek, by railroad express
guard, David A. Trousdale, when the two tried to rob the Galveston,
Harrisburg, and San Antonio Train Number 9 eleven miles east of
Sanderson, Texas. Both men are buried in Cedar Grove Cemetery
a short distance east of Sanderson. The graves are in the extreme
southwest corner of the cemetery and are marked with a single gray
marble stone inscribed with their names. It was placed there in 1985
by the Terrell County Historical Commission.

**469. Kilpatrick, Daniel Boone\*** (1871–1958). He was a brother of Ben
Kilpatrick, "The Tall Texan," of Butch Cassidy's Wild Bunch.
Although he may have given sanctuary to Ben and his friends on
occasion, Boone was not considered an outlaw. He died at his home
at Iraan, Texas, and is buried in Restland Cemetery, 3.6 miles west
of Iraan on the north side of Highway 190. The grave is about fifty
feet directly in front of the entrance and on the left-hand side of the
central drive. A low, engraved stone marks the grave.

**470. King, Sandy\*** (?–January 1, 1881). He was a small-time outlaw
who, along with "Russian Bill," was hanged at Shakespeare, New
Mexico. The two are buried in a single grave at the western edge of
the Shakespeare Cemetery. There is a grave marker. The cemetery
is a short distance south of Lordsburg, New Mexico, to the left of the
dirt road leading to the ghost town of Shakespeare.

**471. Kinney, John William Young\*** (August 31, 1848–August 25,
1919). He was at one time a cavalryman and later a cattle rustler. He
took part in the Lincoln County War in New Mexico and sometime
later served a sentence for cattle rustling. He died at the Pioneer
Home in Prescott, Arizona, of Bright's disease and is buried there in
the International Order of Odd Fellows Cemetery. To locate the

cemetery: from Gurley Street (US 89) in the northeast part of Prescott, turn south on Virginia Street. Follow Virginia and, shortly after the pavement ends, keep left where the dirt road forks. The cemetery is a short distance ahead. Enter the cemetery and go straight ahead. Kinney's white marble, United States military marker is next to the drive on the right.

472. **Kino, Eusebio Francisco** (August 10, 1645–March 15, 1711). Father Kino was a pioneer Jesuit missionary and explorer. He was also a cartographer, a historian, and a mission builder. Father Kino died at Magdalena, Sonora, Mexico, and is buried there. His remains, which were discovered in 1966, were placed in a special crypt, the Father Kino Shrine, and may be seen today.

473. **Kitchen, Peter "Pete"** (circa 1819–August 5, 1895). He was a Texas-Arizona pioneer cattleman. Pete spent his last years in Tucson, Arizona, where he died. Because he was almost penniless, the Arizona Pioneer Historical Society paid his burial expenses. He was buried in the old Tucson Cemetery. When the bodies from this cemetery were later moved to Evergreen Cemetery, the exact location of his grave was lost.

474. **Kloehr, John Joseph*** (1858–March 25, 1927). He owned a livery stable in Coffeyville, Kansas, and when the Dalton Gang attempted to rob two banks there simultaneously, he was one of the civilian defenders that wiped out the gang. Kloehr (pronounced *claire*) was credited with killing three of the gang. He died at Coffeyville and is buried there in Fairview Cemetery, Section O, Lot 48, Plots 1 and 2. The grave is marked and is on the south side of the cemetery, near the top of the hill. A few feet away, a large tomb, partially in the hillside, is that of a brother. Other family members are nearby.

475. **Kohrs, Conrad*** (August 5, 1835–July 23, 1920). He was a Montana cattleman who took over the Grant Ranch near Deer Lodge, Montana. He became extremely wealthy. The Grant-Kohrs Ranch is now a national historic site and is open to the public. Kohrs is buried in Hillcrest Cemetery at Deer Lodge, Montana. A very large, gray marble monument marks his grave. His wife, Augusta

(1849–October 29, 1945), and other family members are also in the Kohrs plot.

476. **Kosterlitzky, Emelio** (November 16, 1853–March 2, 1928). He was born of Russian-German parents and immigrated to America in the early 1870s. He may have served in the United States Cavalry at one time. He later joined the Mexican army and became the head of the famed Rurales. Emelio left Mexico and worked for the United States Department of Justice for a time. He died in Los Angeles, California, and is buried there in Calvary Cemetery.

477. **Kreeger, Louis Michael "Lew"** (December 26, 1848–August 3, 1913). He was a Colorado lawman. He spent more than thirty years as an officer of the law in Las Animas County, Colorado, and the city of Trinidad, Colorado, where he died. Lew is buried in the Catholic cemetery there. I have been unable to locate his grave.

478. **Kuhlman, Fred*** (1853–June 23, 1881). He was murdered in the Red Light brothel at Hunnewell, Kansas. His death came as a result of an argument over one of the girls at the Red Light. Kuhlman is buried in the Caldwell Cemetery at Caldwell, Kansas. He shares a massive granite headstone with George Woods, who owned the Red Light Saloon and who was also murdered. The headstone was placed at the grave site by George's wife, Mag Woods, who was the proprietress of the "dance hall" which occupied the upper floor of the building housing the Red Light Saloon. Kuhlman's grave is on the left, a few feet along the lane leading south from the flagpole. To locate the cemetery and grave: go north from Caldwell on Main Street (State Road 49) and turn left on Avenue G (just past the water tower) to the cemetery. The flagpole can be seen from the maintenance building.

# L

**479. La Framboise, Michel\*** (May 5, 1793–January 25, 1861). He was a fur trapper and trader and worked for both the North West Company and the Hudson's Bay Company. He is buried in a small, unnamed cemetery in St. Paul's Parish, Oregon. There is a bronze plaque, inscribed, "Michael La Framboise, 1786–1861" (name incorrectly spelled, date of birth incorrect). St. Paul, Oregon, is about five miles south of Newberg, Oregon, on State Highway 219. A boulder with a plaque is about 0.1 mile from the St. Paul Church. The cemetery is 0.3 mile from the church, which is also on Highway 219.

**480. Lamar, Mirabeau Buonaparte\*** (August 16, 1798–December 19, 1859). Born in Georgia, he became the second president of the Republic of Texas. He died of a heart attack at his home in Richmond, Texas, and is buried in Richmond Masonic Cemetery. There is a large statue of Lamar at the grave site.

**481. Lamb, Selah Graham\*** (1866–October 16, 1933). After starting out as a cowboy, he became a lawman and served Nevada in that capacity more than thirty years. While attempting to settle a family dispute, he was shot several times by Glenn Hibbs. He died later in the day and was buried in the Winnemucca Cemetery at Winnemucca, Nevada. A small granite stone inscribed "Selah Graham, 1866–1933" marks the grave, which is in the Knights of Pythias Section, Block 14, Lot 6.2. To locate the grave: from the office, take the drive nearest the office down the little hill toward West Winnemucca Boulevard. Lamb's marker is on the left, beside the drive, and is almost hidden by a mass of shrubbery. The marker is on the office side of the shrubbery.

**482.  Lambert, Charles Fred\*** (January 23, 1887–February 3, 1971). He owned the St. James Hotel Saloon in Cimarron, New Mexico, in which, it is said, twenty-six men were killed. Lambert was the last remaining member of the New Mexico Mounted Police when he died. He is buried in Mountain View Cemetery in Cimarron, as is Frank Vance, another member of the New Mexico Mounted Police. There are small, pink marble, ground-level markers for Fred and his wife, Katie Hoover Lambert (1886–1964). Fred's parents, Mary and Henry Lambert, are a few feet away.

**483.  Lambert, Henry (Henri)\*** (October 28, 1838–January 24, 1913). Henry built the St. James Hotel Saloon in Cimarron, New Mexico, and was the father of Fred Lambert, New Mexico lawman. He is buried in Mountain View Cemetery, just south of Cimarron. There is a dark gray marble headstone. His wife, Mary Elizabeth (June 15, 1858–December 8, 1928), is buried beside him.

**484.  Landusky, Powell "Pike"\*** (March 4, 1849–December 27, 1894). Born in Missouri, he became a Montana pioneer. The little town of Landusky, Montana, was named for him. He was shot and killed by Harvey Logan (Kid Curry) in Jew Jake's Saloon. While serving as a lawman, Pike had once arrested Curry. He is buried on a little hill about a mile south of Landusky. The grave is on the east side of the highway, about one-quarter mile from the highway on the Kolczak Ranch (1991). There is a wooden marker, and the grave is surrounded by a little picket fence.

**485.  Lane, George "Clubfoot George"\*** (?–January 14, 1864). Born in Massachusetts, he worked as a cobbler and was a member of Henry Plummer's gang of outlaws. He was hanged by vigilantes at Virginia City, Montana. Four others were hanged with Lane. All five are buried in Boot Hill at Virginia City. Later, in order to prove the location of the graves, his body was dug up and the clubfoot removed. It is on display at one of the Virginia City museums. All graves are marked.

**486.  Lane, James Henry "Jim"\*** (June 22, 1814–July 11, 1866). He was a Union general during the Civil War and was living in

Lawrence, Kansas, when that town was sacked by William Clarke Quantrill. However, he escaped by hiding out. Lane was born in Indiana and had served a term as lieutenant governor of the state. After Kansas became a state in 1861, he served as a Republican United States senator in Washington. He fell into disfavor at home, and when he became implicated in a scandal over Indian contracts, he became despondent and committed suicide near Fort Leavenworth, Kansas. He is buried in the Lawrence Cemetery at Lawrence, Kansas, and a very large monument marks his grave.

**487. Lant, David Barnabas** (September 14, 1874–?). Lant was one of nine children born of Mormon parents at Payson, Utah Territory. He left home at an early age and became a sheepherder before turning to a life of crime. He is best known for his association with the notorious Harry Tracy. After committing several crimes, Lant and Tracy were captured and jailed at Hahns Peak, Colorado. Following an escape they were recaptured and taken to Aspen, Colorado, and jailed. Once again they escaped and sometime afterward the two separated. Little is known of Lant's life thereafter. At least one report has him dying many years later in Utah where he had led a crime-free life as a sheepherder.

**488. Larn, John*** (March 1, 1849–June 24, 1878). He was a Texas gunman and at one time sheriff of Shackelford County, Texas. He was arrested for cattle theft, and while he was in jail in Albany, he was killed by vigilantes. He is buried near the stone house that he built beside the Clear Fork of the Brazos River several miles northwest of old Fort Griffin, Texas. The Putnam family owned and was living in the old Larn home in 1988. It can be reached by traveling a number of miles on dirt roads. Larn's son, Joseph B. Larn, is buried beside him. He was born March 3, 1875, and died September 17, 1875. Another son, William Larn, was at one time a member of the Arizona Rangers. He died at Douglas, Arizona, June 3, 1937, and is buried in Forest Lawn Cemetery, Lot 711, Space 5, in Glendale, California. John's wife was Mary Matthews Larn, a member of the famous Matthews ranching family, descendants of whom still own and operate the Lambshead Ranch northwest of Fort Griffin.

489. **Lassen, Peter\*** (August 7, 1800–April 26, 1859). He was a pioneer of Oregon and California. Lassen Peak and Lassen Volcanic National Park, both in California, were named for him. Lassen was born in Copenhagen, Denmark, and immigrated to the United States in 1828. He was killed by Indians in Nevada and is buried some six miles south of Susanville, California. Both the original monument and a new one mark the grave site. To locate the grave: drive south out of Susanville on Richmond Road about 4½ miles to Wingfield Road. Turn right on Wingfield and drive about 1½ miles to the grave on the left.

490. **Latham, James V.\*** (July 7, 1859–December 17, 1936). He was a Texas Ranger and served under Captain Dan W. Roberts, Captain L.P. Sieker, and Captain Frank Jones. He died at San Diego, Texas, and was buried in the Alamogordo Cemetery at Alamogordo, New Mexico. He is buried in Lot 33, Block 27, which is near the extreme south end of the cemetery between the second and third lanes east of the maintenance building. A large obelisk is just north of the Latham plot, about thirty-five feet from the southernmost drive. A number of family members are also there, and all of the graves are marked.

491. **Lathrop, George\*** (December 24, 1830–December 24, 1915). He was born at Pottsville, Pennsylvania, and became a famous stage driver on the Cheyenne-Deadwood Trail. He died on his eighty-fifth birthday at Willow, Wyoming, and is buried on the south side of Highway 20, about one mile west of Lusk, Wyoming. A large boulder with a bronze plaque marks his grave.

492. **Law, George\*** (?–October 13, 1896). He was a bank robber who was killed in an attempt to rob the bank at Meeker, Colorado. His two confederates, Jim Shirley and "The Kid," were also killed. All three are buried in the southeastern corner of the Meeker Cemetery. There is a marker.

493. **Lawyer\*** (circa 1802–January 3, 1876). He was a Nez Percé chief. Lawyer represented the Nez Percé at the government treaty meetings at Walla Walla, Washington, and during two trips to Washington, D.C. He was the first elder of the First Presbyterian Church at

Kamiah, Idaho. He is buried there behind the little church on US 12. There is a large marker of pink and gray marble.

**494. Lay, William Ellsworth "Elzy"** * (November 25, 1868–November 10, 1934; NOTE: His grave marker incorrectly gives his year of birth as 1869). He was an outlaw and a member of Butch Cassidy's Wild Bunch. Lay was captured, tried, and sentenced to life imprisonment in the New Mexico penitentiary in 1889. He was released in 1906 and led a crime-free life until his death in California. Elzy is buried in Forest Lawn Cemetery in Glendale, California, in Lot 3338. To locate the grave: from the entrance drive past the mortuary and turn right at the "Finding of Moses" statue. Go left when the drive forks and left again at the little "Temple." Turn right on the second drive beyond the temple and drive to the fourth concrete trash receptacle on the right. Park. Go down the hill twelve rows, then left thirty spaces to the ground-level marker.

**495. Lazier, Jules.** See Sheepmen's Mass Grave.

**496. Leavenworth, Henry** * (December 10, 1783–July 21, 1834). Born in Connecticut, he spent all of his adult life in military service. He established Fort Snelling in Minnesota and later became commanding officer at Fort Atkinson, Nebraska. In 1827, he built what would later be known as Fort Leavenworth, Kansas. After being made commander of the entire southwestern military force, he left Fort Gibson in Oklahoma to try to establish peace among the warring Indian tribes. A short time later he developed what was described as "bilious fever" and died within a few days. He is buried in the Fort Leavenworth national cemetery. The largest monument in the cemetery marks his grave.

**497. Ledbetter, James Franklin "Bud"** * (December 15, 1852–July 8, 1937). He was a deputy United States marshal for most of his life and served under Judge Isaac Parker of Fort Smith, Arkansas. He worked with most of the famous lawmen of Oklahoma and Indian Territory such as Bill Tilghman, Heck Bruner, Paden Tolbert, Heck Thomas, and Chris Madsen. "Uncle Bud," as everyone called him, died of a heart attack in Muskogee, Oklahoma, and is buried there

*Left: John Larn, near the old Larn ranch home northwest of Fort Griffin. Below: William Ellsworth "Elzy" Lay, Forest Lawn Cemetery, Glendale, California.*

in Memorial Park Cemetery a few miles west of town. Bud is in Section 2–27, which is diagonally across from the office and about three rows back from the drive. There are ground-level markers for Bud; his wife, Mary J. (March 27, 1856–May 12, 1930); a son, George W. (August 28, 1875–July 2, 1943); and a grandson, Marc Leroy Ledbetter (April 14, 1917–November 5, 1969).

**498. Lee, Daniel W.**\* (June 6, 1810–March 19, 1877). He was the father of Bob Lee, leader of the Lee faction in the Lee-Peacock Feud in northern Texas. He was killed in the feud and is buried in the Old Lee Cemetery south of Leonard, Hunt County, Texas. There is a grave marker. To locate the cemetery: from Leonard, Texas, go west on Highway 78 a little more than two miles to Highway 981. Turn left (south) on 981 for 1.4 miles. Turn left on a dirt road and follow as it turns right, left, right, left, left, and right for 1.8 miles to the cemetery on the left.

**499. Lee, Elizabeth**\* (February 14, 1828–August 18, 1894). She was the wife of Daniel Lee. She is buried in the Old Lee Cemetery south of Leonard, Texas. There are markers for both husband and wife. To locate the cemetery: see Lee, Daniel W.

**500. Lee, Jason**\* (June 28, 1803–March 12, 1845). The Reverend Lee was a Methodist missionary to the Indians in the Northwest. He died in Stanstead, Canada, and his remains were transferred some sixty-one years later to the Methodist mission grounds near Salem, Oregon. The little plot containing Lee, his first and second wives, and other mission workers, is surrounded by a larger cemetery. Trees shade the graves and make photography difficult. The cemetery is at the north end of Twenty-fifth Street in Salem. Lee's first wife, Anna Maria Pittman Lee (1803–1838), was the first white woman to be buried in Oregon.

**501. Lee, John Doyle**\* (September 12, 1812–March 23, 1877). He was a Mormon pioneer in Utah and was convicted of having led the group that perpetrated the Mountain Meadows Massacre in southwestern Utah in 1857. He was executed by a United States Army firing squad in 1877. For years he ran the old Lee's Ferry on the Colorado River in northern Arizona. Lee is buried in the Panguitch Cemetery in Panguitch, Utah. There is a large marker. Lee was excommunicated from the Mormon Church, but on August 20, 1961, he was fully reinstated.

**502. Lee, Oliver Milton*** (November 8, 1865–December 15, 1941). He was a New Mexico cattleman and state senator. He was an enemy of Pat Garrett who, along with many others, believed Lee was responsible for the killing of Colonel Albert J. Fountain and his young son. Lee and two others were tried for the murders but were found not guilty. Lee died in Alamogordo, New Mexico, and is buried in Monte Vista Cemetery in Alamogordo. The large Lee plot contains many Lee family members. The large, gray marble headstones are impressive. The graves are found on the right of the entrance drive not far from the entrance.

**503. Lee, Robert "Bob"*** (?–June 1869). Lee, who had been a captain in the Civil War, was leader of the Lee faction in the Lee-Peacock Feud. He is buried in the Old Lee Cemetery near where he was ambushed and killed. The cemetery is south of Leonard, Texas. There is a large, square granite monument. To locate the cemetery: see Lee, Daniel W.

**504. Lee, Robert "Bob"*** (1869–1912). He was a member of the Wild Bunch and a cousin of the Logan (Curry) brothers. Bob took part in the Wilcox train robbery and was later arrested in Cripple Creek, Colorado. He was tried, convicted of train robbery, and sentenced to ten years in the Wyoming state penitentiary. He was released after seven years and returned to the home of his mother in Dodson, Missouri. He died of Bright's disease in 1912 and was buried in Elmwood Cemetery in Kansas City, Missouri. The grave is marked by a small, ground-level stone and is in the corner of the cemetery bounded by Truman Road and Van Buren Boulevard.

**505. LeFors, Joseph S. "Joe"*** (1865–October 1, 1940). Born in Texas, he became a deputy United States marshal and spent much of his life in some form of law enforcement. Joe is much noted for tricking Tom Horn into confessing crimes that led to Horn's execution by hanging at Cheyenne, Wyoming. LeFors died at his home in Buffalo, Wyoming, and is buried there in Willow Grove Cemetery, Block 51, Lot 8, Space 1. His wife, Nettie W. LeFors (1872–1957), is buried beside him.

**506. Lehmann, Herman\*** (June 5, 1859–February 2, 1932). He was the son of German immigrants who settled in Mason County, Texas. At the age of ten, Herman and his eight-year-old brother Willie were captured by Apache Indians. After five days Willie was released and made his way back home. Herman remained with the Apache and later the Comanche Indians for more than eight years. United States soldiers returned him to his family in 1878, but he maintained ties to Quanah Parker's Comanche family for the rest of his life. Upon his death in 1932, he was buried in the small Loyal Valley Cemetery at the little community of Loyal Valley south of Mason, Texas. Brother Willie (October 30, 1861–September 11, 1951) is also buried there. In 1991 an official Texas state historical marker was placed in the cemetery. Willie's daughter, Ester Lehman (current spelling), was still living about one mile west of Loyal Valley in 1991.

**507. Leonard, Zenas\*** (March 19, 1809–July 14, 1857). Born in Pennsylvania, he went to St. Louis, Missouri, as a young man and entered the fur trade. Zenas was at the Battle of Pierre's Hole and accompanied the Joe Walker Expedition to California. He trapped for Benjamin Bonneville in the Yellowstone and Wind River country and later operated a store and trading post at Fort Osage in Missouri. There he wrote a narrative of his many experiences. He died at Fort Osage and is buried in the old cemetery there beside his wife, Isabel Harrelson (1825–1851), and a daughter, Elizabeth, who died as a child. A ground-level stone marks the graves of Zenas and Isabel, and a white, upright marker indicates the grave of Elizabeth. The graves are near a tall, black marble marker.

**508. Leroy, William "Billy"\*** (circa 1858–May 24, 1881; Note: The last name is sometimes given as LeRoy). His real name may have been Pond or Potter. He was the original "Billy the Kid" and a small-time outlaw. In December 1880, Leroy teamed with the famous Bill

Miner in a successful stagecoach robbery. He and his brother, Sam Pond, were lynched at Del Norte, Colorado. They are buried in Lot 45A in the Del Monte Cemetery. There is no marker. To locate the cemetery and grave: from US 160 at the east end of town, take French Street 1.7 miles to the cemetery. Enter and drive to the lane on the right leading to a maintenance building. Turn right and go about eighty feet. Look to the right to two small stones between the drive and the cement-curbed Wilson plot. The two brothers are buried there.

**509.   Leslie, Frank "Buckskin Frank"** (circa 1842–circa 1922). Little is known of his early life. He was a scout for the army during the days of Geronimo's depredations along the Mexican border. In the late 1870s Leslie was in Tombstone, Arizona Territory, working as a bartender. He gained notoriety as a gunman and killed William Claiborne in a gunfight. He also took part in the killing of Mike Killeen and later shot and killed a woman, Mollie Williams, while he was in a drunken stupor. For this crime he was sentenced to life imprisonment in the territorial prison at Yuma, Arizona. He was pardoned on November 7, 1896, and little is definitely known of his life after that. He was last reported in Oakland, California, in 1922. Some researchers believe he committed suicide shortly after, but details are lacking.

**510.   Lewis, Elmer "Kid"*** (March 1876–February 27, 1896). He was an outlaw who, along with Bill Crawford, attempted to rob the City National Bank in Wichita Falls, Texas. They killed the cashier, Frank Dorsey, and then were captured by a posse led by Bill McDonald. Later they were taken from the jail and lynched. Lewis and Crawford are buried in the same grave in Riverside Cemetery in Wichita Falls. A small headstone with both names marks the grave, which is not far from the grave of the bank employee they killed. To locate the grave: see Crawford, William Foster.

**511.   Lewis, Meriwether*** (August 18, 1774–October 11, 1809). He was a co-leader of the Lewis and Clark Expedition and later served as governor of the Territory of Louisiana for about one and one-half years until his death. While traveling from Louisiana to Washington, D.C., he either committed suicide or was murdered along the Natchez Trace in Tennessee. His death took place in Grinder's Inn. The grave site is just off the Natchez Trace a few miles north of US 64 near Hohenwald, Tennessee. A very large monument marks the grave.

512. **Lewis, William Winslow "Will"*** (September 7, 1855–October 20, 1934). Lewis was born in Carrollton, Kentucky, the son of Dr. John T. and Sarah Bosworth Lewis. He left home and went to Texas in 1871, where he worked on ranches around Burnet, Texas, until May 25, 1874, when he joined Captain C.R. Perry's Company D of the Texas Rangers. Will took part in the Indian fight at Lost Valley near Jacksboro, Texas. He later served under Captain Dan Roberts and Lieutenant F.M. Moore. After leaving the Rangers, he became a businessman at Menard, Texas, where he raised a large family. He died there and was buried in the Pioneer Rest Cemetery. His grave is about halfway up the hill and slightly to the left of the entrance. The large Lewis plot contains several family members including his wife, Nina B. Lewis, two sons, and three daughters.

513. **Lilly, Benjamin Vernon "Ben"*** (December 31, 1856–December 17, 1936). He was a mountain man and noted hunter. He died in Grant County, New Mexico, and is buried in Memory Lane Cemetery in Silver City, New Mexico. To locate the grave: enter the cemetery and turn left to Cypress Lane. Turn right on Cypress and go to the end of the lane. Turn right and then right again on Rose Lane. Continue on Rose Lane to the first intersection on the left. Lilly's grave is fifty feet to the southwest of the intersection. There is a small marker.

514. **Lisa, Manuel*** (September 8, 1772–August 12, 1820). Lisa was a fur trader. He died near St. Louis, Missouri, and is buried there in Bellefontaine Cemetery. His grave is marked by a large, tall monument. His wife, Mary Hempstead Lisa (October 26, 1782–September 3, 1869), and son, Manuel, Jr. (October 12, 1809–June 29, 1826), are buried beside him. A map of the cemetery is available at the office.

515. **Little Raven\*** (circa 1819–1889). He was an Arapaho chief. His tribe and others accepted reservation status as a result of the 1867 Medicine Lodge Treaty. He died at Cantonment, Oklahoma, and is buried on Chief's Knoll in the post cemetery at Fort Sill, Oklahoma. There is a marker.

516. **Little Wolf\*** (circa 1820–October 30, 1904). He was a Northern Cheyenne chief who gained fame as a fierce war leader against other Indian tribes. He took part in the Little Bighorn Battle in 1876 but surrendered a few months later and was sent to Indian Territory, as was Chief Dull Knife. These two led some 300 Cheyennes north from their reservation toward their homeland in Montana. In Nebraska, the group split into two bands with Little Wolf leading his group to Montana, where they wintered with the Sioux of Chief Red Cloud. A short time later he surrendered and was allowed to remain in Montana. He died there and was buried beside his friend Dull Knife in the Indian cemetery at Lame Deer, Montana. Both graves are marked with inscribed brass plates attached to cement bases.

517. **Llewellyn, William Henry Harrison\*** (September 9, 1851–June 11, 1927). While still in his twenties, he was employed by the department of justice to capture Doc Middleton, a notorious outlaw and horse thief. After accomplishing this, he went to New Mexico and became Indian agent for the Mescalero Apaches before turning to law practice and politics. He served with distinction as a member of the Rough Riders during the Spanish-American War. After the war, he became United States attorney for New Mexico. He died at El Paso, Texas, and is buried beside his wife, Ida Mae (1858–1951), in the Masonic Cemetery at Las Cruces, New Mexico. The graves are marked and are in Section A, Block 10, which is between Compress Road and the cemetery office.

518. **Loco\*** (circa 1823–February 2, 1905). He was a Mimbres Apache and served jointly with Victorio as tribal chief. He died at age eighty-two and is buried in the main Apache cemetery near Beef Creek on the Fort Sill, Oklahoma, military reservation. A map showing the location of the cemetery can be obtained at the entrance to Fort Sill.

**519. Logan, Harvey "Kid Curry"** (circa 1875–July 9, 1903). He was a member of the Butch Cassidy Wild Bunch. After holding up a train near Parachute, Colorado, he was cornered and wounded near Glenwood Springs. He shot and killed himself and was buried in the Glenwood Springs Cemetery. The exact location is unknown.

**520. Logan, John "John Curry"\*** (1868–February 1, 1896). He was one of the outlaw Logan brothers and was killed by Jim Winters. Logan and Winters are buried not far from each other at Landusky on the Gill Ranch, a short distance southwest of Zortman, Montana, near the Art Phillips house. Jim was killed, probably by one of John's brothers, on July 25, 1901. There is a small marker at John's grave site. A guide is essential in locating this grave.

**521. Logan, Loranzo Dow "Lonny Curry"\*** (1871–February 28, 1900). He was one of the outlaw Logan brothers. While at his aunt's house in Dodson, Missouri, he was killed in a gunfight with local police and Pinkerton detectives. He is buried in Grave 12, Lot 53, Block 25, in Forest Hill Cemetery in Kansas City, Missouri, near his aunt, Elizabeth Lee. There is an inscribed marker.

**522. Logan, Thomas W.\*** (May 29, 1861–April 6, 1906). He was elected to three terms as sheriff of Nye County, Nevada. While unarmed, he was shot five times and killed by Walter Barieau at the Jewel Resort in Manhattan, Nevada. In one of the most celebrated trials in the history of the state, Barieau was found not guilty. Logan is buried in the Old Tonopah Cemetery, which is just west of the main street in Tonopah, Nevada. The grave is in the extreme northern part of the cemetery and is one of four graves in a group, each surrounded by wrought iron fences. There is an inscribed, low marble headstone set in concrete.

**523. Long, Crockett\*** (1893–July 17, 1932). He was the former chief of police for Madill, Oklahoma, and was an agent of the Oklahoma State Crime Bureau when a gunfight erupted between Long and Wiley Lynn in the Corner Drugstore in Madill, resulting in the deaths of both men. A spectator, Rody Watkins, was also killed. Lynn was the man who had killed officer Bill Tilghman in 1924.

Long is buried in Woodbury-Forest Cemetery on Highway 70 west of Madill. His grave is in Block 2, Lot 23, about two-thirds of the way up the little hill after entering the cemetery. It is on the right of the drive, a few feet from the T.L. Woody marker, which is beside the lane. A small, ground-level stone marks Long's grave.

524. **Long, Jane**\* (July 23, 1798–December 30, 1880). She was the wife of James Long, who led an unsuccessful expedition in an attempt to free Texas from Spanish control. He was killed while his wife awaited his return. She is known as "The Mother of Texas" and was the first woman of English descent to bear a child in the state of Texas. She died near Richmond, Texas, and is buried in the Richmond Cemetery. There is a large monument at her grave site.

525. **Longabaugh, Harry Alonzo "Sundance Kid"**\* (April 19, 1868–?). He was a member of Butch Cassidy's Wild Bunch. Many believe that he was killed along with Butch Cassidy in South America. Others are of the opinion that Longabaugh died in 1955 while using the name "Hiram BeBee." BeBee was almost certainly an imposter; he is buried in the Salt Lake City Cemetery just north of Eleventh Avenue, which crosses the northern portion of the cemetery. There is a small, inscribed marker.

526. **Longley, Campbell**\* (September 30, 1816–September 15, 1907). He was the father of Jim and "Wild Bill" Longley and is buried in the Longley family plot in the Lometa Odd Fellow Cemetery at Lometa, Texas. Lometa is thirteen miles northwest of Lampasas, Texas. There is a marble headstone. His son, Jim, and several other Longleys, are also buried there. To locate the cemetery: see Longley, James Stockton.

527. **Longley, James Stockton "Jim"**\* (1859–April 15, 1938). He was the brother of "Wild Bill" Longley. He died at Lometa, Texas, and is buried in the Lometa Odd Fellow Cemetery. Jim, his wife, Vie, and his father, Campbell, are also buried there, along with many other Longleys. All of the graves are well marked. To locate the cemetery: from US 183, take County Road 2942 at the west end of town and go 0.5 mile to the cemetery. The Longley plot is about thirty feet from this road.

**528. Longley, William Preston "Wild Bill"**\* (October 6, 1851–October 11, 1878). He was an outlaw and gunman who killed many men. He was captured, tried, convicted, and hanged at Giddings, Texas. He is buried at the western edge of the Giddings Cemetery, which is about one mile west of Giddings. For years his grave was marked only by a small petrified stump, but the Texas State Historical Society placed a bronze marker at the grave in 1986. (*Dead Man on the Bayou,* a recent book by Ted Wax, gives evidence that the hanging was faked and that Longley survived and lived in Louisiana for many years using the name "John Brown," dying in 1923 at Plaquemine, Louisiana. In 1992 several graves in the area of the bronze marker were opened in an unsuccessful attempt to locate Longley's body.)

**529. Longstreet, Andrew Jackson "Jack"**\* (circa 1838–July 26, 1928; NOTE: his headstone gives his name as John A. Longstreet). He was a Southerner, but little is known of his early life. His first authenticated presence in the Arizona-Nevada area was in 1880. He mined and ranched in a small way in the desert areas of Nevada. Longstreet was an expert in the use of firearms and killed more than one man. He championed the Indian cause and took an Indian for his wife. Jack died in the Mines Hospital in Tonopah, Nevada, after suffering a stroke. He is buried in the Belmont Cemetery just south of the old ghost town of Belmont, Nevada. His wife, Fannie (1866–1931), is buried beside him. Each grave is marked by a small inscribed headstone. To locate the cemetery and grave: about one mile south of Belmont, a dirt road leads east for 0.5 mile to the cemetery. The Longstreet graves are behind (west of) the Bradley plot, which has a concrete curbing and is surrounded by a tall, wire fence.

**530. "Lottie Deno."** See Thurmond, Charlotte.

**531. Loving, Oliver**\* (December 4, 1812–September 25, 1867). He was a Texas and New Mexico cattleman and trailed cattle to Louisiana, Illinois, and Colorado. With Charles Goodnight, he developed the "Goodnight-Loving Trail." On a trip to Santa Fe, New Mexico, Loving was wounded by Indians. While Goodnight went for help,

Loving made his way to Fort Sumner, New Mexico, but developed gangrene and died. He was buried in the post cemetery. Later Goodnight had the body removed to Weatherford, Texas, and reinterred in Greenwood Cemetery near the corner of Front and Rusk streets. There is a marker.

**532. Lowe, Benjamin "Ben"*** (1868–June 9, 1917). He was a cattleman in western Colorado. Trouble developed between Ben and ex-lawman Cash Sampson, leading to a gunfight in Escalante Canyon in which both men died. Ben left a wife and five children (three daughters and two sons). He is buried in the Delta Cemetery in Delta, Colorado, Block 5, Lot 325, Space 2. Cash Sampson is buried a short distance away. There are large, inscribed markers for both Lowe and Sampson.

**533. Lucas, Orrington "Red"*** (June 21, 1857–March 14, 1955). He was an Oklahoma lawman who took part in the famous gunfight at Ingalls, Oklahoma, between the Doolin Gang of outlaws and deputy United States marshals. He is said to have made over 3,000 arrests without having to kill anyone. Lucas died of heart disease at the age of ninety-seven and is buried in Union Cemetery at Eaton, Indiana, a few miles north of Muncie. His grave is in Section 2, Lot 85. There is no marker, but he is buried next to the marked grave of Emma Butcher.

**534. Lucero, Felipe*** (1867–August 1, 1940). He was sheriff of Dona Ana County, New Mexico, and he and his brother, Jose, were in law enforcement for many years. He is buried in San Jose Cemetery in Las Cruces, New Mexico, which is on Griggs Avenue. To locate the grave: from the Manzanita Street entrance on the west end of the cemetery, the Lucero plot can be seen about 200 feet past the entrance. Three grave markers, side by side, mark the plot. These markers are upright and are easily seen. (NOTE: Most sources give Felipe's grave location as the Masonic Cemetery. This is incorrect. For some reason the Masonic Cemetery records show him to be in the St. Josephs Cemetery, which is also incorrect. He is in San Jose, which is across the street from St. Josephs.) His brother, Jose, who was also a lawman, is buried in the Masonic Cemetery. Felipe died of a heart attack. He was the sheriff to whom Wayne Brazel surrendered when he claimed he had killed Pat Garrett.

**535. Lynn, Wiley U.*** (1888–July 18, 1932). He killed Officer Bill Tilghman while being taken to jail in Chandler, Oklahoma. He also killed and was killed by Crockett Long in a gunfight in the Corner Drugstore in Madill, Oklahoma. Crockett was an agent with the Oklahoma State Crime Bureau. A spectator, Rody Watkins, was also killed during the fight. Lynn is buried in the Woodbury-Forest Cemetery on Highway 70 west of Madill. To locate the grave: enter the cemetery from Highway 70 and drive straight ahead up the little hill. Just over the hill, look to the right for the large Lynn marker. A small, inscribed, ground-level stone marks Wiley's grave.

**536. Lyons, Hayes "Haze"*** (?–January 14, 1864). He was a member of Henry Plummer's gang of outlaws at Bannack and Virginia City, Montana. The gang was known as the "Innocents." He was hanged at Virginia City for the murder of Deputy D.H. Dillingham. Four other gang members, George Lane, Jack Gallagher, Frank Parrish, and Boone Helm, were hanged with him. All five are buried in Virginia City's Boot Hill Cemetery, and all the graves are marked.

**537. Lytle, O. Vernon*** (February 28, 1857–April 17, 1898). He was a member of the posse that captured the bank robbers led by Henry Brown at Medicine Lodge, Kansas, in 1884. He is buried in the Medicine Lodge Cemetery. There is a grave marker.

**M**

**538. McCall, John "Jack"*** (circa 1851–March 1, 1877). He murdered Wild Bill Hickok in Deadwood, South Dakota, on August 2, 1876. He was tried in Deadwood and set free, but later he was tried again at Yankton, South Dakota, convicted and hanged. McCall is buried in the Catholic cemetery there. The grave is unmarked and the exact grave site is not known. In 1984, Father Joseph Holzhauser pointed out a likely grave site for McCall. It is one of two unmarked sites surrounded by grave markers of the 1870s and '80s. The site is in the west-central part of the Sacred Heart Cemetery.

**539. McCanles, David Colbert "Dave"*** (November 30, 1828–July 12, 1861). He was killed by "Wild Bill" Hickok at Rock Creek Station near present-day Fairbury, Nebraska. He was buried near the station, but his body was later removed to the Fairbury Cemetery, where he lies beside his wife, Mary (1832–1907), and two of his children, Clingman (1854–1936) and Elizabeth (1857–1938).

**540. McCanles, William Monroe*** (January 26, 1849–May 17, 1934). Monroe was born in Wautauga County, North Carolina, but came with his parents to Nebraska, where they settled at Rock Creek (now Jefferson County) in 1859. He was at Rock Creek Station when his father, David McCanles, was killed in a fight with Wild Bill Hickok and others. After his father's death, young McCanles worked at odd jobs and helped build the first railroad to Lincoln, Nebraska. He married Martha McCreight (1853–1931) on July 31, 1870; the couple had nine children. In 1884, the McCanles family moved to Kansas, where Monroe later entered the mercantile business and was county treasurer. After his wife died in Kansas City, he lived in

151

Lincoln, Kansas, with his daughter, Mrs. Maude Lyster, until his death. He was buried in the Lincoln Cemetery. To locate the cemetery and grave: from the courthouse in Lincoln, take East Lincoln Avenue a few blocks east to the cemetery on the right. Enter through the brown stone gate and drive to the light brown mausoleum on the left. The McCanles plot a few feet away is marked by a family monument and four individual gravestones.

**541. McCarty, Henry "Billy the Kid"\*** (November 20, 1859–July 14, 1881; NOTE: Some writers give the date of birth as September 17, 1859). He was an outlaw who was also called "Billy Bonney" and "Kid Antrim." He took part in the Lincoln County War in New Mexico and was convicted and sentenced to hang for the murder of Sheriff Pat Brady. He escaped but was later killed by Sheriff Pat Garrett at Fort Sumner, New Mexico, as he entered the dark bedroom of Pete Maxwell. He is buried in the old Fort Sumner post cemetery beside his two friends, Tom O'Folliard and Charley Bowdre. There is a large marker bearing the names of the three outlaws. The headstone is badly chipped, and at one time was stolen. It is now protected by a fence and is also chained to a buried block of concrete. In 1990, an additional marker was placed at the grave site by members of the "Billy the Kid Outlaw Gang."

**542. McCarty, Joseph "Joe"** (August 25, 1854–November 25, 1930). He was a brother of "Billy the Kid," and was sometimes called "Joe Antrim." The Antrim name came from his stepfather, William H. Antrim. Joe died in Denver, Colorado, of apoplexy. His body was turned over to the Colorado Medical School.

**543. McCarty, Thomas "Tom"** (circa 1841–circa 1920). He was an outlaw who, along with his brother Bill, was a member of the Butch Cassidy Wild Bunch. After Bill and his son, Fred, were killed in an attempted bank robbery at Delta, Colorado, on September 6, 1893, Tom escaped, and little is known of his later life. He was known to have lived in Washington State for a time. One report says that he was killed in Montana, another that he was killed in Skagway, Alaska. Bill and Fred are buried in the city cemetery at Delta, Colorado. Their exact grave sites are not known.

*William Jesse "Bill" McDonald, Quanah Memorial Cemetery, Quanah, Texas.*

*Henry "Billy the Kid" McCarty, Tom O'Folliard, and Charley Bowdre, old Fort Sumner post cemetery, Fort Sumner, New Mexico.*

**544. McConnell, Edward Taylor "Bud"*** (November 20, 1845–March
2, 1935). He was an Arkansas lawman. Prior to becoming Johnson
County, Arkansas, sheriff, he had owned a drugstore and a weekly
newspaper, the *Clarksville Enterprise,* which he founded. He led the
posse that brought outlaw Sid Wallace to Clarksville, Arkansas, to
be hanged. After becoming sheriff, he helped to clean up "Bloody
Clarksville." He died at the age of eighty-nine and is buried in the
Oakland Cemetery in Clarksville, Arkansas. To locate the grave:
enter the cemetery through the arch, turn right on the first paved
drive and then left on the next paved drive. After the left turn, look
for a large magnolia tree on the left. Bud's grave is in the third row
of graves from the drive and about thirty feet beyond the magnolia.
His wife, Alice Porter McConnell (November 5, 1865–October 14,
1936), is buried beside him. A low, double headstone of gray granite
serves to mark the two graves.

**545. McCormick, Elizabeth "Frenchy"*** (August 11, 1852–January
12, 1941). Little is known of her past. Some say she ran away from
a convent in New Orleans, Louisiana. She never divulged her
maiden name. She worked as a dance-hall girl in a number of places
before arriving at Tascosa, Texas, where she met Mickey McCormick,
a gambler and livery stable operator. After living together for a time,
they were married. When Mickey died in 1908 (some say 1912),
Frenchy stayed on in Tascosa. She was the last person left when the
town finally folded up. When she died in 1941, she was buried
beside Mickey in the old Casimiro Romero Cemetery a short
distance east of Boy's Ranch. To locate the cemetery and grave:
enter Boy's Ranch at Tascosa and drive straight ahead to the
Anderson House (marked). Bear left here and then right on a dirt
road. Drive straight ahead on the dirt road past two cattle guards and
the water plant on the right. The cemetery is fenced and the gate
locked. The graves can be seen, however, since they are near the
fence on the south side of the cemetery. Two yellowed, upright
marble stones mark the graves.

**546. McDonald, William Jesse "Bill"*** (September 18, 1852–January
15, 1918). He was a Texas Ranger who rose to the rank of captain.
Bill was later United States marshal for the Northern District of

Texas and was serving in that capacity when he died of pneumonia. He is buried in the Quanah Memorial Cemetery in Quanah, Texas. There are a large, impressive headstone and a historical marker.

**547. McHughes, James H. "Jim"\*** (?–July 12, 1937). He was a member of the New Mexico Mounted Police. He died in 1937 and is buried in the Santa Fe national cemetery at Santa Fe, New Mexico, in Section O, Grave 330.

**548. Mackenzie, Ranald Slidell** (July 27, 1840–January 19, 1889). He was a career army officer who gained his greatest fame for his successful campaign against the Indians in the Texas area. Mackenzie attained the rank of brigadier general in 1882, but shortly thereafter, due to mental illness, he was declared unfit for duty. He was placed in an insane asylum in New York. His insanity was said to have been brought about by syphilitic infection, a diagnosis believed by many doctors today to have been incorrect. He died at the home of a relative at the age of forty-eight and was buried on the grounds of the United States Military Academy at West Point, New York. There is a large marker.

**549. McKinney, Andrew\*** (1829–September 17, 1889). He was the father of California badman, Jim McKinney. He is buried in the Porterville Cemetery in Porterville, California. His grave is near the back (north) border of the cemetery, about twenty feet from the fence. There is a flat, inscribed marble marker. His son, Jim, is buried in the space immediately to the north; Andrew's wife, Sarah, is just north of Jim.

**550. McKinney, Charles Brown "Charlie"\*** (1858–December 26, 1886). He served in the Texas Rangers under Captain L.H. McNelly and later under Lieutenant Lee Hall and Captain T.L. Oglesby. He was promoted to lieutenant and placed in command of Company F at Cotulla, Texas, but resigned effective March 1, 1883. He had married Nina Hay in 1882. McKinney and deputy Pete Edwards were ambushed by two men, allegedly George W. "Bud" Crenshaw and James McCoy, while trailing an outlaw; McKinney was killed and Edwards was wounded. Crenshaw was later killed by Rangers, and McCoy was hanged. Charlie is buried in the Cotulla Cemetery in Cotulla, Texas. To locate the grave: from Highway 468, turn into the cemetery and immediately turn right on the first drive. About 100 feet ahead, look to the right to a tall obelisk under a cedar tree. McKinney's grave is just to the south toward the fence. The impressive headstone had been badly damaged by a severe wind storm when I visited the site in July 1989, but according to the caretaker, it has now been repaired.

**551. McKinney, James "Jim"*** (January 3, 1860–April 19, 1903). He was a California and Arizona badman who was known to have killed several men. He was killed in the Joss House gunfight at Bakersfield, California, either by city marshal Jeff Packard or by Bert Tibbet. These two lawmen were also killed in the battle. Jim is buried between his parents, Andrew and Sarah McKinney, in Porterville Cemetery in Porterville, California. The grave is directly north of the office and about twenty feet from the fence on the north side of the cemetery. Jim's grave is unmarked (as was requested by his mother), but it is just north of his father's, which does bear a marker.

**552. McKinney, Thomas Christopher "Kip"*** (March 19, 1856–September 21, 1915). He was a New Mexico lawman and was with Pat Garrett when Garrett killed Billy the Kid. Kip died at Carlsbad, New Mexico, and is buried in the Carlsbad Cemetery, Division G, Lot 10, Space 2. His wife, Theresa Letitia (July 13, 1867–October 30, 1940), is buried beside him.

**553. McLaury, Robert Frank*** (March 3, 1848–October 26, 1881). He and his brother, Tom were born in New York but went to the Southwest as young men. They became members of the "cowboy" element led by the Clanton brothers around Tombstone, Arizona. Frank was killed in the so-called "O.K. Corral" fight by the Earp-Holliday faction and is buried in Tombstone's Boot Hill. There is a marker.

**554. McLaury, Thomas "Tom"*** (June 30, 1853–October 26, 1881). He was the brother of Frank McLaury and another member of the "cowboy" element of Tombstone, Arizona. The two brothers were killed in the gunfight at the "O.K. Corral" by the Earp-Holliday faction. Tom is buried in Tombstone's Boot Hill. There is a marker, which may or may not be at the actual grave site.

555. **McLoughlin, John**\* (October 19, 1784–September 3, 1857). He was a physician who became the Hudson's Bay Company factor in Oregon Territory. After he left the English company, he became a United States citizen and retired at Oregon City, Oregon, where he died. He and his wife, Margaret, are buried beneath the St. John's Roman Catholic Church at Oregon City.

556. **McMillen, Frank**\* (October 9, 1853–July 15, 1881). Frank was killed by the James Gang during a train robbery at Winston, Missouri. A stonemason from Wilton, Iowa, he was shot through a window of the train and died instantly. Conductor William H. Westfall was also killed. McMillen is buried in the Oakdale Cemetery in Wilton. To locate the cemetery and grave: from the main highway (West Fifth Street) in Wilton, turn south on Story Avenue for about four blocks to the cemetery on the right. Enter and turn left at the large, brick-lined ditch; pass the little maintenance building on the right and stop. The grave is a few feet south of the two very large oaks some fifty feet southwest of the maintenance building. It is marked by a pink marble obelisk, broken to symbolize a life cut short by death. The stone is inscribed but is difficult to read.

557. **McNelly, Leander H.**\* (March 12, 1844–September 4, 1877). He was a Texas Ranger and held the rank of captain. He commanded a special Ranger force along the Mexican border that disposed of a number of outlaws. Forced to retire due to illness, he returned to his former home at Burton, Texas. He died there and is buried in the Burton Cemetery. The very tall monument marking his grave was paid for by Captain Richard King of the famous King Ranch in Texas.

558. **McSween, Alexander A.**\* (June 15, 1837–July 19, 1878). He was born in Canada and in the 1870s was a lawyer and store owner in Lincoln, New Mexico. McSween and John Henry Tunstall opposed

the Murphy-Dolan faction in the Lincoln County War. McSween was killed in the five-day battle at Lincoln and is buried behind the old Tunstall store beside his partner, Tunstall, who had been killed a short time before. There are two markers, but they probably are not at the actual graves.

**559. McSween, Susan.*** See Barber, Susan McSween.

**560. Maddox, George** (?–circa 1898). He was a member of Quantrill's Raiders. Later, in the 1890s, he served as a guard at the Missouri state penitentiary at Jefferson City. His place of burial is unknown.

**561. Madsen, Christopher "Chris"*** (February 25, 1851–January 9, 1944). Born in Denmark, he came to the United States and served as a soldier and later as a lawman in Oklahoma Territory. He was a deputy United States marshal and, along with Bill Tilghman and Heck Thomas, formed the trio known as the "Three Guardsmen." Madsen died at Guthrie, Oklahoma, and was buried at Yukon, Oklahoma. His grave is in Frisco Cemetery, and there is a ground-level marker. To locate the cemetery: from Yukon, which is a few miles west of Oklahoma City, go north on Highway 4 for four miles. Turn left for 2$^1$/2 miles to the cemetery on the right.

**562. Majors, Alexander*** (October 4, 1814–January 13, 1900). In partnership with William H. Russell and W.B. Waddell, he organized a freighting and staging firm. Later they started the famed Pony Express. Majors died in Missouri and is buried in Union Cemetery in Kansas City, Missouri. Beside him is his wife, Katherine Stalcup Majors (September 26, 1820–February 13, 1856). There is a large marker. A map can be obtained from the Union Cemetery office showing the location of Majors' grave, as well as those of other well known individuals.

**563. Maledon, George I.*** (June 10, 1830–May 6, 1911). He served as hangman for Judge Isaac Parker, the "Hanging Judge," of Fort Smith, Arkansas. He hanged more than eighty men on the Fort Smith gallows. It is said that he took up the job of hangman after his daughter was killed by outlaws. Maledon had served with the Union

Army in the First Arkansas Federal Battery. He died at the soldiers' home in Johnson City, Tennessee, and is buried there in the national cemetery. His grave is in the fourth row, left side of Section E. There is a United States military marker.

564. **Mangas*** (?–February 9, 1901). He was a Mimbreno Apache and a scout for the army. He was the son of Chief Mangas Coloradas. Mangas is buried on Chief's Knoll in Fort Sill military cemetery at Fort Sill, Oklahoma. The grave is marked.

565. **Manning, Charles*** (December 25, 1881–July 2, 1914). He was an outlaw and came to the little town of Cokeville, Wyoming, around 1910. On July 2, 1914, Manning and two others, Albert Meadors and Clarence Stoner, attempted to rob a train in the Blue Mountains of Oregon, about twenty miles from La Grande. Manning was shot and killed by George McDuffie, a deputy sheriff who was on the train. Manning's body was returned to Cokeville and buried in the Cokeville Cemetery, which is just north of town. There is a grave marker. The house in which the Mannings lived was still standing and in good condition in 1986.

566. **Manning, Frank*** (circa 1846–November 14, 1925). He was a brother to Doc and Jim Manning of El Paso, Texas. Frank died in the Arizona state hospital in Phoenix, Arizona, and is buried in the state hospital cemetery there. The grave is unmarked. The state hospital cemetery is surrounded by a high fence and the gates are always locked. Visitors must be accompanied by a public relations officer of the hospital.

567. **Manning, George Felix "Doc"*** (October 27, 1837–March 9, 1925). Doc and his brother, Jim, killed ex-marshal Dallas Stoudenmire in a fight at El Paso, Texas. George died in Flagstaff, Arizona. He is buried there in the Masonic Section, Tract E, Lot 2, of Citizens Cemetery. This is on the west side of the cemetery near the fence, beyond which is a large, eight-story hospital. There is a marker. His wife, Sarah Ellen (February 21, 1858–January 27, 1942), and several children are also buried here.

**568. Manning, James "Jim"\*** (circa 1839–May 27, 1915). Jim and his brother, Doc, killed ex-marshal Dallas Stoudenmire in a fight in El Paso, Texas. Both Mannings were acquitted. After living in Arizona and Washington State, Jim moved to California, where he died of cancer. He is buried in Section B, Lot 108, Space 4, of Forest Lawn Memorial Park in Glendale, California, beside his wife, Leonora (1864–1923). The grave is marked. To locate the grave: from the entrance go straight ahead to the drive just beyond the mortuary. Turn right and curve right. At the first cross-drive, go straight ahead to the next cross-drive. Turn left and park. Look along the concrete curb for Lot 108. From this marker, go ten spaces away from the drive to the ground-level markers.

**569. Maples, Daniel "Dan"\*** (January 17, 1846–May 5, 1887). He was a deputy United States marshal and was killed by Ned Christie. He is buried in the Bentonville Cemetery in Bentonville, Arkansas. To locate the grave: enter the cemetery just south of the Baptist church. The Maples plot is on the right, under a scraggly pine tree (just across the gravel drive from the large DeShong monument). The graves of four Mapleses are here: Dan; his wife, Maletha Maples (March 31, 1847–December 17, 1929); Dan's son, George Maples (September 4, 1881–January 1, 1961); and George's wife, Emma Maples (May 22, 1883–May 12, 1958). To locate the cemetery: from US 71, turn east on Central Avenue for two blocks to the cemetery on the right.

**570. Marshall, James Wilson\*** (October 8, 1810–August 10, 1885). Born in New Jersey, he became a prospector and discovered gold at Sutter's Mill in California, leading to the California Gold Rush of 1849. When he committed suicide in 1885, he was penniless. He is buried in a California state park at Coloma, California. There is a very tall and impressive monument.

**571. Marshall, John E. "Curly"\*** (?–November 24, 1872). He was a small-time Kansas outlaw and horse thief. He is buried in Highland Cemetery, Wichita, Kansas, in Section 1, Lot 95, Grave 6. During the Civil War he served in Company L, Second Missouri Cavalry. There is a small United States military marker.

**572. Martin, Robert A.C.*** (1830–April 29, 1872). Martin was the cashier who was killed by the James Gang in the bank robbery at Columbia, Adair County, Kentucky. He was buried on May 2, 1872, in Grove Hill Cemetery in Shelbyville, Kentucky, Section E, Lot 128. His wife, Hester A. Martin (1837–1918), is buried beside him. There is a large headstone.

**573. Mason, Barney*** (October 29, 1848–April 11, 1916). He was born in Virginia but went to New Mexico at the age of thirty. He became a good friend of Pat Garrett. In 1880 he married Juana "Jenny" Madril (1866–1929), and Garrett married Apolonia Gutierrez in a double wedding at Anton Chico, New Mexico. The old church in which they were married still stands in excellent condition. When Garrett was elected sheriff of Lincoln County, he hired Mason as a deputy. Barney was a member of the posse which killed Tom O'Folliard and later captured Billy the Kid, Billy Wilson, Tom Pickett, and Dave Rudabaugh at Stinking Springs, New Mexico. After serving a prison sentence of less than a year for stealing a calf, Mason moved his wife and five children to Bakersfield, California. He died there of a cerebral hemorrhage and was buried in Union Cemetery, Block 976, Lot 6. After his wife died, Barney was reinterred in Block 1067, Lot 4. He now lies beside Juana and other family members in marked graves.

**574. Massie, William Rodney*** (1831–January 29, 1910). Captain Massie operated a river boat on the Mississippi. When he died in 1910, he still carried the bullet that had killed Wild Bill Hickok. It had passed through Hickok's head, lodged in Massie's arm, and was never removed. Massie died in St. Lukes Hospital in St. Louis, Missouri, of "incarcerated hernia" at age seventy-nine. He is buried beside his wife, Fannie K. Massie (1842–1924) and a son, Henry L. Massie (1872–1929), in Block 216, Lot 1611, in Bellefontaine Cemetery in St. Louis, Missouri.

**575. Masterson, Edward John "Ed"** (September 22, 1852–April 9, 1878). He was a brother of Bat and Jim Masterson. While a deputy marshal of Dodge City, Kansas, he was shot and killed by Jack Wagner in the Lady Gay Saloon. He was originally buried in the Fort

Dodge military cemetery, but his body was later removed to Prairie Grove Cemetery and finally to Maple Grove Cemetery in Dodge City. No marker was placed on the grave, and the exact location is not known.

**576. Masterson, James P. "Jim"*** (September 16, 1855–March 31, 1895). Jim was a lawman, as were his two brothers, Bat and Ed. Jim had also been a buffalo hunter and saloon owner. As a deputy United States marshal, he took part in the famous gunfight at Ingalls, Oklahoma, involving the Doolin Gang and deputy United States marshals. He died of "quick consumption" and is buried at Wichita, Kansas, in Highland Cemetery, Section 2, Lot 70, Space 6. Buried in the same lot are his father, Thomas (1824–January 12, 1921); his mother, Catherine (1832–March 6, 1908); two brothers, George (1860–November 1, 1892) and Thomas, Jr. (1858–November 10, 1941); and a sister, Emma "Minnie" (1862–February 20, 1881). Not all of the graves are marked.

**577. Masterson, Bartholomew "Bat"** (November 26, 1853–October 25, 1921; NOTE: His name is sometimes given as William Barclay). He was a Kansas lawman. Prior to that he was a buffalo hunter and took part in the Battle of Adobe Walls. After serving as a deputy United States marshal, a city policeman, and a county sheriff, he moved to New York City and became a sports writer. He died there of a heart attack and is buried in Woodlawn Cemetery in the Bronx. The cemetery is at 233rd Street and Webster Avenue, adjacent to Van Cortland Park. There is a marker.

**578. Mather, David "Mysterious Dave"** (August 10, 1851–?). He was a gunman who sometimes served as a lawman in Kansas and elsewhere. He killed Tom Nixon in Dodge City, Kansas, but was not convicted. Mather moved throughout the West and little is known of his later life or his death.

**579. Mathews, Jacob Basil "Billy"*** (May 5, 1847–June 3, 1904). Born in Tennessee, he served in the Confederate Army during the Civil War. After the war he mined for a time and then took up ranching in New Mexico. He later moved to Lincoln, New Mexico, and became associated with James J. Dolan. Sheriff Pat Brady deputized Mathews, and it was Mathews' posse that killed John Tunstall. After Brady's death, Sheriff George W. Peppin retained Mathews as a deputy, and he took part in the five-day battle at Lincoln. Later he resumed ranching for a time before moving to Roswell, New Mexico, where he served as postmaster for several years. Billy died there and was buried in South Park Cemetery, Lot 11, South Masonic Circle. There is a very large marker. The grave is in the southwest quadrant of the circle. His wife, Cora (1867–1952), is buried beside him. The marker is the largest on Masonic Circle.

**580. Mathewson, William\*** (January 1, 1829–March 22, 1916). He was the "Original Buffalo Bill" and was a noted army scout. He is buried in Highland Cemetery in Wichita, Kansas. His grave and large monument are in the south central part of the cemetery. It is easily located because of its size.

**581. Maxwell, C.L. "Gunplay"\*** (?–August 23, 1909). He was a noted Utah horse thief and small-time outlaw. He served a prison sentence for bank robbery, but it was commuted before he served all of the eighteen-year term. He was killed on the streets of Price, Utah, in a gunfight with a man called "Shoot-em-up Bill" and is buried in the Price Cemetery. There is a large stone monument adjacent to one of the drives recognizing Maxwell and other Utah gunfighters, but the exact location of their graves is unknown.

**582. Maxwell, Electa B.\*** (May 8, 1842–May 5, 1912). She first married Sheriff Henry Plummer, who led a large band of outlaws in southwestern Montana. After a few months she left him and went to Vermillion, South Dakota, to live with her sister, a Mrs. Vail. Later she married James Maxwell and they had three children. James also had six children by a previous marriage. Electa and James, along with several of their children, are buried in Union Cemetery in Wakonda, South Dakota, which is a few miles north of Vermillion. To locate the cemetery and graves: in Wakonda, drive west on Ohio Street. The street bears right and ends at a cross-street. Turn left and go 0.5 mile. Turn left on a dirt road and go about two miles to the cemetery on the right. The Maxwell plot is in the southeast quadrant of the cemetery. The graves are marked with large, upright stones.

**583. Maxwell, Ella "Cattle Kate"** (1861–July 20, 1889). She was also known as Kate Averill and Ella Watson. She was a "soiled dove" who traveled throughout most of the West. In Wyoming, she lived with James Averill, a saloon owner. Many believed that she was taking stolen cattle for her favors. As a result, a group of cattlemen, led by A.J. Bothwell, Tom Sun, and several others, hanged both Averill and Ella in Spring Creek Gulch in Wyoming. They were buried nearby, but the graves are now covered by a lake. No one was ever convicted of the murders.

**584. Maxwell, Lucien Bonapart\*** (September 14, 1818–June 25, 1875). He was a cattleman of New Mexico and Colorado. In his younger days he took part in one of John C. Frémont's expeditions as a hunter. He gained control over the enormous Beaubien-Miranda Land Grant through his marriage to Maria de la Luz Beaubien. His holdings amounted to more than 1,700,000 acres in Colorado and New Mexico. He had fine homes at both Fort Sumner and Cimarron, New Mexico. Maxwell is buried in the old Fort Sumner post cemetery near the grave of Billy the Kid. There is a very large marker.

**585. Maxwell, Pedro "Pete"\*** (April 27, 1848–June 21, 1898). He was the son of Lucien Maxwell. It was in his bedroom that Pat Garrett shot and killed Billy the Kid. After his father's death, Pete lost all of the Fort Sumner, New Mexico, holdings through gambling and poor management. His is buried in the old Fort Sumner post cemetery near his father. There is a marker.

**586. Mayer, Frank H.\*** (May 28, 1850–February 12, 1954). He was born in New Orleans, Louisiana, and became one of the most noted buffalo hunters in the West. He died at age 103 and is buried in Fairview Cemetery at Fairplay, Colorado. To locate the cemetery and grave: from Fairplay, drive north on US 285 about 0.8 mile. Turn right (east) on a gravel road for 0.6 mile to the cemetery. Keep right on entering the cemetery and drive to the south end. Circle to the left. As you climb the slight rise, a little lane angles to the left. Alone on the right is the pink marble stone, about eighteen inches high, marking Mayer's grave.

**587. Meagher, Michael "Mike"\*** (April 3, 1842–December 17, 1881).
He was marshal of Wichita, Kansas, mayor of Caldwell, Kansas, in
the 1870s, and also a deputy United States marshal. He was killed
in Caldwell by a group of five cowboys, and is buried in Highland
Cemetery in Wichita beside his father, Timothy (May 16, 1812–
December 27, 1871). To locate the grave: from Hillside Street, turn
west into the cemetery just north of Ninth Street. Drive straight
ahead to within about sixty feet of the far (west) side of the cemetery.
The grave is on the left, next to the drive. There is a ten-foot-tall,
marble marker.

**588. Medina, Mariano.** See Modena, Mariano.

**589. Meek, Joseph Lafayette "Joe"\*** (February 7, 1810–June 20, 1875).
He was a mountain man who trapped and explored throughout the
Northwest as well as California. Meek settled about four miles north
of Hillsboro, Oregon, where he died. He was first buried on his farm
but later his remains were reinterred in the Tualatin Plains Presbyterian Church Cemetery (known locally as "The Old Scotch Church").
His wife and other family members are nearby. To locate the
cemetery: from Hillsboro, Oregon, at the junction of Oregon Highway 8 and First Street, go north on Glencoe Road 4.5 miles to Scotch
Church Road. Turn right and go 0.5 mile to the Tualatin Plains
Presbyterian Church. The Meek grave is to the right of the church
and is marked by a tall obelisk with an inscription and a historical
marker. Joe's wife, Virginia (1824–March 5, 1900), and daughter,
Lizzie W. Meek (August 27, 1861–July 23, 1876), are buried
nearby.

**590. Meeker, Nathan Cook\*** (July 12, 1817–September 29, 1879). He
was Indian agent at the White River Ute Indian reservation in
Colorado and was killed by a group of Ute Indians under Chief
Douglas. Seven other agency personnel were killed also. Meeker
is buried in the Linn Grove Cemetery in Greeley, Colorado. A large,
pink marble stone marks his grave. The inscription on the stone
incorrectly gives his year of birth as 1814.

**591. Middleton, David Charles "Doc"\*** (February 9, 1851–December

27, 1913). He was a noted horse thief whose real name was James
M. Riley. Born out of wedlock, he began his horse stealing career
at the age of fourteen. He was sent to prison for fourteen years but
escaped twice. After the second escape he used the name, "David
C. Middleton." After forty-five months in the Nebraska state
penitentiary, Middleton was released and later operated saloons in
South Dakota and Wyoming. He died of pneumonia and is buried
in the Douglas Cemetery in Douglas, Wyoming, in Section 3, Block
2, Lot 3, Space 2. There is a ground-level marker of gray granite.

592. **Middleton, Harry**\* (?–September 19, 1887). He was killed by the
Tewksbury faction in the Pleasant Valley War in Arizona and is
buried in the Young Cemetery just north of Young, Arizona, and on
the west side of the road leading to Heber, Arizona. There is a small,
ground-level marker among the weeds.

593. **Milam, Benjamin Rush "Ben"**\* (October 20, 1788–December 7,
1835). He was a Texas hero killed by Mexican forces in the siege
of Bexar. Ben is buried in San Antonio, Texas, near the center of
Milam Square, which is bounded by West Commerce, West Houston, North San Saba, and Santa Rosa Avenue. There is a large grave
marker and, a few feet away, a very tall monument.

594. **Miles, Nelson Appelton** (August 8, 1839–May 15, 1925). He was
a career army officer who gained fame through his many victories
over the Indians in the West. He rose to the rank of brigadier general.
Miles died at Washington, D.C., during the playing of the national
anthem at the Ringling Brothers Circus and is buried in one of the
two mausoleums at Arlington National Cemetery. The mausoleum
is at the end of Miles Drive in Area IV, Section 3.

595. **Miller, Clelland D. "Clell"**\* (December 17, 1849–September 7,
1876). He was a member of the James-Younger Gang. Clell was
killed in the bank robbery attempt at Northfield, Minnesota, and is
buried beside his father, Moses W. Miller (May 26, 1798–January
3, 1879) in the Muddy Fork Cemetery about three miles north of
Kearney, Missouri, on State Highway 33. In the family plot there is
a central marker about seven feet tall dedicated to Clell and other

family members. In 1991, Clell's grave was marked by a regulation Confederate States of America military headstone. A brother, Francis M. Miller (July 22, 1853–September 24, 1874), is also buried there.

**596. Miller, James B. "Killing Jim"*** (October 25, 1861–April 19, 1909). He was a paid killer who was known to have killed more than a dozen men. Many believe that he killed Pat Garrett. In April of 1909, he ambushed and killed Gus Bobbitt, a prominent citizen of Ada, Oklahoma. Miller and the three men who hired him to do the killing, J.C. Allen, Jesse J. West, and Berry Burwell, were arrested and placed in the Ada jail. A mob composed of Bobbitt's friends took the four men from the jail and hanged them in an unused barn. Miller's body was taken to Fort Worth, Texas, and buried in Oakwood Cemetery, Block 101, Lot 14, Space 1. His wife, Sarah Francis, was the daughter of Mannen and Mary Ann Clements. Sarah Francis and Mary Ann are buried in the same plot as Miller.

**597. Miller, Sarah Francis "Sallie"*** (October 12, 1871–October 7, 1938). She was the wife of James B. Miller and the daughter of Mannen Clements. She is buried in Oakwood Cemetery in Fort Worth, Texas. She lies beside her husband in Block 101, Lot 14.

**598. Mills, John G.*** (?–July 4, 1883). He was one of several men killed in the Fourth of July shootout in Grand Lake, Colorado (see Day, Barney, for details). Mills is buried in the Grand Lake Cemetery, and the grave is marked by a ground-level, marble stone. To locate the cemetery and grave: from the spur road leading from US 34 into Grand Lake, take US 34 north and then turn left on the second road (marked "to Columbine Lake"). Take the second gravel road on the right and go up the hill to the cemetery. Mill's grave is behind the plot which is enclosed by a white picket fence.

**599. Milner, Moses Embree "California Joe"*** (May 8, 1829–October 29, 1876). He was chief of scouts under Lieutenant Colonel George Armstrong Custer. Milner was killed by Tom Newcomb at Fort Robinson, Nebraska, and was first buried in the Fort Robinson post cemetery near Crawford, Nebraska. Later his remains were reinterred in the Fort McPherson national cemetery about twelve miles southeast of North Platte, Nebraska. There is a United States military marker.

**600. Milton, Jefferson Davis "Jeff"** (November 7, 1861–May 7, 1947). At various times he was a Texas Ranger, a deputy sheriff in New Mexico, chief of police in El Paso, Texas, and an express messenger for Wells, Fargo. He retired in 1930 and died in Tucson, Arizona. In his book, *Jeff Milton: A Good Man With A Gun,* J. Evetts Haley stated that Milton's body was cremated and the ashes scattered over the desert.

**601. Miner, William "Bill"*** (December 27, 1846–September 2, 1913; NOTE: Some writers give his year of birth as 1843 or 1847). He was born in Ingham County, Michigan, near Onondaga, and became an outlaw and train robber at an early age. He committed his first stage robbery in 1869, starting him on a career in crime that was to last forty years. Miner spent most of his life in various prisons, from which he made several escapes. His last robbery was in 1911, when he robbed a Southern Railway express car near Gainesville, Georgia. He was sentenced to twenty years in prison but made two escapes, the last when he was almost sixty-five years of age. He died in the Georgia state penitentiary at Millegeville, Georgia, and was buried in Millegeville's cemetery on Memory Hill. A map showing the location of the grave is available at the cemetery office. A few years ago, a small marker was placed at the grave by Georgia historian Dr. James C. Bonner. It is inscribed, "Bill Miner, The Last of the Famous Western Bandits, Born 1843. Died in the Millegeville State Prison Sept. 2, 1914." The actual year of his death was 1913.

**602. Mitchell, Luther H.*** (1815–December 11, 1878). He was a homesteader and was killed near Callaway, Nebraska along with Ami Ketchum, in 1878. The two were killed by wealthy cattleman, I.P. "Print" Olive. Their bodies were partially burned after having been hanged and shot. Mitchell's body was taken to his former home at Central City, Nebraska, and buried in the Central City Cemetery in Lot 89. To locate the cemetery and grave: from US 30 in Central City, turn north on Highway 14 and go about one mile to the

*Burton Mossman, Mount Washington Cemetery, Independence, Missouri.*

*James B. "Killing Jim" Miller, Oakwood Cemetery, Fort Worth, Texas.*

cemetery on the right. Enter through the main entrance and go straight ahead (about 0.3 mile) until the main paved drive turns left toward the Civil War memorial directly ahead. On turning left, count the trees on the left until the fourth tree is reached. Just across the paved lane on the right and adjacent to the lane is the ground-level, gray marble marker. There is also a metal Civil War marker.

603. **Modena, Mariano\*** (circa 1812–June 25, 1878). He was a mountain man and the founder of Loveland, Colorado. Born in Taos, New Mexico, around 1812 (other dates given are 1810 and 1817), he served as a guide and scout and was a good friend of Kit Carson. He married a Flathead Indian woman called "John." Modena traded a Frenchman voyageur named Papa several horses for John, who would a short time later give birth to the Frenchman's son, Louis. Modena and John had four children of their own. They settled in Colorado on the Big Thompson River, where Modena operated a trading post. After John's death, he lived with another Indian woman for a time before marrying Susan Howard. He died in 1878 and was buried beside his first wife, John. To locate the grave: go west of Loveland on US 34. Shortly after passing Rist Bensen Lake on the right, turn left on Namaqua Road (County Road 19E), cross the railroad tracks and then Big Thompson River. On the left, just beyond the river bridge, is a park and picnic area. The Modena graves are behind a stone wall; the remains were moved there a number of years ago from their original burial place near the school which is a short distance beyond the park on the right. There is a metal plaque on the wall.

604. **"Molly B'Dam."** See Hall, Maggie.

605. **Monk, Henry "Hank"\*** (1833–February 28, 1883). He was a famous stagecoach driver in Nevada and California. Monk died in Carson City, Nevada, and is buried there in the western part of Lone Mountain Cemetery. There is an inscribed granite marker as well as the old original headstone.

606. **Mooar, J. Wright\*** (August 10, 1851–May 1, 1940). He and his brother, John, were two of the most famous buffalo hunters in the

West. J. Wright once killed a pure white (albino) buffalo, a statue of which is on the courthouse grounds in Snyder, Texas. The tanned hide is still in the possession of a descendant who lives about eight miles from Snyder. J. Wright is buried beside his wife, Julia (1852–1921), in the "old" Snyder Cemetery. To locate the cemetery and grave: from Twenty-third Street, take E Street north to the cemetery. Enter through the arch and drive to the second cross-lane. Turn left and go to the third cross-lane and turn right. Look for the McDonnell plot of his wife's family. The graves of J. Wright and Julia are marked with ground-level headstones.

**607. Mooar, John Wesley\*** (June 12, 1846–May 24, 1918). Born in Vermont, John was the brother of J. Wright Mooar. The two became famous in the buffalo hunting and hide business and later engaged in cattle ranching near Colorado City, Texas. John died and is buried in the Colorado City Cemetery, which is on the north side of Business 20 on the east side of town. His grave is on the east side of one of the north-south drives near a corner. His wife, Margaret Adams McCollum Mooar (1862–1918), is beside him. Also buried in this cemetery are three Texas Rangers whose graves bear official Texas historical markers.

**608. Morrow, David "Prairie Dog Dave"\*** (April 14, 1837–October 18, 1893). He worked at times as a lawman around Dodge City, Kansas. Morrow died at the state soldiers' home at Fort Dodge, Kansas, and is buried in Maple Grove Cemetery on the west side of Dodge City beside his wife, Mary E. Morrow (February 4, 1852–April 20, 1913). There is a small United States military marker which reads "David Morrow—Co. 'C', 1st. Cal. Cav." To locate the grave: from the front entrance of the office, look to the left toward the large Grand Army of the Republic monument. The grave is about 100 feet behind this monument. Morrow's grave is near a large tree with two large limbs forking about twenty feet above the ground. The marker is just before the cross-drive.

**609. Morse, Harry Nicholson** (February 22, 1835–January 11, 1912). Born in New York, he settled in California, where he served as sheriff of Alameda County from 1864 to 1878. Morse had been a sailor for four or five years before going to California in 1851. He did some mining and engaged in the hotel business, and in 1855, married Virginia E. Heslep. After fourteen years as sheriff, he started his own detective agency. He died of apoplexy in Oakland, California, and is buried there in Mountain View Cemetery. The grave is marked.

610. **Mossman, Burton\*** (April 30, 1867–September 5, 1956). Mossman was an Arizona lawman and at one time he was the manager of the Hashknife Outfit (Aztec Land and Cattle Company) near Holbrook, Arizona. Later he organized and led the Arizona Rangers. He died at Roswell, New Mexico, and is buried in Mount Washington Cemetery in Independence, Missouri, Block 2, Lot 742. The grave is marked with a dark marble stone.

611. **"Mother Featherlegs"\*** (?–1879). She operated a "house of joy" in eastern Wyoming. She is buried in a remote area several miles south of Lusk, Wyoming. The grave, which is marked, is accessible only by poor ranch roads across cattle range. A guide or detailed map is essential to locating the grave, which is protected by a heavy pipe fence. She was murdered by "Dangerous Dick" Davis for a $1,500 cache.

612. **Mullan, John** (July 31, 1830–December 28, 1909). He was an explorer and road builder. John graduated from West Point in 1852 and was chosen to lay out and build a road from Walla Walla, Washington, to Fort Benton, Montana. The military road, started in July 1859, was completed to Fort Benton in 1860. The road was some 624 miles long. Later Mullan practiced law in Washington, D.C., where he died near the age of eighty. He is buried in a cemetery at Annapolis, Maryland.

613. **Murphy, Lawrence Gustave\*** (1831–October 20, 1878). He served in the Civil War, attaining the rank of major. After leaving the army, he entered into a partnership with Emil Fritz and they opened a store in Lincoln, New Mexico. When Fritz became ill and returned to Germany, James Dolan became associated with Murphy. Murphy drank heavily and eventually Dolan moved him to Santa Fe,

New Mexico, where he died of cancer. He is buried in the Santa Fe national cemetery, and there is a large marker at his grave. To locate the grave: enter the cemetery through the main gate and drive straight ahead to an adobe service building at the back of the cemetery. Turn right here and go about fifty yards to a tall, brown sandstone marker on the left, which is next to Governor Charles Bent's white marble marker.

**614. Nation, Carry Amelia Moore*** (November 25, 1846–June 9, 1911). She was a social reformer and campaigned throughout the West against the use of alcohol and tobacco. Using her little hatchet, she smashed bars in half a dozen states. She died at Leavenworth, Kansas, and is buried in the Belton Cemetery in Belton, Missouri. The grave is in the southeast part of the cemetery. There is a large headstone.

**615. Nation, David*** (1827–October 1903). He was the divorced husband of Carry Nation. He died in Medicine Lodge, Kansas, and is buried in the Medicine Lodge Cemetery. His grave is marked by a small stone, about one foot in height, which is about twenty feet from the flagpole near the little office building. The Medicine Lodge Cemetery is beside US 281 some eight blocks north of the junction with US 160.

**616. Neiman, Charles Willis "Charley"*** (March 24, 1861–July 7, 1947). He was sheriff of Routt County, Colorado, from 1895 to 1905, and had spent many years as a cowboy before becoming a lawman. His most noteworthy accomplishment was the capture of outlaws Harry Tracy and David Lant. When the two escaped from jail at Hahns Peak, Colorado, Neiman led a posse in below-zero weather and recaptured the pair the next day. They later escaped again, this time from the Aspen, Colorado, jail. Neiman married Ruby Carle (1877–1965) in 1890 and they had several children. He died at Steamboat Springs, Colorado, in 1947 and was buried in the Yampa Cemetery at Yampa, Colorado. To locate the cemetery: from the Yampa River bridge at Yampa, go north on Highway 131 for 2.2 miles. Turn left on a gravel road for 0.5 mile to the cemetery. Neiman's grave is beside the right-hand branch of the cemetery drive and on the right. The grave is marked by a large, pink marble headstone.

617. **Nelson, John Young**\* (1869–1957). He was a sergeant of Indian Scouts in South Dakota and was the son of the more famous scout, John Nelson (1826–1903). Both father and son are buried in the Episcopal Cemetery at Pine Ridge, South Dakota. There is a United States military headstone.

618. **Nevill, Charles L.**\* (April 6, 1855–June 13, 1906). Born in Alabama, he grew up in Texas. He spent eight years as a Texas Ranger and carried the rank of captain when he left the force. Nevill was the man to whom the fatally wounded Sam Bass surrendered after the gun battle at Round Rock, Texas. He was a member of the first party to successfully negotiate the Rio Grande canyons by boat. He was elected sheriff of Presidio County, Texas, in 1882 and served for eight years. Nevill died at San Antonio, and was buried there in city cemetery number six. To locate the grave: after entering the cemetery, you can see the Nevill headstone to the right, about seventy feet from the entrance drive. There is a very large marble monument. His wife, Sallie E. Nevill (1860–1915), is beside him.

619. **Newcomb, George "Bitter Creek"** (circa 1867–July 20, 1895; NOTE: Some writers give the date of his death as May 1, 1895). He was a member of Bill Doolin's Gang. There is some question about the date and circumstances of his death. Most writers agree that he was killed by the Dunn brothers for the reward. Charlie Pierce, another gang member, was killed at the same time. Most authorities say that Bitter Creek was buried at Ten Mile Flat, west of Norman, Oklahoma, by his parents. I have talked to many people at Ten Mile Flat and none of them had ever heard of his burial place. One elderly lady suggested that the Canadian River, in changing its course, may have destroyed the grave site.

620. **Nickell, William "Willie"**\* (May 4, 1887–July 18, 1901). He was killed by a rifle bullet allegedly fired by Tom Horn and is buried in

Lot 950 of Lakeview Cemetery in Cheyenne, Wyoming. The grave is about 150 feet directly north of the small sandstone service building with a red tile roof on the west side of the cemetery. The marker, four or five feet tall, is of gray marble and is inscribed with the name "Nickell" at the base. There is another almost identical marker a few feet away. Willie's father, Kels P. (1855–1929), and mother, Mary (1865–1936), are buried beside him.

**621. Nixon, Thomas Clayton "Tom"*** (circa 1835–July 21, 1884). When George Hoover, mayor of Dodge City, Kansas, appointed Bill Tilghman city marshal, he also appointed Tom Nixon as assistant (or deputy) marshal. Nixon had also served as assistant under three or four other city marshals. Nixon married Cornelia Houston and they had three children, Albert, Howard Tracy, and Jessie. Tom was shot and killed by "Mysterious Dave" Mather on the streets of Dodge and was buried in the post cemetery at old Fort Dodge. His headstone was uncovered years ago during road work at the cemetery and is now displayed in the Dodge City Museum near the exit which leads from the building out into Dodge's Boot Hill.

**622. Nolin, Charles*** (1852–August 19, 1876). He was a Pony Mail carrier on the Sidney-Deadwood Gold Trail who was killed and scalped by Indians at what is today Sturgis, South Dakota. He was buried at the spot where he was killed. On June 7, 1889, local citizens reinterred his remains in Bear Butte Cemetery on the east side of Sturgis. A large boulder bearing a bronze plaque marks his grave in Section 2, about fifty feet from the flagpole. To locate the cemetery: from downtown Sturgis, take Sherman Street east for several blocks to a dead end at the cemetery.

**623. Norfleet, J. Frank*** (1865–October 15, 1967). When he was beaten out of more than $100,000 by stock-market con men, the Texas rancher started a search for the men responsible. The search lasted four years and covered more than 32,000 miles in the United States, Canada, Mexico, and Cuba. The five men were eventually caught along with some thirty others including lawmen and bankers who had been, in some way, involved in the fraud. All received long prison sentences. Norfleet died at the age of 102 at Hale Center,

Texas. His remains were placed in the mausoleum of Restlawn Memorial Park in Lubbock, Texas. His wife, Mattie E. Norfleet (1871–1972), died at the age of 101 and is beside her husband in Hope Sanctuary, C-4, C-1, and C-2. Two of their children are buried in the Norfleet plot in the Hale Center Cemetery.

**624. North, Frank J.**\* (March 10, 1840–March 14, 1885). Frank was the brother of Luther North. He was a Pawnee scout leader and carried the rank of major. While touring with Buffalo Bill's Wild West Show, he fell from a horse and was severely injured. Frank retired and moved to Columbus, Nebraska, where he died of asthma. He is buried beside his brother, Luther, in the Columbus Cemetery. There are large monuments at each grave.

**625. North, Luther Hedden** (March 6, 1846–April 18, 1935). He was a plainsman and army scout. North scouted for George A. Custer on his Black Hills exploring expedition in 1874. He died at his home in Columbus, Nebraska, and is buried beside his brother, Frank, in the Columbus Cemetery. Large monuments mark both graves.

# O

**626. Oakley, Annie\*** (August 13, 1860–November 3, 1926). She was probably the world's premier markswoman. An automobile accident in Florida in 1922 put an end to her career as a sharpshooter. She died in Greenville, Ohio, and her husband, Frank C. Butler, died eighteen days later on November 21, 1926. Both are buried in the Brock Cemetery in northern Darke County, Ohio. The graves are marked.

**627. Oatman, Lorenzo\*** (1835–October 8, 1901). He was a member of the Oatman family, all of whom—except Lorenzo, Olive, and Mary Ann—were massacred by Indians in Arizona on March 19, 1851. Lorenzo was left for dead and the sisters were captured. Lorenzo spent several years searching for his sisters and finally, after Mary Ann had died, he and Olive were reunited. Since the massacre Olive had believed that Lorenzo had been killed with the other members of her family. He died at Red Cloud, Nebraska, and was buried in the Red Cloud Cemetery. There is a marker.

**628. Oatman, Olive Ann.** See Fairchild, Olive Ann Oatman.

**629. O'Day, Thomas "Tom"** (1862–November 22, 1930). He was an outlaw who, for a time, rode with the Wild Bunch which included Kid Curry and the Sundance Kid. Tom took part in the Belle Fourche, South Dakota, bank robbery and after spending six years in the Wyoming state prison at Rawlins, he worked as a cowboy for the rest of his life, mostly in Iowa and South Dakota. He died following a wagon accident which resulted in injury and exposure to freezing temperatures. The accident occurred near his home at

178

White Horse, South Dakota. His sister had his body removed from its original grave and reinterred in Pleasant Hill Cemetery in Dunlap, Iowa. Many family members are here, but there is no marker for Tom. He is probably buried in the unmarked space beside his parents, Thomas (1822–1881) and Margaret (1832–1911).

630. **O'Folliard, Thomas "Tom"*** (1858–December 19, 1880). He was an outlaw and good friend of Billy the Kid. Tom was shot and killed by lawmen led by Pat Garrett. He was with the Kid and others at the time. He is buried beside Billy the Kid and Charlie Bowdre in the old Fort Sumner post cemetery. There is a large marker inscribed with the names of the three friends.

631. **Ogden, Peter Skene*** (February 1790–September 27, 1854). He was a fur trader and explorer and at one time was chief factor for the Hudson's Bay Company at Fort Vancouver, Washington. He died at Oregon City, Oregon, and is buried there in Mountain View Cemetery. There is a large, granite, upright marker.

632. **O'Hara, John "Jack"*** (August 14, 1852–February 14, 1884). He was a deputy sheriff of Lawrence County, South Dakota, and was a member of a posse that tried to arrest George Axelby and members of his outlaw gang at Stoneville, Montana Territory (now Alzada, Montana). The resulting gunfight proved fatal for O'Hara and four others. Axelby, a former Hashknife cowboy, eluded capture and later disappeared in Mexico. O'Hara was buried in Section 8, Block B, Lot 27, of the Spearfish Cemetery in Spearfish, South Dakota. There is a slender, inscribed, gray marble obelisk at the grave.

633. **Old, William "Billy"*** (circa 1874–April 28, 1914). He was a member of the Arizona Rangers and rose to the rank of lieutenant, second in command only to Captain Harry Wheeler. He may have been the son of the William Old(s) who was killed at the Battle of Adobe Walls in the Texas panhandle. He was killed by his wife, some say in a fit of jealousy, and is buried in the old Pearce Cemetery at Pearce, Arizona. There is a large monument which was placed there by his many friends.

634. **Olinger, Robert Ameridth "Bob"** (1841–April 28, 1881). He was a deputy United States marshal and was killed, along with James W. Bell, by Billy the Kid when the Kid escaped from jail in Lincoln, New Mexico. He was buried in the Fort Stanton post cemetery at Fort Stanton, New Mexico. There is no marker.

635. **Olive, Isom Prentice "Print"*** (February 7, 1840–August 16, 1886). He was a Texas, Nebraska, and Kansas cattleman. Print led some of his men in the lynching (and burning of the bodies) of Ami Ketchum and Luther Mitchell. He was convicted of murder, but legal maneuvering finally freed him at the cost of almost everything he owned. He was killed by Joseph Sparrow at Trail City, Colorado, and is buried beside his wife, Louisa E. (1845–April 25, 1892), and son, William Prentice, in Maple Grove Cemetery in Dodge City, Kansas, Block 6, Lot 29, Grave 5. There is a large marker.

636. **Olive, James "Jim"*** (May 21, 1804–July 10, 1882). He was the father of Print Olive. He is buried beside his wife, Julia Ann Brashear Olive, in the Lawrence Chapel Cemetery near Thrall, Texas, which is some eight miles east of Taylor, Texas. There is a headstone.

637. **Olive, Julia Ann Brashear*** (May 15, 1820–December 20, 1883). She was the wife of James Olive and the mother of Print. She is buried beside her husband in the Lawrence Chapel Cemetery near Thrall, Texas. James and Julia are between two of their sons, Bob and Jay. The graves are marked.

638. **Olive, Robert Allen "Bob"*** (January 9, 1855–November 27, 1878). A brother of Print Olive, Bob was deputized to bring in Ami Ketchum and Luther Mitchell for cattle theft, but in an ensuing gunfight he was shot and killed by Mitchell. His body was returned to Texas and was buried in the Lawrence Chapel Cemetery near Thrall, Texas. There is a marker.

639. **Olive, Thomas Jefferson "Jay"*** (circa 1842–August 20, 1876). He was a brother of Print Olive and was a Texas rancher. On the night of August 1, 1876, he was shot in a gunfight at the Olive Ranch

and died as a result. He is buried in the Lawrence Chapel Cemetery near Thrall, Texas. The grave is marked.

640. **Olive, William Prentice "Willie"**\* (October 9, 1868–September 8, 1887). He was the son of Print and Louisa E. Olive. Willie was shot from ambush and killed by Joe Hodge and a man named Henderson in the Oklahoma Strip. He is buried beside his parents in Maple Grove Cemetery in Dodge City, Kansas. The grave is in Block 6, Lot 29. There is a marker.

641. **Olney, Joseph Graves "Joe"**\* (October 19, 1849–December 3, 1884). He was a Texan by birth, but after getting into trouble there for rustling cattle and shooting a man, he moved into Arizona Territory, where he became friends with Johnny Ringo and Curly Bill Brocious. Joe ranched near Bowie, Arizona, and died from a fall from a horse. Joe is buried in Desert Rest Cemetery at Bowie beside his wife, Agnes Jane Olney (October 31, 1850–October 3, 1887). Other family members are also buried in the large Olney plot, which is beside the plot of James "Jim" Tevis, the founder of Bowie. A very large, marble headstone marks the graves of Joe and Agnes. To locate the cemetery and grave: from the center of the little town of Bowie, go north for 0.3 mile on North Central Avenue to the cemetery on the left. Walk west and to the right of two rows of tall cedars to two plots surrounded by wrought iron fences. To the right is the Tevis plot and to the left the Olney plot.

642. **Omohundro, John Baker "Texas Jack"**\* (July 26, 1846–June 28, 1880; NOTE: Omohundro's middle name is usually given as "Burwell" but the family Bible gives "Baker"). He was a noted scout who later became a showman with Buffalo Bill Cody's Wild West Show. He died at Leadville, Colorado, and is buried in Evergreen Cemetery in Leadville. To locate the grave: from downtown Leadville, take Eighth Street west and turn right on James. Enter the cemetery through the stone gate. Turn left along the eastern border of the cemetery for about 150 yards. The grave is in back of the George Stuart marker on the right. There is a headstone, which was placed there by Buffalo Bill Cody some years after Texas Jack's death.

**643. O'Neill, William Owen "Buckey"** (February 2, 1860–July 1, 1898). He was a lawman, cowboy, miner, newspaperman, soldier. Buckey was captain of Troop A of the First United States Volunteer Cavalry (the "Rough Riders") in the Battle of San Juan Hill in the Spanish-American War. He was killed in action and was buried nearby. On May 1, 1899, his body was removed and taken to Arlington National Cemetery in Virginia and reinterred with full military honors. There is a marker.

**644. Orchard, Harry\*** (March 18, 1866–April 13, 1954). Born in Ontario, Canada, his real name was Albert E. Horsley. He served a long prison term for killing ex-governor Frank Steunenberg of Idaho. Harry was the "hit man" for W.D. "Big Bill" Haywood and other union agents from Denver who were trying to organize local miners. He almost exclusively used high explosives in his assassinations. Orchard is buried in Morris Hill and Pioneer Cemetery in Boise, Idaho. The grave is marked with a flat, bronze marker in Section C, Block 8, Grave 1.

**645. Orrick, John C., Jr.** See Arrington, George Washington.

**646. Ormsby, William** (1814–May 12, 1860). He was a former army major. He led an expedition against the Paiute Indians at Pyramid Lake in Nevada and was killed along with more than half of the 103 men he led. Ormsby was buried at Carson City, Nevada. In 1885, his remains, along with those of his wife, Margaret, were removed to Oakland, California.

**647. Osborne, John E.\*** (June 19, 1858–April 24, 1943). Osborne was born in New York and was a graduate of the University of Vermont, where he studied medicine. He went to Rawlins, Wyoming, in the early 1880s and was appointed surgeon for the Union Pacific Railroad. He later became the largest sheep owner in the state. Osborne entered politics and served one term as territorial governor. He married Selina Smith of Princeton, Kentucky, and they had one daughter, Jean Curtis. When a mob at Rawlins lynched outlaw "Big Nose" George Parrott, Osborne removed skin from Parrott's body and had it tanned and made into a pair of shoes and other articles. The shoes may be seen today at the Carbon County Museum in Rawlins. Osborne died in Rawlins but was buried in a very large and elaborate marble vault in the Princeton Cemetery at Princeton, Kentucky. The grave is easily found because of the vault's size.

— CEDAR HILL CEMETERY

**648. Ouray\*** (1833–August 27, 1880; NOTE: Some give his year of birth as 1820). He was a chief of the Ute Indian Nation and was a friend to the white man. He died of kidney disease and is buried in the Indian cemetery at Ignacio, Colorado. There is a large marker. His wife, Chipeta, is buried in a small park beside US 550 south of Montrose, Colorado. For years she refused to tell where her husband was buried.

**649. Outlaw, Baz (or Bass) L.** (circa 1865–April 5, 1894). He rose to the rank of first sergeant in the Texas Rangers, but later he began to drink heavily, leading to the acceptance of his resignation by Captain Frank Jones. On April 5, 1894, in El Paso, Texas, Baz killed Ranger Joe McKidrict, who was attempting to arrest him for creating a disturbance in a house of ill repute. Constable John Selman then shot and killed Outlaw. Baz is buried in El Paso's Concordia Cemetery in an unmarked grave.

**650. Owens, Commodore Perry\*** (July 29, 1852–May 10, 1919). He was an Arizona lawman whose greatest fame came from a gunfight in Holbrook, Arizona, in which he killed Andy Cooper (real name Blevins), Mose Roberts, and Sam Blevins and wounded John Blevins. Owens fired only five shots. He died of paresis of the brain near Flagstaff, Arizona, and is buried there in Citizens Cemetery, Tract J, Block A, Lot 13, Space 2. The grave is opposite the mausoleum and has a chain link fence around it. The grave can be seen from the cemetery supervisor's office.

# P

**651. Packard, Thomas Jefferson "Jeff"\*** (1863–April 20, 1903). He was marshal of Bakersfield, California, and was killed by Jim McKinney and Alfred Hulse in the Joss House gunfight in Bakersfield. Also killed were Jim McKinney and lawman Will Tibbet. Packard is buried in Union Cemetery in Bakersfield. The grave is in the Benevolent and Protective Order of Elks Section, Main, Block 135, Lot 3. There is a black marble stone about one foot tall.

**652. Packer, Alferd (or Alfred)\*** (January 21, 1842–April 23, 1907). He became known as the "Colorado Cannibal." He was one of six men who attempted to travel from Montrose, Colorado, to the San Juan Mountains in 1874 after gold was discovered there. Only Packer made it through the winter snows. The remains of the five men who perished were later found, and Packer was accused of killing them and eating parts of their bodies to survive. After two trials and an escape, he was given a forty-year sentence on August 5, 1886. He was released on January 10, 1901. He is buried in the Littleton Cemetery, Littleton, Colorado. The grave is marked and is on Lilac Lane.

**653. Packer Victims Gravesite\*** In 1874, Alfred Packer killed the five men buried here after they became trapped by heavy snow and lack of food. Packer survived by eating parts of his victims. The grave site is about 2¹/₂ miles east of Lake City, Colorado, and about 600 yards north of State Highway 149. The burial site is enclosed by an iron fence, and a natural rock bears a bronze plaque which reads, "This tablet erected in memory of Israel Swan, George Noon, Frank Miller, James Humphries, and Shannon Bell who were murdered on this spot early in the year 1874 while pioneering the mineral resources of the San Juan country."

**654. Padda-wah-ser-man-oh.** See Ten Bears.

**655. Parker, Ann C. Gillies\*** (July 12, 1847–May 1, 1905). She was the mother of Butch Cassidy and is buried beside her husband, Maxmillian Parker, in the Circleville Cemetery in Circleville, Utah. The grave is near the center of the cemetery, which is just north of town.

**656. Parker, Arthur** (November 6, 1869–July 5, 1890). He was a brother of Butch Cassidy and was killed in a fall from a horse during Fourth of July races. He is supposedly buried in the Telluride Cemetery in Telluride, Colorado. His sister, Lula Parker Betenson, said that she visited his grave there. I have been unable to locate a marker.

**657. Parker, Cynthia Ann\*** (1827–circa 1870; NOTE: Many writers give the year of her death as 1865). She was captured by a band of Kiowa-Comanche Indians in 1838 and became the wife of Chief Peta Nocona (Nacona, Nakona) and bore him three children, including the famous Quanah Parker. Cynthia Ann lived with the Indians for more than twenty years before being set free by a group of Texas Rangers. She was returned to her people, along with her infant daughter, Topsannah (Prairie Flower), but was heartbroken and died in 1870. She was buried southeast of Poyner, Texas, but Quanah Parker later had her body moved to the Fort Sill military cemetery in Fort Sill, Oklahoma. Her grave is on the Chief's Knoll and is beside Quanah Parker and Topsannah. There is a marker. To locate the original grave site in Fosterville Cemetery in Henderson County, Texas: from Highway 175 near Poyner, Texas, go three miles south on Highway 131. Turn left on a dirt road for 0.7 mile. Turn left on a poor road and, when the road forks, keep right on an even worse road. Go 0.2 mile to the first gate, then about 200 feet to a second gate. About 100 yards from the second gate, a trail leads left for about 250 feet to the cemetery. Cynthia Ann's original grave is straight ahead. There still remains a marker composed of stone and concrete. Do not attempt to reach this grave site in bad weather.

*Left: Quanah Parker (tall obelisk) and Cynthia Ann Parker (immediate left of obelisk), Fort Sill post cemetery, Fort Sill, Oklahoma.*

*Right: Isaac Charles Parker, national cemetery, Fort Smith, Arkansas.*

**658. Parker, Isaac Charles*** (October 15, 1838–November 17, 1896).
He was the federal judge at Fort Smith, Arkansas, who had jurisdic-
tion over Oklahoma and Indian territories. He sentenced 162
persons to death by hanging and as a result, he was known as the
"Hanging Judge." During the thirty-one years that he was a judge,
eighty men were actually hanged. Parker died at Fort Smith and is
buried in the national cemetery. There is a marker.

**659. Parker, Quanah*** (circa 1845–February 23, 1911). He was a
Comanche chief and the son of Cynthia Ann Parker and Peta Nocona
(Nacona), a chief. He died at his home near Cache, Oklahoma, and
was buried nearby. His body was later removed to Fort Sill,
Oklahoma, and reinterred in the Fort Sill post cemetery where he
now lies on Chief's Knoll. A very large monument marks his grave.
His mother and sister are buried beside him.

**660. Parker, Robert LeRoy "Butch Cassidy"** (April 13, 1866–?).
Parker was the leader of a band of outlaws known as the "Wild
Bunch." He took the name "Cassidy" from an outlaw whom he
knew briefly as a youngster. Although he robbed both trains and
banks, he was never known to have killed anyone. Details of his
death are questionable. Some say he was killed in South America,
while others say he escaped from South America and died in
Washington State many years later.

**661. Parker, Maxmillian "Maxi"*** (June 8, 1844–July 28, 1938). He
was the father of Butch Cassidy. Both Maxi and his wife, Ann C.
Gillies Parker, are buried in the Circleville Cemetery in Circleville,
Utah. The cemetery is on the north side of town. To locate the
cemetery and grave: from US 89 north of Circleville, turn west on
100 E for 0.5 mile to the end of the pavement. Turn left (south) on
400 N for about 0.6 mile to the cemetery. Enter the gate, go past a
small black building on the left, and stop at two cedar trees close
together and just beyond the black building. The graves of the
Parkers are about twenty feet to the right and in line with the two
cedars. There are several markers for other members of the family.
Butch's sister, Lula Parker Betenson, is buried in the extreme

southeast corner of the cemetery. The names and dates of birth and death of those buried here are:

Ann C. Gillies Parker (July 12, 1847–May 1, 1905).
Lula Parker Betenson (April 5, 1884–May 5, 1980).
Jean A. Parker (October 16, 1871–April 8, 1960).
Mark D. Parker (October 4, 1886–June 7, 1932).
Eb Parker (June 19, 1879–October 22, 1957).
Joseph R. Parker (May 25, 1894–January 19, 1962).
Joseph A. Betenson, Lula's husband (June 29, 1887–July 8, 1948).
Nina G. Eckland (January 26, 1889–January 1, 1923).

Lula, Jean A., Mark D., Eb, Joseph R., and Nina G. were brothers and sisters of Butch Cassidy.

**662. Parkhurst, Charley Darkey\*** (1812–1879). Parkhurst was a stagecoach driver in California. When Charley died, it was discovered that Charley was a woman. She was the first woman to vote in the United States (November 3, 1868). She is buried in the Old Pioneer Cemetery (sometimes referred to as the "Oddfellow Cemetery") in Watsonville, California. To locate the grave: drive around the cemetery to locate two yellow brick structures about 100 feet apart. Parkhurst's grave is about midway between the two yellow structures. There is a large, inscribed marker in a nicely kept plot.

**663. Parmer, Allen H.\*** (May 6, 1848–October 27, 1924). He was the husband of Susan James Parmer, who was the sister of Jesse and Frank James. Parmer once rode with Quantrill's Raiders. He died in Wichita Falls, Texas, and is buried there in Riverside Cemetery beside his wife, Susan, and several of their children: Allen, Jr. (October 16, 1885–January 21, 1887); Robert A. (December 19, 1872–drowned July 9, 1883); a daughter called "Tot" on her headstone (December 25, 1886–October 6, 1892); and an infant son (died March 2, 1889). The graves are in the northeast quadrant of the cemetery beside a dirt lane passing between rows of cedars. All of the graves have markers, including an eight-foot obelisk beside a cedar tree for Susan. The house in which the Parmers lived in Archer City, Texas, burned about 1985 or 1986.

**664. Parmer, Susan James\*** (November 25, 1849–March 3, 1889). She was the sister of Jesse and Frank James. Susan died in Archer City, Texas, as a result of complications arising from childbirth. She is buried in Riverside Cemetery in Wichita Falls, Texas. Graves of Susan, her husband, Allen, and four children are in the plot, which is in the northeast quadrant of the cemetery beside a dirt lane leading between rows of cedars. The grave is marked by an eight-foot marble obelisk very close to a cedar tree. The children are listed under Parmer, Allen H.

**665. Parrott, George "Big Nose"\*** (?–March 22, 1884; Note: The last name is sometimes spelled "Parrotte"). He was an outlaw. Parrott and his gang attempted to rob a Union Pacific train and were trailed by Deputy Sheriff Robert Widdowfield and railroad detective Tip Vincent. The lawmen were ambushed and killed by Parrott and members of the gang. Two years later, Parrott was arrested in Montana and returned to Rawlins, Wyoming. A mob took Parrott from the jail and hanged him from a telegraph pole. Dr. John E. Osborne, who later became governor of Wyoming, made a death mask of Parrott and also removed skin from his body and had a pair of shoes and a bag made from it. The shoes are now on exhibit at the Carbon County Museum in Rawlins, as are other items relating to Parrott. The top part of Parrott's skull was sawed off and is currently exhibited in the Union Pacific Railroad Museum in Omaha, Nebraska. The rest of Parrott's remains were buried in a barrel. Sixty-nine years later they were dug up during construction work and identified.

See p. 182

**666. Patron, Juan Batista** (1850–April 9, 1884). Patron had studied law and had served in the New Mexico territorial legislature, where he was speaker of the house in 1878. He was a friend of the Tunstall-McSween faction during the Lincoln County War in New Mexico. He was killed by M.E. Maney (Mike Manning) in Puerto de Luna and buried nearby in Santa Rosa, New Mexico.

**667. Payne, David L.\*** (June 29, 1836–November 28, 1884). Payne was born in Indiana but went to Kansas when he was twenty-two years of age. He held various jobs such as hunter, scout, guide, and soldier, serving with the Fourth Kansas during the Civil War. He served as a Kansas legislator on two occasions and in 1868, he was commissioned captain of Company D of the Eighteenth Kansas Cavalry. After spending some time in Washington, D.C., he returned to Caldwell, Kansas, and began activities devoted to opening the unassigned lands in Indian Territory to homesteaders. Payne led numerous invasions of "Boomers" into the unassigned lands and was arrested on each occasion. His continued agitation resulted in an earlier opening of Oklahoma than would have occurred otherwise. His popularity resulted in the naming of a county for him. He died and is buried at Wellington, Kansas. His grave is in Block 80, Lot 13, which is in the northwest quadrant of the Wellington Cemetery. A six-foot square, black marble monument, bearing American flags on two sides, marks the grave.

**668. Peacock, James*** (August 5, 1824–June 21, 1914). He was a soldier in both the Mexican and Civil wars. Originally from Kentucky, he went to Missouri in 1830. At Independence he served as city marshal and deputy marshal. In 1882, he was elected mayor of Independence. Trouble developed between Peacock and "Jim Crow" Chiles, a Missouri badman who had been a member of Quantrill's Raiders. The climax came on September 21, 1873, when a gunfight erupted between the two men. As they grappled for a pistol, Chiles' twelve-year-old son, Elijah, shot Peacock in the back, but the officer was able to draw his own pistol and kill Chiles. Peacock's fifteen-year-old son, Charles, then shot Elijah, who died four days later. Peacock survived and lived to the age of eighty-nine. He died of natural causes and was buried in Woodlawn Cemetery in Independence in Lot 5 of Block 8. His wife, Minerva, and several children are beside him.

**669. Peacock, Lewis*** (?–June 14, 1871). He was the leader of the Peacock faction in the Lee-Peacock Feud in Texas. He was killed by a member of the Lee faction, probably Dick Johnson. He is buried in the old Pilot Grove Cemetery at Pilot Grove, Grayson County, Texas. To locate the grave: enter the cemetery and walk straight ahead to the back (east) side. A small, ground-level, marble stone marks the grave. It was placed there in the 1980s. For more than 100 years the grave was marked only by two bois d'arc sticks which are now in the possession of K.A. Jinkins, who lives a short distance west of the cemetery on the south side of the road.

670. **Pearce "The Kid"**\* (?–October 13, 1896; NOTE: His real name is unknown). "Pearce" was the name given him by the press. He was one of the three bank robbers shot and killed at Meeker, Colorado, during an attempted hold-up. The three are buried in the southeast corner of the Meeker Cemetery. There is a marker.

671. **Peppin, George Warden "Dad"**\* (October 1841–September 18, 1904). He became sheriff of Lincoln County, New Mexico, after Sheriff Pat Brady was killed by Billy the Kid. He served as leader of the Murphy-Dolan faction during the five-day battle at Lincoln, New Mexico. Peppin died in Lincoln and is buried beside his second wife and two children in the Lincoln Cemetery a short distance east of town beside US 380. Only Dad Peppin's grave is marked. The headstone is a United States military, white marble marker. A low concrete curbing surrounds the plot, which is in the western part of the cemetery. Peppin was a stone and brick mason by trade. His old home still stands in Lincoln and was in the process of being restored in 1989.

672. **Pfeiffer, Albert H.**\* (1822–April 6, 1881). Born in the Netherlands, he came to the United States as a young man. He drove freight wagons from St. Louis to Santa Fe, a city in which he later married. Pfeiffer became an officer in the New Mexico militia and, as a lieutenant colonel, served under Colonel Kit Carson in the campaign to round up the Navajos and put them on a reservation. Pfeiffer once represented the Ute Indian tribe in a knife fight with a Navajo brave for exclusive rights to the mineral waters at Pagosa Springs, Colorado. He killed his adversary and became a hero to the Utes. His wife and child were killed by Apaches in 1863. In 1881, Pfeiffer died at Grainger, Colorado, and was buried west of Del Norte, Colorado. To locate the grave: from US 160 nine miles west of Del Norte, turn north on County Road 16 for 1.4 miles. Then turn left and go 0.5 mile on County Road 15 to a large historical marker on the right. The grave is about 250 feet up the hill near a clump of scrub oaks. It is

surrounded by a white picket fence. Pfeiffer's grandson, A. Myrwood Goodman (1912–1966), is also buried there.

673. **Philip, James "Scotty"*** (April 30, 1858–July 23, 1911). He was a South Dakota rancher who was born in Scotland and came to the United States in 1874. Scotty is credited with helping to save the buffalo from extinction. He died on his ranch and is buried just a short distance from his home, which is west of Pierre, South Dakota. There is a marker in the family cemetery, which is to the left of the road leading to the ranch.

674. **Phillips, John "Portugee"*** (April 8, 1832–November 18, 1883). He was noted for his winter ride from Fort Phil Kearny to notify Fort Laramie of the Fetterman Massacre. During the ride of some 200 miles, one of his feet was frozen, resulting in later amputation. He died at Cheyenne, Wyoming, and is buried there in Lake View Cemetery. His grave is in Lot 30, on the outer perimeter of a circle 200 feet in diameter in the southeast part of the cemetery. It is marked by a fifteen-foot, gray marble monument with a large cross on top. Several of his children are buried in the Phillips plot: Mamie L. (died January 15, 1883, age 11 years, 11 months, 8 days), Johnny (died June 1, 1879, age 2 months, 5 days), Georgia (died June 22, 1879, age 2 months, 22 days), and Maud Ellen (died January 18, 1876).

675. **Phy, Joseph "Joe"*** (May 22, 1845–June 1, 1888). He was killed in a gunfight with Sheriff Pete Gabriel in Florence, Arizona. At one time he had been Gabriel's deputy and friend. Gabriel was also seriously wounded in the fight, and at first it was believed that his wounds would prove fatal. However, he eventually recovered. Phy was buried with Masonic rites in the Florence Cemetery south of town in Block 7, Lot 3, Grave 2. To locate the cemetery and grave: drive south from Florence about one mile on US 89. Turn right (west) on a paved road just after passing over a large canal. Continue on this road for 0.6 mile as it curves to the left to the cemetery. Turn right after entering the cemetery and go to the third major lane. The grave is on the corner of this lane. The inscribed marker is about three feet high, and the stone has yellowed with age.

**676. Pickett, Thomas "Tom"\*** (May 27, 1856–May 14, 1934). He was a member of Billy the Kid's Gang in New Mexico. After the death of Billy the Kid, Pickett left New Mexico and spent most of the remainder of his life in Arizona. He died at Pinetop, Arizona, a few days short of his seventy-eighth birthday, and is buried in Desert View Cemetery in Winslow, Arizona, Lot 6, Block 29, Subdivision A. His grave marker says, "In charge of government stables, Fort Apache, 1908." The metal marker is about eight inches by six inches.

**677. Pierce, Abel Head "Shanghai"\*** (June 29, 1833–December 26, 1900). He was a famous Texas cattleman, and his huge ranch was near Blessing, Texas. Pierce is buried in the Hawley Cemetery just east of Blessing. Before he died he had a large figure of himself carved to be placed over his grave. The cemetery is one mile north of State Highway 35. His brother, Jonathan Edward, is buried beside him but with only a modest headstone.

**678. Pierce, Charlie\*** (?–May 1, 1895; Note: His headstone gives his date of death as May 5, 1895, and spells his name "Pearce"). He was a member of Bill Doolin's Gang and was a good friend of "Bitter Creek" Newcomb. He, along with Bitter Creek, was assassinated by brothers Bee and John Dunn at the Bee Dunn Ranch near Ingalls, Oklahoma, for the $5,000 reward. Pierce is buried near Bill Doolin in the Summit View Cemetery at Guthrie, Oklahoma. There is a grave marker.

**679. Pierce, William Hartwell\*** (September 3, 1833–February 27, 1862). He was a physician and was killed by the Peacock faction during the Lee-Peacock Feud in Texas. He is buried beside his father, Benjamin Pierce (December 29, 1793–March 1, 1881), in the Old Pilot Grove Cemetery at Pilot Grove, Grayson County, Texas. As you enter the cemetery, the grave is on the left-hand side, just over the small rise. To the left of the Pierce graves are several Clement graves, including a "Mannan Clement." Benjamin's headstone is badly broken. To locate the cemetery: from Whitewright in Grayson County, go south 4.5 miles on Highway 160 and turn right on Highway 121 for about a mile to the first of two cemeteries on the left.

**680. Pike, Albert** (December 29, 1809–April 2, 1891). Pike was a fur trapper. He served in the Mexican War and was at the Battle of Buena Vista. In the Civil War he was an Arkansas brigadier general and fought in the Battle of Pea Ridge. He moved to Washington, D.C., where he died. Pike is buried in Oak Hill Cemetery in Washington.

**681. Pike, George*** (circa 1855–1908). He was a Wyoming cowboy and horse thief with a likable personality. When he died a marble headstone inscribed with a verse was placed at his grave by a former employer. He is buried in the Douglas Cemetery in Douglas, Wyoming.

**682. Pitts, Charlie*** (?–September 21, 1876). He was a member of the James-Younger Gang and was also known as Samuel Wells. He was killed by a posse a few days after the attempted bank robbery at Northfield, Minnesota. His body was turned over to Dr. Henry F. Hoyt, who used the skeleton in his Chicago office for many years. The Bank Museum in Northfield has a skeleton believed to be that of Pitts on exhibit.

**683. Pleasants, Henry Clay*** (March 23, 1828–November 7, 1899). As judge of the Twenty-third District Court in Texas, he was instrumental in bringing law to DeWitt County during the Taylor-Sutton Feud. He was a graduate of the University of Virginia and practiced law in Virginia before going to Clinton, Texas, in 1854. He was a judge for forty years. He is buried in Hillside Cemetery in Cuero, Texas. To locate the cemetery and grave: from US 87 in Cuero, take Valley Street northeast to the cemetery on the right. Enter the cemetery from the Valley Street entrance, turn left and go to the second paved drive. Turn right and go to the first large group of trees on the left. Henry's headstone is on the corner along with an official Texas historical marker. His wife, Ann Eliza (September 2, 1837–September 17, 1918), is beside him.

**684. Plenty Coups*** (1848–May 3, 1932). He was a Mountain Crow Indian chief who was always a friend of the whites. He died at Pryor, Montana, and is buried in the Indian cemetery near his home, which still stands. There is a grave marker. An Indian museum is also located at Pryor.

**685. Poe, John William\*** (October 17, 1850–July 17, 1923). He was a Texas and New Mexico lawman and was with Pat Garrett at Fort Sumner, New Mexico, when Garrett killed Billy the Kid. Poe succeeded Garrett as sheriff of Lincoln County, New Mexico. His wife, Sophie, wrote a book, *Buckboard Days,* about his experiences. He died either of pneumonia or by suicide. He is buried beside his wife, Sophie M. Poe (1863–1954), in South Park Cemetery in Roswell, New Mexico. To locate the grave: from the office, drive straight ahead into the cemetery to the circle. From the middle of the circle, look forty-five degrees to the right and ahead. The graves are side by side and are easily found. They are in Block SMC, Lot 51.

**686. "Poker Alice."** See Ivers, Alice.

**687. Potter, Andrew Jackson\*** (April 3, 1830–October 20, 1895). Potter was born in Missouri and as a youngster rode race horses. He joined an expeditionary force and went to New Mexico and then in 1851, he left for California with a group of Mormons. Potter next moved to San Antonio, Texas, where he became a freighter. In 1853 he married Emily Guin, and they eventually had fourteen children, eight boys and six girls. Shortly after he married, he was converted to the Methodist religion and obtained a license to preach. In 1861 he drove a herd of cattle to Kansas, after which he returned to Texas. Potter served in the Confederate Army throughout the Civil War as chaplain of the Twenty-sixth Texas Cavalry. When the conflict was over, he helped found numerous frontier churches. He dropped dead in the pulpit of Tilman Chapel, Texas, and was buried in Bunton Cemetery, a short distance from Lockhart, Texas. A square, white marble stone, about four feet tall and set on a concrete base, marks his grave. It is about fifty feet from the east boundary of the cemetery and about two-thirds of the way from the south to the north boundary.

**688. Pourier, John "Big Bat"\*** (October 5, 1841–circa September 7, 1932). He was a scout for the United States Army. He died of natural causes at his Horsehead Ranch near Manderson, South Dakota, and is buried in the Red Cloud Cemetery about two miles west of Pine Ridge, South Dakota. The cemetery is on the south side of US 18, at the entrance to the Indian mission. He is buried beside his son, Joseph Pourier (July 29, 1878–September 15, 1907). There is an inscribed headstone. Many descendants of Big Bat still live in Manderson, South Dakota.

**689. Power, John Grant\*** (September 11, 1891–April 5, 1976). He was the brother of Tom Power. Tom and John, along with Tom Sisson, received life sentences for killing Sheriff Robert F. McBride and two deputies, Martin Kempton and Kane Wootan, in a shootout in the Galiuro Mountains of Arizona. The Power brothers were paroled after forty-one years in prison. John died of influenza at Klondyke, Arizona, and is buried beside his brother in the Klondyke Cemetery. Sisson died in the Arizona state prison in Florence. To locate the cemetery: see Power, Thomas.

**690. Power, Thomas J., Jr. "Tom"\*** (1894–September 12, 1970). He was the brother of John Power. Tom died of a heart attack at the Joe Bull Ranch at Sunset, Arizona, and is buried along with other family members in the Klondyke Cemetery at Klondyke, Arizona. To locate the cemetery: the caretaker lives in the last house before reaching the Klondyke store. Permission to visit the cemetery must be obtained here. From the Klondyke Road enter the gate leading to the ranch house, pass around the house, and through another gate. Keep right on the poor dirt road as it passes to the right of a hill and then climbs the hill to the cemetery on the left. The poor dirt road continues past the cemetery, so it is necessary to keep a sharp lookout for the cemetery. There are about a half dozen or so graves with headstones surrounded by cactuses. Buried here are: the Power boys' father, T.J. "Old Man" Power, Sr., who was killed in the shootout in 1918 at the age of fifty-four ("Shot down with his hands up in his own door"); their grandmother, Martha Jane "Granny" Power ("1915—Killed in a run away horse and buggy accident"); and their sister, Ola May Power ("1917—Poisoned by an unknown person").

**691. Power, William "Bill"*** (?–October 5, 1892). He was also known as "Joe Evans" and "Tom Evans" and was a member of the Dalton Gang. He was killed in the attempted robbery of two banks simultaneously in Coffeyville, Kansas, and is buried beside Grat and Bob Dalton in Elmwood Cemetery in Coffeyville. A marker includes the three names, Bob Dalton, Grat Dalton, and Bill Power. The marker is in the row of graves next to the railroad tracks.

**692. Powers, John Hall*** (December 25, 1863–February 5, 1902). At one time he was sheriff of Johnson County, Arkansas. When four outlaws dynamited the bank vault in Clarksville, Arkansas, Powers rushed to the bank and was fatally wounded in the ensuing gunfight. Prior to becoming sheriff, he and Bud Ledbetter had served as deputies under Bud McConnell. The citizens of Clarksville raised $1,500 to erect a large monument at Powers' grave. It is the largest in Clarksville's Oakland Cemetery. To locate the grave: enter the cemetery through the arch and follow the paved drive to the first paved drive to the left. Turn left here and go a short distance to the large, impressive monument on the left.

**693. Prairie Flower "Toh-Tsee-Ah" or Topsannah*** (1858–1863). She was the daughter of Cynthia Ann Parker and Chief Peta Nocona. She died shortly before her mother and was buried in Fosterville Cemetery in Henderson County, Texas, a few miles southeast of Poyner. Her body was later removed, and she now lies beside her mother and brother, Quanah Parker, on Chief's Knoll in the post cemetery at Fort Sill, Oklahoma.

**694. Preese, Thomas William "Billy"*** (February 11, 1856–February 2, 1928). He was sheriff of Uintah County, Utah, and took part in the chase and capture of outlaw Harry Tracy. He died of dropsy and is buried in the family plot in Rock Point Cemetery near Vernal, Utah. There is a headstone. To locate the cemetery: in Vernal, Utah, go west on Main Street (US 191) to 500 West. Turn right (north) and go 0.5 mile on 500 West to 500 North. Follow the curve to the left (west). Go one mile from the curve on 500 North and then turn right (north). Go 1.95 miles until you see a church steeple on the left. Just before reaching the church, turn left (west) and follow the curving road for 0.9 mile, and then turn right (north) for 0.15 mile to the cemetery. Preece's grave is directly across the paved drive from the flagpole. Many members of the Preece family are buried here. Billy Preece's grave marker gives the year of birth as 1854. This is incorrect. The actual year is 1856.

**695. Price, Sterling*** (September 14, 1809–September 29, 1867). He was a Confederate major general in the Civil War and took part in many battles including Wilson Creek and Pea Ridge. Price had also served during the Mexican War as a colonel under General Stephen Watts Kearny, and he was a one-term governor of Missouri. He died in St. Louis, Missouri, and is buried there in Bellefontaine Cemetery. There is a large monument at his grave. A map of the cemetery can be obtained at the office.

**696. Pridgen, Oscar Fitzgerald "O.D."*** (June 13, 1853–July 11, 1944). He was active in the Sutton-Taylor Feud in DeWitt County, Texas, and served for a few months in the Texas Rangers. He is buried in Oakwood Cemetery in Austin, Texas. To locate the grave: enter the cemetery from Navasota. Go past the office on the left and turn right on the first narrow drive. Follow the drive as it curves right, then left. After the left-hand curve, go about seventy-five feet and look for the gray marble marker on the right. His wife, Mary Alice (March 8, 1860–September 22, 1948), is buried beside him.

**697. Proctor, Ezekiel "Zeke"*** (July 4, 1831–February 28, 1907). He was a wealthy half-Cherokee Indian. He died of pneumonia and is buried in the Proctor family cemetery (now called the Johnson Cemetery) which is located on the right hand side of *old* Oklahoma State Road 33, five miles west of Siloam Springs, Arkansas. His headstone is the largest in the cemetery. There are many other Proctors buried here.

**698. Provost, Etienne** (1785–July 3, 1850). He was a mountain man for whom Provo, Utah, was named. Provost died in St. Louis, Missouri. His funeral services were held in the St. Louis Cathedral, and he was interred in the cathedral burial grounds. Later his body was reburied in Calvary Cemetery in St. Louis. The exact location is not known.

**699. Pryor, Nathaniel Hale "Nate"** * (circa 1775–June 1, 1831). He was a member of the Lewis and Clark Expedition, and Pryor, Oklahoma, is named for him. Nate died at his trading post about 3¹/₂ miles south of present-day Pryor and was originally buried there. In 1982, the Mayes County Historical Society had his remains moved to the Pryor Cemetery. He now rests in a beautiful plot on the south side of the highway which bisects the cemetery. The grave is just beyond a little hill and is covered by a very large, inscribed stone giving biographical information on Pryor. A low chain fence surrounds the grave.

**700. Puneney, Walter C. "Walt"** * (May 1, 1870–April 19, 1950). He was a friend of Butch Cassidy and other members of the Wild Bunch, but there is no proof that he was a regular member of that gang. The only crime with which he was ever charged was being an accomplice in robbing the bank in Belle Fourche, South Dakota. He was arrested, tried, and found not guilty when witnesses placed him many miles from the scene of the robbery. Walt left Frankfurt, Kansas, where he was born and went to Wyoming at the age of eighteen. He ranched at various locations in the state, and in 1893, he was appearing as top rider and roper with Buffalo Bill Cody's show in St. Louis, Missouri. In 1907, he married Alice Walker. They had three daughters, Nellie, Gladys, and Florence. Puteney was of French Huguenot ancestry and originally the family name was "de Puntenney." After coming to America, the family shortened the name. Walt's father, Eli, had settled in Frankfurt, Kansas, where he became a well-to-do and respected citizen. Walt underwent major surgery at the Mayo Clinic in 1949 and died a few months later in Pinedale, Wyoming. He was buried there in Pinedale Cemetery. For many years prior to his death he had operated the Cowboy Saloon in Pinedale. To locate the grave: from the east end of Pinedale, take Highway 111 north toward Fremont Lake to the cemetery on the left. Enter the cemetery, drive past the maintenance buildings, and turn right on a gravel drive. About halfway down the drive, look about fifty feet to the right for four spruce trees forming a small square. Puteney's grave is under the spruce on the left. There is a small, pink marble, ground-level marker inscribed "Walter Puteney."

# Q

**701. Quantrill, Kate King\*** (1848–1930). Kate gained notoriety when she left home and ran away with William Clarke Quantrill at the age of fourteen. A prominent member of Quantrill's command, Fletcher Taylor, said that he loaned his horse to Kate so that she and Quantrill could ride six miles to a minister to be married. No proof of this has surfaced. Kate rode with the guerrillas and accompanied her lover when he went to Texas. She was left behind when Quantrill rode to his death in Kentucky. Kate supposedly ran a brothel in St. Louis, Missouri, for a time before marrying a man named Wood. When that marriage broke up, she married again, this time to a man named Head. She spent her last years in the Jackson County, Missouri, old folks home, where she was known as Sarah Head. Kate died at age eighty-two and was first buried in the little cemetery at the old folks home. Later her remains were reinterred in the Slaughter Cemetery north of Blue Springs, Missouri, beside her parents, Robert and Malinda King, and her brother, Francis. Her grave is marked by a low, pink marble, inscribed stone. To locate the cemetery: from Blue Springs take State Road 7 north to Pink Hill Road. Turn east on Pink Hill Road for 2.1 miles and turn left (north) on Slaughter Road. Go 0.4 mile to a gravel lane and turn right (a little pond will be on the left after turning). Stop at the house on the left for permission to visit the cemetery, which is 0.5 mile from Slaughter Road. The grave is in the easternmost part of the cemetery.

**702. Quantrill, William Clarke\*** (July 31, 1837–June 6, 1865). He was a captain in the Confederate Army during the Civil War and led a band of guerrillas whose most infamous act was the sacking of Lawrence, Kansas. He was killed in Kentucky and was originally buried in the St. John's Catholic Cemetery in Louisville, Kentucky. His body was later taken to Dover, Ohio, where he was born, and buried in the Dover Cemetery. There is a grave marker. Some of his bones were not buried, and the Dover Museum has what is believed to be his skull. Other bones, supposedly those of Quantrill, are stored at the Kansas State Historical Society in Topeka, Kansas.

**703. Queton\*** (1850–1931). He was a Kiowa leader and is buried in the Rainy Mountain Cemetery in Oklahoma. To locate the cemetery: see Gotebo.

**R**

**704. Rae, Nick.** See Ray, Nick.

**705. Raidler, William "Little Bill"** (circa 1866–?). He was a member of the Dalton and Doolin gangs and took part in the bank robbery at Southwest City, Missouri, in which banker J.C. Seabourn was killed. After serving a prison sentence, he returned to Oklahoma and led a clean life until his death some years later. His grave site is unknown.

**706. Rand, Theodore P.*** (?–December 27, 1902). He was a Pony Express rider. Rand died at Atchison, Kansas, and is buried in the Oak Hill Cemetery in Atchison in Division East, Block 1, Lot 12, Grave 6. He is twenty graves south of the flagpole on the east side of the drive and two rows in from the drive. There is no marker. To locate the cemetery: in Atchison, go west on Main Street (Highway 9) to Seventeenth Street. Turn right to the cemetery on the left. The entrance is off Atchison Street.

**707. Rash, Madison M. "Matt"*** (January 4, 1865–July 8, 1900). He ran a small herd of cattle in Brown's Park, Colorado, and also acted as foreman of the Bassett Ranch. He and Ann Bassett were probably lovers. Matt was shot at his cabin by Tom Horn, who a short time later killed Isom Dart, a friend of Matt's. Rash was originally buried near his cabin; later his father, Samuel, and brother, James, moved the body to the Acton Cemetery at Acton, Texas. He was reinterred near the grave of his aunt, Mrs. Davy Crockett. A large marble obelisk marks his grave. Inscribed on the stone is the following: "M.M. Rash, Born Jan. 4, 1865. Murdered in his cabin on Cold

Spring Mt., Routt County, Colo., July 8, 1900. A dutiful son, a faithful friend, a worthy citizen." Matt's mother, Mary Ann Rash (January 17, 1837–January 24, 1877), and father, Samuel A. Rash (October 17, 1830–March 23, 1910), are buried nearby.

**708. Rath, Charles** (circa 1836–July 30, 1902). He was a Dodge City, Kansas, pioneer and hide dealer. He founded Rath City, Texas, a town that no longer exists. He died in Los Angeles, California, and is buried there in Rosedale Cemetery in Section C, Lot 112, Portion 3 NW.

**709. Rath, Ida Ellen (Ellen Drinkwater)*** (November 10, 1884–May 21, 1971). She was an author and the daughter of Charles Rath, Dodge City pioneer. She is buried in Maple Grove Cemetery in Dodge City, Kansas, in the West Grand Army of the Republic Section, Lot 1, Block 72.

**710. Ravalli, Antonio*** (May 16, 1811–October 2, 1884). Father Ravalli was a Jesuit missionary to the Indians of the Northwest. He designed and helped build the St. Mary's Mission Church at Stevensville, Montana. After serving in Idaho and Washington, he returned to Montana, where he died. He is buried at Stevensville near the old Mission Church. A very tall monument marks his grave.

**711. Ray, Nick*** (1864–April 9, 1892). He was a small-time rustler who worked with Nate Champion on the KC Ranch near Kaycee, Wyoming. Nick and Nate were killed by the Johnson County "Invaders." He is buried beside Champion in the Willow Grove Cemetery at Buffalo, Wyoming. There is a small marker.

**712. Rayner, Hamilton Polk** (June 6, 1860–April 12, 1932). He was a lawman in several Kansas and Texas towns. He died at Wichita Falls, Texas, but was taken to El Paso, Texas, for burial. I do not know the final disposition of his remains.

**713. Red Cloud*** (September 20, 1822–December 10, 1909). He was a highly respected chief of the Oglala Sioux and led many war parties along the Bozeman Trail. He is buried in the Red Cloud Cemetery about two miles west of Pine Ridge, South Dakota. The cemetery is on the south side of US 18 at the entrance to the Pine Ridge Indian mission. There is a large marker at his grave, which is on the east side of the cemetery near the wire fence. The famous Red Cloud Prayer Circle is a short distance from the cemetery.

**714. Reed, James Edward "Eddie"\*** (February 22, 1871–December 14, 1896). He was the son of Belle Starr and Jim Reed. After serving a short prison sentence for selling liquor, he became a deputy United States marshal. In 1896, he killed the two Crittenden brothers, Dick and Zeke, in a gunfight at Fort Gibson, Oklahoma. Eddie was killed in Claremore, Oklahoma, by two bartenders. He is buried in the Cochran family cemetery about six miles south of Claremore, near Tiawah. A small obelisk marks his grave. The marker was turned over when I visited the grave site in 1984. The marker incorrectly gives 1877 as the year of his birth. To locate the cemetery: from Tiawah, Oklahoma, drive 1.7 miles south on Highway 88. Turn right on Yoachum Road. Go 0.7 mile and turn right on a narrow dirt road. Go 150 yards and park. The grave is in a small clump of trees about 100 feet to the left, in the middle of a field. The little cemetery is on private property.

**715. Reed, Pearl\*** (July 19, 1887–July 27, 1970). She is possibly the daughter of Rose Pearl Reed and the granddaughter of Belle Starr. She is buried in the Calvary Cemetery in Douglas, Arizona, not far from the grave of Rose Pearl Reed. There is a marker.

**716. Reed, Rose Pearl\*** (1868–July 6, 1925). She was the daughter of Belle Starr and Jim Reed, who were married in 1865 at Decatur, Collins County, Missouri. After running a house of ill repute for a number of years in Fort Smith, Arkansas, she moved to Douglas, Arizona, where she died. She is buried there in Calvary Cemetery, Lot 7, Section K. There is a low, dark gray marker.

**717. Reed, Nathaniel "Texas Jack"\*** (March 23, 1862–January 7, 1950). He was an outlaw of Texas, Oklahoma, and California. Reed was wounded by Bud Ledbetter and later gave himself up. He served a prison sentence, and after his release, he became an evangelist and preached for forty-one years. Reed died at his home in Tulsa, Oklahoma, and was buried in the cemetery at St. Paul, Arkansas, in an unmarked grave. The cemetery caretaker, however, knows the location.

**718. Reid, Frank H.*** (1844–July 20, 1898). He killed, and was killed by, "Soapy" Smith in a shootout in Skagway, Alaska. Both men are buried in a small cemetery just west of Skagway. A marked trail leads to the graves, both of which are marked.

**719. Reni, Jules.** See Beni, Jules.

**720. Reno, Frank*** (June 27, 1837–December 12, 1868). He was one of the four train-robbing Reno brothers. Frank, along with his three brothers, John, Simeon, and William, committed the first train robbery in America on October 6, 1866. After a number of other crimes, Frank, Simeon, and William were arrested and jailed at New Albany, Indiana. A mob of vigilantes invaded the jail and hanged the three, as well as a man named Anderson. The three Reno brothers are buried in the Seymour Cemetery in Seymour, Indiana. The brothers had served in the Civil War, and their graves are marked with standard United States military headstones and surrounded by a wrought iron fence.

**721. Reno, John** (?–January 1895). He was one of the Reno brothers who committed the first train robbery in America. John served a prison sentence, was pardoned in 1888, and died in Columbus, Indiana, in January 1895. The location of his grave is unknown.

**722. Reno, Marcus Albert*** (November 15, 1834–April 1, 1889). A native of Illinois, Reno was graduated from West Point and entered active military service in July 1857. His early service included tours of duty in Washington State as well as Oregon. During the Civil War he was a member of the Army of the Potomac and was breveted brigadier general. Following the war he joined the Seventh Cavalry as a major and was with Lieutenant Colonel George Armstrong Custer at the Battle of the Little Bighorn. When Custer split his command into three groups prior to the battle, Reno led one of the

*Red Cloud, Red Cloud Cemetery, Pine Ridge, South Dakota.*

*Charles Henry Rich, Miamiville Cemetery, Miamiville, Ohio.*

groups. His conduct during the fight was questionable. Later, after Custer and his immediate command were annihilated, Reno was severely criticized for not going to Custer's aid. In 1877, Reno was court martialed and dismissed from the service for "conduct unbecoming an officer." He died of cancer in 1889 and was buried in Glenwood Cemetery in Washington, DC. In 1967, a board of review reversed the court martial findings and changed his discharge to honorable. Some time later his remains were reinterred in the Custer Battlefield National Cemetery in Section C, Grave 1459. As a brevet brigadier general, Reno is the highest ranking officer in the cemetery and is also the only Seventh Cavalry officer buried there.

**723. Reno, Simeon*** (August 2, 1843–December 12, 1868). He was one of the Reno brothers who committed the first train robbery in America. See Reno, Frank.

**724. Reno, William*** (May 15, 1848–December 12, 1868). He was one of the Reno brothers who committed the first train robbery in America. See Reno, Frank.

**725. Reynolds, Glenn*** (December 19, 1853–November 2, 1889). He was sheriff of Gila County, Arizona, in the late 1880s. He was born near Albany, Texas, and was of the Reynolds family associated by marriage with the Matthews family who started the famous Lambshead Ranch not far from Albany, Texas. Glenn was killed by Apache Indians (among them, the "Apache Kid") who were being taken from Globe, Arizona, to the territorial prison at Yuma, Arizona. He is buried in the Globe Cemetery. To locate the cemetery and grave: from US 60 in Globe, turn south on Hackney Avenue. A short distance from US 60, the road will branch three ways. Take the center of the three branches and enter the cemetery on a very narrow, one-lane drive with tall trees on either side. Continue up the hill on the paved drive. The Reynolds graves are on the right, beside the paved drive and just beyond the Masonic symbol, which is on a tall metal post on the right. The grave is covered by a red sandstone slab with a marble inset inscribed with name and dates of birth and death. Glenn's infant son, George (March 10, 1888–January 23, 1889), is buried beside him. His grave is also marked.

**726. Rhodes, John (Tewksbury)*** (October 3, 1887–November 26, 1973). John Rhodes was born a few weeks after his father, John Tewksbury, was killed by members of the Graham faction during the Pleasant Valley War in Arizona. After Tewksbury was killed, his wife, Mary Ann Crigger Tewksbury, married John Rhodes, Sr. John (Tewksbury) Rhodes became a cattleman and was a rodeo performer for almost fifty years. Together with his son, Tommy, he won World Championships in team roping in 1936 and 1938. He last competed at age seventy. He died at Tucson and is buried in the Mammoth Cemetery at Mammoth, Arizona, as are his wife, Bessie P. (1883–1968), and his son, Tommy (1915–1981). The cemetery is on a hillside above Highway 77 on the southwest side of Mammoth. The grave is easily found in the small, well-kept cemetery.

**727. Rhodes, Mary Ann Crigger Tewksbury*** (October 28, 1862–December 23, 1950). During the Pleasant Valley War in Arizona, Mary Ann watched as her husband, John Tewksbury, and his friend, William Jacobs, were shot and killed near the Tewksbury home by members of the Graham faction. When hogs began to eat the bodies, she defied the guns of the Grahams to drive the animals away and cover the victims. A few weeks later she gave birth to her second child, a boy. Later Mary Ann married her dead husband's friend, John Rhodes. Mary Ann and her second husband had six children of their own. John Rhodes, Sr., died in 1919, but his wife lived until 1950, dying in Florence, Arizona. She is buried in Valley Memorial Cemetery, which is on the north side of Highway 287 between Florence and Coolidge, Arizona. Her grave is in Section 4, Block 8, Lot 2, Grave 8. Her ground-level headstone rests under a large pine tree in the southeast corner of the cemetery.

**728. Rich, Charles Henry "Charlie"*** (?–?). Rich dealt "Aces and Eights" to Wild Bill Hickok in the No. 10 Saloon in Deadwood, South Dakota, on August 2, 1876. Hickok was holding those cards when he was shot and killed by Jack McCall. The actual cards were the ace and eight of spades, the ace and eight of clubs, and the jack of diamonds. Rich had traveled throughout the West and was a good friend of Hickok. He was a native of Ohio and upon his death was buried in the Miamiville Cemetery at Miamiville, Ohio, a few miles northeast of Cincinnati. There is a large black marble marker with the "Dead Man's Hand" inscribed at the top. There is also a historical marker just inside the cemetery entrance. To locate the cemetery: from I-275, which circles Cincinnati, take Exit 54 (Ward's Corner Road) and drive southwest to Miamiville. Turn right on State Road 126, which is not marked at this intersection. Drive about one-half mile to the cemetery on the right. The grave can be seen from the cemetery entrance.

**729. Richey, Anna "Queen Ann"\*** (1890–1922). She owned a ranch in western Wyoming and was once tried for cattle rustling but was acquitted. Anna died of poisoning under strange circumstances. She is buried at the top of the hill in the South Lincoln Cemetery in Kemmerer, Wyoming. The cemetery is a short distance west of town. There is a large, dark gray marble marker on a lighter colored base. To locate the grave: enter the cemetery and immediately turn right and drive to the next lane on the left. Turn left and drive straight ahead to the highest point in the cemetery. Anna's grave is on the left, a few feet from the drive.

**730. Ridge, John\*** (1803–June 22, 1839). He was a Cherokee Indian leader and was the son of Major Ridge. The two Ridges, Elias Boudinot, and Stand Watie were leaders of the Cherokee faction favoring the selling of tribal lands in Georgia, North Carolina, and Tennessee, and taking up reservation lands in Indian Territory. After their removal to Oklahoma, the two Ridges and Boudinot were assassinated by the Cherokee faction which opposed them. John Ridge is buried in the Polson Cemetery in northeastern Oklahoma. This cemetery is best reached from Southwest City, Missouri, by a good dirt road. There is a grave marker.

**731. Ridge, Major\*** (circa 1771–June 22, 1839). Major Ridge, his son John, Elias Boudinot, and Stand Watie led a Cherokee Indian faction which favored selling tribal lands and taking up reservation lands in Oklahoma. A rival Cherokee faction assassinated the two Ridges and Boudinot. Major Ridge is buried in the Polson Cemetery in northeastern Oklahoma. The cemetery is best reached from Southwest City, Missouri, by a good, graded dirt road. There is an inscribed marker.

**732. Riggs, Barney K.**\* (December 18, 1856–April 3, 1902; NOTE: the 1900 Census gives his year of birth as 1844). Riggs was a Texas gunman and was killed in Fort Stockton, Texas, by his son-in-law, Buck Chadborn (1880–March 30, 1966). He is buried in the old Fort Stockton post cemetery. There is an inscribed marker set on a concrete base. Barney and his first wife, Vinnie, had a son, William Earl Riggs. Barney married his second wife, Annie Stella Frazer Johnson, on September 23, 1891. They had four children, Barney K., Jr. (born May 1892), Ernest M. (born June 8, 1894), Eva (born April 1896), and George (born February 15, 1898). Annie had six children by a previous marriage to James Johnson: Nata (born January 1885), Emily (born October 1886), and Myrtle (born November 1887) were living with the Riggses in 1900. Another of Annie's daughters, sixteen-year-old Mary Jane Johnson, married Tom Riggs, a brother of Barney. There were also two boys, James Johnson and Thomas Johnson.

**733. Riley, John Henry**\* (March 19, 1841–February 10, 1916; NOTE: Riley's headstone incorrectly gives his birthdate as May 12, 1850). He was born in Ireland but came with his parents to America when he was twelve years old. He served in the Union Army from 1861 to 1864 and came to New Mexico with Brigadier General James Henry Carleton's (1814–1873) California Column. He was originally associated with the Murphy-Dolan faction which opposed the Tunstall-McSween group during the Lincoln County War. Prior to the beginning of hostilities, Riley moved to Colorado Springs, Colorado, where he died of pneumonia and Bright's disease. He is buried in Section 4, Block 3, Lot 15, in Mount Olivet Cemetery in Denver.

**734. Ringo, John "Johnny"**\* (May 3, 1850–July 14, 1882). He was a Texas and Arizona gunman. In Tombstone, Arizona, he joined "Curly Bill" Brocius and a group of "cowboys" who opposed the Earp brothers. Circumstances surrounding his death are not clear. The official report ruled suicide, but most authorities opt for either "Buckskin Frank" Leslie or Wyatt Earp as his killer. His body was found beside West Turkey Creek, a short distance west of the Sanders Ranch house in southeastern Arizona. He is buried there in a marked grave. To locate the Sanders Ranch: from US 666, drive east on Highway 181 for twelve miles. Where 181 turns sharply left, go about four miles straight ahead on the gravel West Turkey Creek Road to the Sanders Ranch on the left. The grave is a short distance west of the ranch house beside West Turkey Creek.

**735. Riordan, Archibald Wilder "Arch"** (June 30, 1869–March 16, 1937). He was at one time marshal of Buffalo Gap, South Dakota, and later mayor of Hot Springs, South Dakota. At the time of his death he was retired, after having owned a bottling works. The cause of his death was "general debility—hyper-static pneumonia and senility." He died in Lutheran Hospital in Hot Springs, and his funeral services were held at the Masonic temple. His body was shipped to Denver, Colorado, for cremation.

**736. Rising, Dan Clarence "Johnny Granada"*** (December 1, 1844–September 30, 1909). He was a Pony Express rider who rode under the name "Johnny Granada." He died at Wetmore, Kansas, and is buried there in the Wetmore Cemetery. The grave is on the right of the entrance drive, a short distance from the entrance. There is a gray marble marker engraved "Pony Express." His father, N.H. Rising (1818–1875); his mother, Mary E. Rising (1822–1888); and several sisters are also buried in the Rising plot.

**737. Rivet, Francois*** (circa 1757–February 28, 1847). He was a member of the Lewis and Clark Expedition. He was a boatman and went only as far as Fort Mandan in what is today North Dakota, where the expedition wintered. He went to Oregon several decades later. He is buried at St. Paul Parish in the Willamette Valley of Oregon. There is a marker alongside Highway 219 about 0.1 mile from the St. Paul Catholic Church. The old cemetery has been destroyed and there are no individual markers.

**738. Robert, Sallie Chisum*** (1858–1934). She was the daughter of James Chisum and the niece of John Chisum. She married William Robert but the marriage was not successful and they were later divorced. She lived with her Uncle John and took over running the house at the South Springs Ranch. She was very popular and at dances in the area frequently danced with Billy the Kid. After the death of John Chisum, she and John's brothers, James and Pitzer, stayed on at the "Jinglebob" Ranch. Eventually the ranch holdings were dissolved and she spent her last days at Roswell, New Mexico. Sallie is buried in South Park Cemetery at Roswell. Her grave is on the Masonic Circle, Lot 45, which is in the southwest quadrant of the circle. In the same plot is John's brother, Pitzer Chisum.

**739. Roberts, Andrew L. "Buckshot"**\* (?–April 4, 1878). During the Lincoln County War, he opposed the faction led by Dick Brewer and Billy the Kid. He killed Brewer in the gunfight at Blazer's Mill southwest of Lincoln. Roberts was also shot and died a few hours later. Both he and Brewer were buried on a little hill at Blazer's Mill. In 1991 the graves were marked with wooden crosses and Roberts' with a marble stone.

**740. Roberts, Daniel Webster "Dan"**\* (October 10, 1841–February 6, 1935). He was a captain in the Texas Rangers during the Mason County War. Roberts was born in Mississippi, but his parents took him to Texas at the age of two. He died in Austin, Texas, and is buried in the state cemetery there. There is a large headstone near the top of the hill.

**741. Roberts, James Franklin "Jim"**\* (circa 1858–January 8, 1934). As a young man he took part in the Pleasant Valley War in Arizona and later became a lawman at Clarkdale, Arizona. He died of a heart attack in 1934 and is buried beside his wife, Permelia Kirkland Roberts, in Valley View Cemetery, which is west of Clarkdale, Arizona. The graves are in Section A, West $^1\!/_2$, Lot 7. A large, black marble stone with the single word "Roberts" marks the plot. Jim is buried between the marker and the grave of Charles Young Webb.

**742. Roberts, Mose (or Mote)**\* (?–September 15, 1887). He was wounded in a gun battle by Commodore Perry Owens at the Blevins house in Holbrook, Arizona, on September 4, 1887, and died eleven days later. Roberts is buried in the Holbrook Cemetery beside Andy Cooper (Blevins) and Sam Blevins who were also killed by Owens. Holbrook Cemetery is at the corner of Navajo Boulevard (Highway

77) and Iowa. To locate the grave: enter the cemetery at the first entrance on Iowa. The graves are just inside and to the left of the entrance and are marked by a flat, sandstone slab inscribed with the three names.

**743. Roberts, Ollie L. "Brushy Bill"*** (December 31, 1868–December 27, 1959). In his later years he claimed to be Billy the Kid but these claims have been proven false. Some writers have proposed that he was the noted outlaw, Jesse Evans, who played a prominent role in the Lincoln County War, but his known date of birth shows this to be impossible. Roberts died in 1959 and was buried in a cemetery just north of Hamilton, Texas. To locate the grave: coming south toward Hamilton on Highway 281, turn left on the fourth drive leading into the cemetery. Stop immediately at the oak tree on the left. The grave is in the first row of graves next to the highway and about forty feet from the oak. An inscribed, flat, cement marker is at the grave site, which has a concrete curbing.

**744. Rockwell, Orrin Porter*** (June 28, 1813–June 9, 1878). He was a leader of the "Sons of Dan," sometimes referred to as the "police force of the Mormon Church" and sometimes called "The Avenging Angels." Although accused of several murders, he was never convicted. Rockwell died of a heart attack in Salt Lake City, Utah, and is buried there in the city cemetery (C-5-9). There is a marker.

**745. Rogers, Diana (Tiana)*** (circa 1800–November 17, 1838). Some say she was the Cherokee Indian wife of Sam Houston; others disagree. When Houston left Indian Territory for Texas, she did not go with him. She is buried on Officer's Circle in the Fort Gibson national cemetery at Fort Gibson, Oklahoma. There is a small marker bearing the incorrect name "Talahina."

**746. Rose, Albert "Al"*** (October 24, 1841–November 1, 1887). He was killed by the Tewksbury faction in the Pleasant Valley War in Arizona and is buried in the Young Cemetery just north of Young, Arizona. The cemetery is on the west side of the road leading to Heber, Arizona. A small marker among the weeds is inscribed with the dates of his birth and death.

**747. Rose, Louis Moses** (circa 1785–1857). He was the only man to leave the Alamo prior to the battle. He worked at Nacogdoches, Texas, until 1842. Some say he died at or near Loganport, Louisiana. Tom Allen, in his book, *Those Buried Texans,* says that Rose is buried in Greenhill Cemetery near Mount Pleasant, Texas. I visited Greenhill Cemetery in 1990 but was unable to locate a marker for Rose.

**748. Ross, John*** (October 3, 1790–August 1, 1866). He was a Cherokee Indian leader in Oklahoma who opposed the Ridges, Elias Boudinot, and Stand Watie on matters relating to reservation status for the Cherokees. He is buried in the Ross Cemetery near Tahlequah, Oklahoma. There is a large, inscribed marker.

**749. Royal, Andrew Jackson*** (November 25, 1855–November 21, 1894). He was sheriff of Pecos County, Texas, and a very controversial figure. After leaving office, he was assassinated by unknown persons. He is buried in the old Fort Stockton post cemetery at Fort Stockton, Texas. There is a large marker.

**750. Rudd, William L.*** (August 10, 1845–January 9, 1941). He was variously known as "Little Red," "Colorado Chico," or "Will." Born in England, he went to Texas at an early age. Rudd was a Texas Ranger under Lee Hall and was in DeWitt County during the Taylor-Sutton Feud. Later he became sheriff of Karnes County, Texas. He lived at Yorktown for a number of years and died there in 1941. Rudd is buried in Westside Cemetery at Yorktown. To locate the cemetery and grave: from Highway 72 in Yorktown, turn north on Mehnert Street (Highway 119) and drive to Twelfth Street. Turn left (west) to the cemetery on the right. Enter the cemetery through the first entrance and go about seventy-five feet. Watch for the Rudd marker on the left in front of a tree. This is the Harper plot. The Harpers buried here were the parents of Rudd's wife, Evylin (November 11, 1858–December 1, 1939), who is buried beside her husband.

**751. Rusk, David Vance "Dave"*** (January 19, 1839–April 13, 1897). He was a deputy United States marshal for Judge Isaac Parker in

Oklahoma Territory. He is buried in Oak Hill Cemetery in Siloam Springs, Arkansas. To locate the cemetery and grave: from Arkansas 68 Bypass, turn north on Holly Road to Oak Hill Cemetery on the left. The grave is in the extreme southern part of the cemetery near West Central Avenue, which is the southern boundary. A large, dark marble marker with the single word, "Rusk," marks the plot. A separate marker is at the grave of Dave Rusk. Also in the Rusk plot are several other family members.

**752.  Russell, William Hepburn*** (January 31, 1812–September 10, 1872). He was a member of the Russell, Majors and Waddell Stage Company. The company also started the Pony Express. After he withdrew from the business, he lived for a time in New York. He died at Palmyra, Missouri, at the home of his son, John Russell, and is buried in the Palmyra Cemetery just north of the city. There is a large marker bearing the Pony Express symbol at the grave.

**753.  "Russian Bill."** See William Rogers Tettenborn.

**754.  Rynning, Thomas H. "Tom"*** (1866–June 18, 1941). He was a cavalry lieutenant in the Spanish-American War and later became head of the Arizona Rangers. Rynning was born in Christiana, Norway, but came to the United States at the age of two. He died in California and is buried in the Fort Rosecrans national cemetery in San Diego, California. The cemetery is bisected by Catalina Boulevard, which leads to Cabrillo National Monument. Rynning's grave is on the east side of Catalina, directly across from the national cemetery office. A small, white marble, standard United States military headstone marks the grave which is on the right of the entrance drive, Officers' Section A, Grave 12).

**755. Sacajawea\*** (circa 1780–April 9, 1884; NOTE: some believe that she died in 1812 in North Dakota). She was a Shoshone Indian girl, who accompanied the Lewis and Clark Expedition along with her husband, Touissaint Charbonneau, the expedition's interpreter. She is buried in the Wind River Cemetery near Fort Washakie, Wyoming (not the Fort Washakie Cemetery). The Reverend J. Roberts officiated at her burial. In this cemetery are the graves of Bazil, her adopted son, and other descendants. All of the graves are marked.

**756. St. John, Silas P.\*** (April 21, 1835–September 15, 1919). He was a Butterfield Stage Company employee who lost an arm at Dragoon Springs, Arizona, in a fight with Mexican workers who tried to kill him. He recovered and lived for many years thereafter in San Diego, California, where he is buried in Mount Hope Cemetery, Division 7, Section 6, Row 8, Grave 17. To locate the grave: enter the cemetery from Market Street and drive straight ahead past the office on the left. Turn right on the first drive and then left on the next drive. Park when even with the large eagle monument on the left. The grave is a little to the left of that monument. A large, marble stone bears an engraved plaque honoring St. John. A map of the cemetery can be obtained at the office.

**757. St. Vrain, Ceran\*** (May 5, 1802–October 28, 1870). St. Vrain was a frontiersman, trapper, and trader. He ran a grain mill and had a home at Mora, New Mexico. At one time he was a partner in the famous Bent brothers' trading empire. He married four times and fathered a child by each wife. He died at Mora and is buried in the little St. Vrain Cemetery about one-half mile south of Mora. It can be reached by parking at the school on the south side of Mora and walking due south to the cemetery, which is surrounded by a fence. There is a large marker. NOTE: Do not confuse this cemetery with the Mora Cemetery, which is also south of Mora but is right beside the highway.

**758.   Salazar, Yginio**\* (February 14, 1863–January 7, 1936). He fought with Billy the Kid during the Lincoln County War in New Mexico, against the forces of Lawrence Murphy and James Dolan. He was wounded in the five-day battle in Lincoln, New Mexico, but played dead and later recovered from his wounds. Salazar is buried in the Lincoln Cemetery beside his wife, Isabel (September 3, 1869–May 15, 1935). The cemetery is just east of town on Highway 380. The grave, with a large, gray marble marker, is just inside and to the left of the entrance to the cemetery. Below his name are the words, "Pal of Billy the Kid."

**759.   Sampson, Cassius "Cash"**\* (1871–June 9, 1917). He served at various times as sheriff of Delta County, Colorado, brand inspector, and deputy United States marshal. Trouble developed between Cash and Ben Lowe, leading to a gunfight in Escalante Canyon, which is in western Colorado between Delta and Grand Junction. Both men were killed in the fight. Sampson is buried in the Delta Cemetery in Delta, Colorado, Block 2, Lot 173, Space 2. There is a marker. Lowe is also buried there.

**760.   Samuel, Archie Peyton**\* (July 26, 1866–January 26, 1875). He was the half-brother of Jesse and Frank James and the son of Dr. Reuben Samuel and Zerelda Samuel. Archie was killed when an explosive device was thrown in the window of the Samuel home by Pinkerton detective agents in 1875. He is buried a few feet from Jesse in the Mount Olivet Cemetery at Kearney, Missouri. There is a ground-level marker a few feet from the grave of Jesse James and other family members.

**761.   Samuel, Reuben**\* (January 12, 1829–March 1, 1908). He was a medical doctor and the third husband of Zerelda Cole James Samuel, the mother of Jesse and Frank James. Before coming to Missouri, the Samuel family had lived in the northwestern part of Arkansas. He is buried in the Mount Olivet Cemetery in Kearney, Missouri, beside his wife, Zerelda. There is an inscribed marker at the grave site.

762. **Samuel, Zerelda Cole James\*** (January 29, 1825–February 10, 1911). She was the mother of Jesse and Frank James and the wife of Dr. Reuben Samuel. Zerelda died while traveling on a Pullman sleeper at the age of eighty-six. She is buried in Mount Olivet Cemetery at Kearney, Missouri, beside her husband, Reuben, and sons, Jesse and Archie. There is an inscribed headstone.

763. **Sandoz, Jules Ami "Old Jules"\*** (1858–November 1928). He was a pioneer Nebraska cattleman and the father of author Mari Sandoz. He died at Alliance, Nebraska, and is buried there in the Alliance Cemetery, where he rests beside his fourth wife, Mary Sandoz (1867–1938). Both graves are marked.

764. **Sandoz, Mari Susetta\*** (May 11, 1896–March 10, 1966). She was the noted author of numerous books dealing with the West. Mari died of cancer in New York City and is buried on the old Sandoz farm about twenty-three miles south of Gordon, Nebraska, on a hillside less than one mile from the farmhouse built by Jules and still occupied by Mari's sister, Lula, in 1978. The grave is on the left (north) side of the narrow road which leads from Highway 27 to the farmhouse. It is about one-quarter mile from the farm road and is best reached by foot. There is a marker.

765. **Sarber, John Newton\*** (1838–October 2, 1905). He was United States marshal for the Western District of Arkansas during the early 1870s. A native of Pennsylvania, Sarber had served the Union Army in a Kansas cavalry unit during the Civil War and at one time was stationed at Clarksville, Arkansas. When the war was over, he made Clarksville his home and married a native girl, Susan Rose. Once while Sarber was conducting a hanging at Fort Smith, Arkansas, a bolt of lightning struck the gallows just as the trapdoor was sprung. A minor panic ensued. Sarber's son, Frank, would later be a member of the posse that killed outlaw Ned Christie. Sarber is buried in Lot

124 in Oakland Cemetery in Clarksville, Arkansas. A six-foot-tall, marble obelisk marks his grave.

**766. Sarpy, Peter A.** (November 3, 1805–January 4, 1865). He was a mountain man and fur trader. He died in Plattsmouth, Nebraska, and his body was taken to St. Louis, Missouri, for burial in Calvary Cemetery.

**767. Satank "Setangya"\*** (circa 1810–June 6, 1871). He was a Kiowa chief and one of the leaders of the Indians who took part in the Warren Wagon Train Massacre in Texas. He was captured, and as he was being taken to Texas for trial, he attempted to escape and was killed. His body was left by the roadside, but later his son gathered up the remains and today the chief rests on Chief's Knoll in the Fort Sill post cemetery at Fort Sill, Oklahoma. There is a marker.

**768. Satanta "White Bear" or "Set-tainte"\*** (circa 1830–October 11, 1878). He was a Kiowa chief and, along with others, took part in the Warren Wagon Train Massacre near Graham, Texas. He was tried in Jacksboro, Texas, and sentenced to death, but the sentence was later commuted to life imprisonment. After Governor Edmund J. Davis of Texas paroled both Satanta and Big Tree, Satanta was arrested again for other raids and imprisoned at Huntsville, Texas. He committed suicide by leaping from a second-story window of the state prison. He was first buried in the prison's Joe Byrd Cemetery in Huntsville, where a marker still indicates his first grave. Later his remains were removed to Fort Sill, Oklahoma, where they now lie on Chief's Knoll in the Fort Sill post cemetery. There is a marker.

**769. Scarborough, George Adolphus\*** (October 2, 1859–April 6, 1900). He was a Texas and New Mexico lawman who first served as a Jones County, Texas, sheriff and later as a deputy United States marshal. He killed John Selman on April 6, 1896, after Selman had killed John Wesley Hardin in 1895. Scarborough and lawman Walt Birchfield were ambushed as they were trailing outlaws in the Chiricahua Mountains. Scarborough was shot through the thigh and was later taken to a hospital in Deming, New Mexico, where his leg was amputated. He died a short time later as a result of the injury. He is buried in the International Order of Odd Fellows section of the Deming Cemetery in Deming, New Mexico. The cemetery is about three miles east of Deming on the south side of US 80. A white obelisk with black letters marks the grave.

770. **Schieffelin, Edward Lawrence "Ed"\*** (October 8, 1847–May 14, 1897; NOTE: the tombstone incorrectly gives the date of death as May 12, 1897). He discovered silver at Tombstone, Arizona. Schieffelin died in Oregon, but his body was returned to Tombstone for burial about two miles west of town. To locate the grave: follow Allen Street west past the Tombstone Cemetery to the large pyramid of stone that marks the grave.

771. **Schonchin "Old Chief"\*** (circa 1797–August 10, 1892). He was the older brother of Schonchin John. After he became chief of the Modoc tribe, he kept his followers on the Klamath Indian reservation and took no part in the Modoc War. He died at age ninety-five on the reservation and is buried in the Chief Schonchin Cemetery. A plaque at his grave reads, "Head Chief of the Modocs, His Courageous Loyalty to His Treaty Obligations Kept the Bulk of His Tribe From the Warpath and Saved the Klamath Settlement 1872–1873." To locate the cemetery: from Beatty, Oregon, go five miles west on Highway 140 to the Sprague River Junction. Turn right (north) and go 1.2 miles. Turn right (east) on a gravel road for 0.7 mile to the cemetery. Winema, daughter of Old Chief Schonchin, and her husband, Frank Riddle, are also buried there. All of the graves are marked.

772. **Schonchin John\*** (circa 1829–October 3, 1873). He was a Modoc Indian leader and the brother of Old Chief Schonchin. Along with Captain Jack, he was one of the small group of Modocs who took part in the Modoc Indian War. He was tried for murder, found guilty, and hanged at Fort Klamath, Oregon, along with Captain Jack and two other Modocs. The four are buried near the museum at Fort Klamath. The graves are marked.

773. **Scott, James.** See Bloody Basin Gravesite.

**774. Scott, Walter Edward "Death Valley Scotty"*** (September 20, 1872–January 5, 1954). With funds provided by wealthy insurance man Albert M. Johnson, he built the fabulous "Scotty's Castle" in the northern part of Death Valley, California. Scotty is buried on the little hill just north of the castle. A trail leads to the marked grave site. Scotty and his little dog are buried side by side.

**775. Scott, William "Bill"*** (January 17, 1854–November 12, 1913). He was a member of June Peak's Company B of the Texas Rangers and took part in the chase of Sam Bass in north Texas. He later served in Captain George W. Arrington's Company C as well as the commands of Captain Lee Hall and Captain T.L. Oglesby. After leaving the Rangers for about two years, he reenlisted in Company F and in 1886 was promoted to captain. In 1887 he married Georgia Lynch and shortly thereafter resigned from the Ranger service. He worked as a railroad contractor in Mexico before finally returning to Waelder, Texas, where he died from a fall on a downtown street. He is buried in the Masonic Cemetery in Waelder. A large pink marble headstone marks his grave. The cemetery is north of town on State Road 1296. Scott's grave is about 100 feet from the entrance and a little to the right of center.

**776. Scurlock, Josiah Gordon "Doc"*** (January 11, 1850–July 25, 1929). He was a member of Billy the Kid's Gang in New Mexico. After receiving a pardon for crimes committed in New Mexico, he moved to Texas, where he raised a family. He died of heart failure at age seventy-nine in Eastland, Texas, and is buried in the Eastland Cemetery near the entrance. There is a large granite marker for "Doc" and his wife, Antonia (June 13, 1860–November 27, 1912). Also buried here are his son, William Scurlock (April 14, 1893–May 6, 1933), and William's wife, Liddie E. (August 19, 1882–August 15, 1952).

**777. Seabourn, Joseph C.*** (June 25, 1848–May 14, 1894; NOTE: the name is sometimes incorrectly spelled "Seaborn"). He was a merchant who was killed by the Doolin Gang in the bank robbery at Southwest City, Missouri. Seabourn is buried in the Southwest City Cemetery, which is on the west side of Highway 43, just north of town. His grave is at the extreme back of the cemetery and is marked by a pink marble obelisk. There is also a United States military marker. A number of relatives are buried here. All use the spelling "Seabourn."

**778. Seger, Charles W.*** (January 20, 1866–December 29, 1887). He was an inhabitant of Brown's Park on the Utah-Colorado border. When Joseph Melvin Tolliver was defeated in a wrestling match by Seger, Tolliver stabbed him with a knife and Seger died the next day. He is buried on a little hillside on the south side of the Green River, a short distance from the residence of the area's Utah wildlife ranger. Seger's brother is buried beside him, and the graves are elevated and surrounded by fieldstones. The grave is in Brown's Park, just across the Colorado line in Utah.

**779. Seguin, Juan Nepomuceno*** (October 27, 1806–August 27, 1890). Although of Spanish ancestry, he fought with Texans in 1835 at the siege of Bexar. Seguin was later mayor of San Antonio, Texas. He died in 1890 at Nuevo Laredo, Mexico. His remains were returned to Seguin, Texas, in September 1974 and reinterred in a special plot just south of Seguin.

**780. Selman, John Henry** (November 16, 1839–April 6, 1896). He was both an outlaw and lawman. He had been in partnership with John Larn in Shackelford County, Texas, prior to Larn's death at the hands of vigilantes. Selman was not seen in Shackelford County again. Among others, he killed Bass Outlaw and John Wesley Hardin. He was shot and killed by George Scarborough in El Paso, Texas, and is buried in an unmarked grave near Hardin in Concordia Cemetery in El Paso. The exact location of the grave is not known.

**781. Selman, John Marion, Jr.*** (January 30, 1875–March 31, 1937). He was the son of John Selman and served as a city policeman under his father in El Paso, Texas. He was also a veteran of the Spanish-American War. He died in Rockdale, Texas, and is buried in Old South San Gabriel Cemetery near Bertram, Texas. To locate the cemetery: from Bertram, go east on Highway 29 for 4.2 miles. Turn right (south) and go 1.6 miles. Turn left (east) and go 0.5 mile to the cemetery on the right. Selman's grave is about forty feet from the road and is marked.

782. **Seng, Marvin B.**\* (August 22, 1900–October 11, 1923). He was the fireman on the train which was held up by the D'Autremont brothers at Tunnel 13 near the Oregon-California border. Seng and three other members of the train crew were killed. He is buried in the Dunsmuir Cemetery on the south side of Dunsmuir, California. A pink marble stone on a granite base marks the grave. His parents, Henry (1865–1933) and Dolly Seng (1868–19 ?), are in the family plot.

783. **Serra, Junipero**\* (November 14, 1713–August 28, 1784). Father Serra was a Franciscan missionary. He is credited with founding several missions in California. He died in California at Mission San Carlos and is buried in the sanctuary of San Carlos. His burial site is marked.

784. **Setangya.** See Sitting Bear.

785. **Set-tainte.** See Satanta.

786. **Set-imkia.** See Stumbling Bear.

787. **Severns, Harry.** See Harry Tracy.

788. **Shadley, Lafayette "Lafe"**\* (June 6, 1844–September 3, 1893). He was a deputy United States marshal. Lafe was killed in the gunfight at Ingalls, Oklahoma, between lawmen and the Doolin Gang and is buried in the Mount Hope Cemetery in Independence, Kansas, Section 111-F. A large marker is at the grave site. His wife and child are also in the Shadley plot. About fifteen feet away and also marked by an impressive headstone is the grave of Coffeyville city marshal Charles T. Connelly, who was killed by members of the Dalton Gang when they attempted to rob two banks simultaneously at Coffeyville, Kansas.

789. **Shanley, Edward P.**\* (1868–October 2, 1906). He was sheriff of

Gila County, Arizona, and is buried in the Benevolent and Protective Order of Elks Section of the Globe Cemetery in Globe, Arizona. The grave is on the left of the paved drive, part way up the hill and to the east of the grave of Al Sieber. Shanley hanged Zack Booth, killer of sheepmen Juan Vigil and Wiley Berry near Gisela, Arizona.

790. **Shannon, George, Jr. "Peg-Leg"** (1784–August 30, 1836). He was a member of the Lewis and Clark Expedition. After returning from the expedition, he lost one of his legs as a result of a wound suffered at the hands of unfriendly Indians. He later became a lawyer in Palmyra, Missouri. He died of a heart attack and is buried just north of Palmyra on private property on the west side of the old US Highway 61. The grave is not marked, according to the man who owns the property. A Missouri historical marker which once stood near the highway has disappeared in recent years.

791. **Shea, Cornelius "Con"** * (June 12, 1840–May 20, 1926). Shea was born in the province of Ontario, Canada. His parents, Jeremiah and Eliza Shea, had emigrated from Ireland. As a young man, Con headed west to the gold mining town of Silver City, Idaho. He soon decided to enter the cattle business and brought several herds of cattle from Texas to the Idaho-Oregon area. On one of the drives, several families from Texas came to the Northwest with him. Driving a wagon the entire way was fifteen-year-old Marietta ("Etta") McIntyre. A short time later, she became Mrs. Con Shea. The Sheas had four children, Thomas, Albert, Emma, and Ida. Con built the Idaho Hotel in Silver City, and one of his brothers ran it for some time. The hotel was still standing as of 1991. After becoming wealthy, the Sheas moved to Santa Rosa, California, where Con entered the real estate business and became a millionaire. He died in Santa Rosa and was buried in Holy Cross Cemetery in Colma, California. A huge monument marks his grave in Section I, Row 3, Area 5, Plot 4. Several other member of the Shea family are nearby.

792. **Sheepmen's Mass Grave Near Ten Sleep, Wyoming.** Joe Allemand, Joe Emge, and Jules Lazier were murdered by cattlemen April 2, 1902. To locate the mass grave: from Highway 16 at Ten Sleep, Wyoming, go south on Norwood Road (Highway 434) for 7.2

*Right: John "Johnny" Ringo, Sanders Ranch, Cochise County, Arizona.*

*Left: Cornelius "Con" Shea, Holy Cross Cemetery, Colma, California.*

miles. Turn left on a gravel road (Spring Creek Road) and go 4.4 miles (pass the Taylor Ranch en route). Turn left on a dirt road for 1.4 miles. The grave is a few feet from the road on the right. The small stone marker with the three names inscribed is surrounded by a pole fence which was in poor repair in 1986. Just beyond the graves is the Rome Hill Ranch. The total distance from Highway 16 is thirteen miles.

793. **Sheets, John W.*** (October 3, 1818–December 7, 1869). At age fifty-one, Sheets was killed by the James-Younger Gang in the 1869 Gallatin, Missouri, bank robbery. His wife, Mary G. Sheets (1834–1878), is buried beside him in the Gallatin Cemetery, which is beside the Baptist Church. The grave is at the back (west side) of the cemetery, and the five-foot obelisk is turned at a forty-five degree angle to the other headstones. To locate the cemetery: turn west off Highway 13 onto Richardson Street and go about four blocks to the cemetery on the right.

794. **Shepherd, George Washington*** (January 5, 1840–February 23, 1917). He was born in Jackson County, Missouri, and became a member of Quantrill's Raiders. Later he rode with the James-Younger Gang and served a prison sentence for the Russellville, Kentucky, bank robbery. He once shot Jesse James for the reward but succeeded only in wounding him. Shepherd died at Lee's Summit, Missouri, and is buried there near the middle of Lee's Summit Cemetery. There is an engraved headstone. His wife, Mary Jane Waters Shepherd (July 4, 1856–July 15, 1935), is buried beside him. George's cousin, Oliver Shepherd (spelled "Shepard" on his headstone), is buried nearby.

795. **Shepherd, Oliver B.*** (November 25, 1842–April 4, 1868; Note: The name is spelled "Shepard" on the headstone). He was a member of Quantrill's Raiders and was one of the first persons buried in the Lee's Summit Cemetery at Lee's Summit, Missouri. A 2$\frac{1}{2}$-foot, upright, white marble headstone marks his grave. The inscription says he was "assassinated." He was a cousin of George Shepherd.

796. **Sheridan, Philip Henry "Phil"** (March 6, 1831–August 5, 1888).

A West Point graduate, Sheridan entered the military service in 1853 and remained as a career officer until his death some thirty-five years later. He saw service in the Northwest. During the Civil War he served with distinction and rose to the rank of major general. Following the Civil War, Sheridan was involved in problems dealing with the Indians, for whom he had little sympathy. He died in Nonquitt, Massachusetts, a few days after he attained the rank of four-star general. He is buried in Arlington National Cemetery in Area II in front of the Custis-Lee mansion. The cemetery's Sheridan Drive is named in his honor.

797. **Shibell, Charles A.*** (August 14, 1841–October 21, 1908). He was sheriff of Pima County, Arizona, from 1876 to 1882. After that he was county recorder for twenty years. He died of dengue fever and is buried at Tucson, Arizona, in Block 33, Section C, Lot 154, of Evergreen Cemetery, which is on the west side of Oracle Road, north of the city. There is a marker. His son, Charles B., Jr. (?–April 26, 1945), and daughter, Mercedes Shibell Ghould (December 14, 1875–September 13, 1965), are buried beside him. To locate the graves: enter the cemetery through the Oracle entrance. Drive to the first cross-drive. Park. Block 33 was on the left as you entered the cemetery. Starting at the northwest corner of the block, count six rows of graves toward Oracle Road, then six or seven graves to the right (south). There are three Shibell graves in the plot and all have markers.

798. **Shields, John** (1769–December 1809). At age thirty-five, he was the oldest member of the Lewis and Clark Expedition. He was related to Daniel Boone, and after returning from the expedition, he trapped with Boone for a year. He later trapped with Daniel's brother, Squire Boone, Jr., in Indiana. He died in Indiana and is probably buried in the Little Flock Baptist Burying Grounds south of Corydon, Indiana.

799. **Shirley, James "Jim"*** (?–October 13, 1896). He was an outlaw and was killed along with two confederates when the three attempted to rob a bank at Meeker, Colorado. All three outlaws are buried in the southeast corner of the Meeker Cemetery. There is a marker.

**800. Shonsey, Michael "Mike"\*** (September 6, 1866–August 5, 1954). He was born in Canada but came to Wyoming at an early age. He worked as a cowboy and was affiliated with the big cattle outfits in the Johnson County War. He was foreman of the NH Ranch and directed the Invaders to the KC Ranch, where they killed Nate Champion and Nick Ray. Later Mike killed Nate's twin brother, Dudley, in a gunfight. Shonsey moved to Nebraska, where he lived at Clarks for many years. He died at nearly eighty-eight at Council Bluffs, Iowa, and was buried in the Central City Cemetery in Central City, Nebraska. There is a very large, black marble headstone. Descendants of Mike Shonsey still live at Clarks, Nebraska. There has been a "Michael Shonsey" in each of the last five generations. Mike is buried in Block C, Lot 192, Grave 1. To locate the cemetery and grave: in Central City take Highway 14 north for 1.2 miles and turn right into the cemetery. Drive straight ahead to the first paved cross-drive and turn left. Follow the paved drive as it turns right and continue until there is a gravel road and graves on the left. Stop and look to the right. The Shonsey plot is near a tree about forty feet from the drive. Several Shonseys are buried here, including Mike's wife, Olive Belle (January 22, 1866–November 11, 1905), and several sons and daughters.

**801. Shores, Cyrus Wells "Doc"\*** (November 11, 1844–October 18, 1934). He was one of the most famous of all Colorado lawmen. He died in Gunnison, Colorado, and is buried there beside his first wife, Agnes Hoel (1850–1908), and a son, C.W., Jr. (1885–1918), in the Gunnison Cemetery, which is just east of town. Doc's grave is marked by a large, gray marble headstone. His parents are also buried there in the Shores plot.

**802. Short, Charles Edward "Ed"\*** (July 29, 1864–August 23, 1891). He was an Oklahoma lawman who killed, and was killed by, "Black Face Charley" Bryant, while taking Bryant to jail by train. Short is buried in the Osgood Cemetery in Osgood, Indiana. His grave is marked by a large, white marble marker set on a concrete pedestal. To locate the cemetery: in Osgood, go west on Railroad Avenue. Pass the U.S. Shoe Company on the right. Take the first paved street beyond the shoe company to the right for one-half mile to the cemetery on the left. The grave is about ninety feet east of the maintenance building.

**803. Short, John Luke*** (February 19, 1854–September 8, 1893). He was a gunman and gambler and was a member of the Dodge City Peace Commission. He later moved to Texas, where he killed "Long-Haired Jim" Courtright in a gunfight at Fort Worth. Luke died at a health spa at Geuda Springs, Kansas. He is buried in Oakwood Cemetery in Fort Worth, not far from the grave of Courtright. There is a small, yellowed, upright marker at Short's grave. To locate the grave: from the office, go to the second drive and turn left. The grave is about halfway to the next drive and on the right. The grave is in Block 20, Lot 17, Space 3. Luke's parents, J.W. and Hettie, are buried in the cemetery at Ben Ficklin, a ghost town near San Angelo, Texas.

**804. Sieber, Albert "Al"*** (February 29, 1844–February 19, 1907). He was a well-known scout during the Southwest Indian wars. He was killed by a falling boulder while supervising a work detail during the building of the Roosevelt Dam in Arizona. He is buried in the Grand Army of the Republic section of the Benevolent and Protective Order of Elks enclosed area of the Globe Cemetery in Globe, Arizona. A large, grayish-tan sandstone monument marks the grave. The Benevolent and Protective Order of Elks enclosed area is about one-quarter of the way up the hill. The grave marker can be seen to the left as the paved drive passes under the Benevolent and Protective Order of Elks sign.

**805. Sieker, Edward Armon, Jr. "Ed"*** (1853–April 17, 1901). Ed and three of his brothers served in Company D of the Texas Rangers. He was born in Baltimore, Maryland, and raised in Virginia. He went to Texas and enlisted in Company D of the Rangers on May 25, 1874. He served under Captain C.R. Perry, Lieutenant F.M. Moore, and Captain Dan Roberts and rose to the rank of sergeant before he retired from the Rangers. Two years later he married Sarah J. Gay (1860–1940) and engaged in the cattle and oil business until his death in 1901. He is buried in Pioneer Rest Cemetery at Menard, Texas. The grave is by the drive to the left of the entrance. There are large headstones for Ed and his wife on the right of the drive, just as it curves to the right.

806. **Silcott, Jane "Indian Jane"**\* (1842–January 17, 1895).  She was a full-blood Nez Percé Indian and the daughter of Chief Timothy. Jane led Captain E.S. Pierce across the Blue Mountains and into Idaho, where gold was discovered at present-day Pierce.  She died in 1895 of burns suffered when her clothing caught fire from an open fireplace.  Jane was buried on the hillside north of Lewiston, Idaho, and in 1902, her husband, John Silcott, was buried beside her in an unmarked grave.  A tall marble shaft marks her grave.  To locate the grave: go north across the Clearwater Bridge and turn left at the first traffic light.  Go to Eighteenth Street and turn right a few blocks to *old* US 95.  Turn left on old US 95 and left again on Down River Road.  Continue to the first road to the left leading toward the river. Turn left and park off the road.  Walk to the left, parallel to the river, to the second ridge.  The graves, surrounded by a low stone or concrete wall, are near two tall power poles and are across from the railroad bridge which spans the river there.

807. **Simpson, William Ray**\* (March 4, 1862–October 30, 1940).  He owned a hardware store in Delta, Colorado.  When brothers Tom and Bill McCarty and Bill's son, Fred, attempted to rob the bank at Delta, Simpson used his Sharps rifle to kill Bill and Fred.  Tom escaped.  In later life, Simpson and his family moved to California, where he died at age seventy-eight.  He now rests in Crypt 6205, Sanctuary of Refuge in the Great Mausoleum of Forest Lawn Cemetery at Glendale, California.

808. **Sisson, Thomas J. "Tom"**\* (June 9, 1869–January 23, 1957).  He was an ex-cavalryman and army scout.  He joined the service in St. Louis, Missouri, and was later mustered out at Fort Grant, Arizona. He was in the Power cabin in 1918 when the Power boys, John and Tom, killed Sheriff Robert F. McBride and Deputies Martin Kempton and Kane Wootan.  Although the Power boys testified that Sisson did not fire a shot, he was nevertheless sentenced to life imprisonment at the Arizona state prison in Florence.  After thirty-eight years in prison, he died there in 1957.  He was buried in the Florence city

cemetery. The grave is marked by a United States military marker. To locate the grave: enter the cemetery, which is south of Florence and go straight ahead to the end of the drive. The grave is on the right, directly in back of the Meadows plot. Sisson had asked not to be buried in the prison cemetery.

809. **Si-tanka.** See Big Foot.

810. **Sitting Bear "Setangya"*** (?–June 8, 1871). He was a Kiowa chief and was a signer of the Medicine Lodge Treaty. He is buried on Chief's Knoll in the post cemetery at Fort Sill, Oklahoma.

811. **Sitting Bull*** (March 1834–December 15, 1890). He was a Hunkpapa Sioux leader. In his later life he encouraged the Ghost Dance craze, and when Indian police tried to arrest him at his home, he was shot and killed by Lieutenant Bullhead and Sergeant Red Tomahawk. He was originally buried at Fort Yates, North Dakota. His body was supposedly exhumed and taken to a site near Mobridge, South Dakota, and reinterred there. A very tall monument marks the grave, which is covered by a thick layer of concrete. The original grave site is marked and can be seen to the left as you enter Fort Yates, North Dakota. To visit the site where Sitting Bull was killed, check with the owner of the trading post at Little Eagle, northwest of Mobridge, South Dakota. A guide and a four-wheel-drive or pick-up truck are essential. The site is marked.

812. **Slack, John B.** See Arnold, Philip.

813. **Slade, Joseph Alfred "Jack"*** (1829–March 10, 1864). Slade was born in Carlyle, Illinois, of well-to-do parents. His father was a United States senator and had founded the town of Carlyle. After killing a man in Illinois, young Slade moved west, where he became a frontiersman and stage station operator. He was most noted for having killed Jules Beni (or Reni). Slade cut off Jules' ears and carried one of them on his watch chain for years. He was hanged in Virginia City, Montana, by vigilantes after engaging in a drunken spree and threatening the townspeople. His wife, who arrived in town shortly after he was hanged, had his body placed in a lead-lined

casket filled with alcohol. Some time later she took the remains to Salt Lake City, Utah, and buried them in the Mormon city cemetery on July 20, 1864. The grave is in Block B, Lot 6, Grave 7, and is marked with a small, bronze, ground-level marker.

**814.** **Slaughter, Gabriel Webster "Gabe"** * (August 3, 1852–March 11, 1874). During the Taylor-Sutton Feud in Texas, Gabe and his friend, Bill Sutton, were killed by Jim and Bill Taylor as they were boarding the steamer *Clinton* at Indianola, Texas. Bill Taylor shot Gabe in the head, killing him instantly; Jim Taylor shot Sutton as he was running away. Slaughter was the grandson of Governor Gabriel Slaughter of Kentucky and was also related to Judge Henry Clay Pleasants of Clinton, Texas. He had taken no part in the feud up to that point. Gabe is buried a few feet from Bill Sutton in Evergreen Cemetery in Victoria, Texas. To locate the grave: enter the cemetery, which is at Vine and Red River, through the Vine Street entrance. Immediately walk to the left-hand fence. Turn right and follow the fence a short distance to the grave. Bill Sutton is buried a few feet away.

**815.** **Slaughter, John "Johnny"** * (1850–March 25, 1877). He was a stagecoach driver who was killed by Robert "Little Reddy" McKimie. McKimie, along with Sam Bass and two others, was attempting to rob Slaughter's coach near Deadwood, South Dakota. Johnny was the son of J.N. Slaughter, city marshal of Cheyenne, Wyoming. He was buried in the Lakeview Cemetery at Cheyenne on April 4, 1877. The grave is marked.

**816.** **Slaughter, John Horton** * (October 3, 1841–February 16, 1922). He was a lawman and rancher in Texas and Arizona. His ranch headquarters, some twenty-three miles east of Douglas, Arizona, is now a state park. He died at Douglas and is buried beside his wife, Cora Viola Slaughter (September 18, 1860–April 1, 1941), in Calvary Cemetery in Douglas. The grave is on the west side of Rose Lane and is the tenth grave directly south of the tall flag pole. There is a large marker.

**817.** **Smalley, Edwin J. "Ed"** * (June 27, 1868–November 21, 1937). He was the Laramie County, Wyoming, sheriff who officiated at the hanging of Tom Horn in Cheyenne, Wyoming, November 20, 1905. He died in Cheyenne and is buried there in Lakeview Cemetery. To locate the grave: enter the cemetery from Twenty-fourth Street. Drive past the office and stone building and turn left and then right, going around the circle some fifty feet. Turn left at the Clark marker. Go past the cross-lane to the circle with a very tall obelisk. Turn right. Smalley's grave is on the left, about forty feet from the last turn. He is buried beside his wife, Edith A. Smalley (December 21, 1880–May 18, 1959); his mother, Mary J. Smalley (May 16, 1850–July 16, 1916); and his father, Benjamin H. Smalley (August 2, 1846–December 5, 1915). Large markers are at each of the graves.

**818. Smith, Erastus "Deaf Smith"\*** (April 19, 1787–November 30, 1837). He was a scout and a soldier in the War for Texas Independence. He died at Richmond, Texas, and is buried there. Although a marker was placed in the vicinity of his grave, the exact location is unknown.

**819. Smith, Henry Street\*** (1857–October 17, 1955). Many believe that he was Billy the Kid. He died at the Pioneer Home in Prescott, Arizona, and is buried in the Pioneer Home Cemetery in the northwest part of the city. The grave is in the lower part of the hillside cemetery, a few rows from the fence. A small, flat, inscribed, marble stone marks the grave. To locate the cemetery: from Gurley Street, turn north on Grove Avenue which, as it bears left, becomes Miller Valley Road. Follow Miller Valley Road until the road forks. Take the left fork, which is Iron Springs Road. The cemetery is on a steep hill on the right, immediately after passing a shopping center on the right. A paved drive leads to the top of the hill and a parking area.

**820. Smith, Henry Weston "Preacher Smith"\*** (January 1828–August 20, 1876). He was a pioneer Methodist minister and was the first preacher in the Black Hills of South Dakota. He was killed by Indians about five miles from Deadwood, South Dakota, and is buried in Mount Moriah Cemetery in Deadwood near Wild Bill Hickok. The grave is marked. A large historical marker on US 14 denotes the spot of his death five miles west of Deadwood. A brochure showing the location of a number of historical graves in the cemetery is available at the ticket office. A small fee is charged to visit the cemetery.

821. **Smith, Hyrum\*** (February 9, 1800–June 27, 1844). He was the brother of Joseph Smith, Jr., the founder of the Mormon Church. He was killed by a mob at Carthage, Illinois, along with Joseph. Both Hyrum and Joseph were buried secretly in a freshly dug basement at the site of the Nauvoo House at Nauvoo, Illinois. After being reburied in still another secret place, Hyrum, Joseph, and Joseph's wife, Emma, were all three reinterred in 1928 in the yard of Joseph's first Nauvoo home across the street from the Nauvoo House. A large slab covers the three graves.

822. **Smith, Jefferson Randolph "Soapy"\*** (1860–July 8, 1898). He was born in Newnan, Georgia, but spent most of his life moving throughout the West as a gambler and con man. He killed and was killed by Frank Reid in a gunfight in Skagway, Alaska. Both men are buried a few feet apart in a cemetery a short distance west of Skagway. Both graves are marked, as is the trail to the cemetery.

823. **Smith, Joseph, Jr.\*** (December 23, 1805–June 27, 1844). He was the founder of the Church of Jesus Christ of Latter Day Saints (Mormon). He and his brother, Hyrum, were assassinated at Carthage, Illinois, by a mob. Both were twice secretly buried in different places in Nauvoo, Illinois. Their third and final resting place was in the yard of Joseph's first Nauvoo home, across the street from the Nauvoo House. The graves of Joseph, Hyrum, and Joseph's wife, Emma, are covered by a large slab.

824. **Smith, Thomas James "Bear River Tom"\*** (June 12, 1840– November 2, 1870). Originally from New York, Tom Smith became a Kansas lawman. Although he rarely used a gun, he brought order to the wild town of Abilene. In addition to his duties as town marshal, he also served as deputy sheriff of the county. Smith was killed while trying to arrest Andrew McConnell and Moses Miles at their dugout several miles from Abilene. McConnell shot him, and then Miles almost decapitated him with an axe. Tom was buried in

the Abilene Cemetery. Some thirty-four years later, his remains were reinterred in a more prominent part of the same cemetery. On Memorial Day, May 30, 1904, the citizens of Abilene dedicated a large natural boulder marking the grave site. It stands beside one of the main driveways.

**825. Smith, Winchester.** See Arnold, Mason.

**826. Snipes, Benjamin "Ben"\*** (July 3, 1835–January 12, 1906). Born in North Carolina, Snipes moved with his family to Tennessee and then to Iowa when he was twelve years old. At age seventeen, he worked his way to Oregon in search of his older brother, George. After finding George, Ben entered the cattle business and, in time, became known as the "Cattle King of the Northwest." His 125,000 cattle roamed over a range in Washington and Oregon about the size of England. He pioneered the Caribou Trail, over which he drove cattle to the gold-rich Fraser River country in British Columbia. Snipes' parents later joined him in Oregon. In 1864, Ben married Mary Parrott (1846–1920). A son, Ben, Jr., was born in 1870; he would die tragically at sea at age twenty-one while on his way to the goldfields of Alaska. The Snipes' final years were spent at The Dalles, Oregon, and the family home still stands today. Ben died there in 1906. He was buried in the International Order of Odd Fellows Cemetery at The Dalles. Later, his wife was buried beside him. To locate the cemetery and grave: from US 30 westbound in The Dalles (Second Street) turn left on Union Street and go to Tenth. Turn right and go several blocks and turn left on Cherry Heights Road. Then turn left into the Odd Fellows Cemetery and drive straight past the office. Bear right on reaching the mausoleum. After passing the last mausoleum building, turn right on a gravel lane with graves on the left. Continue past the Manchester marker to the next row of graves and then walk about ninety feet to the Snipes plot. The large, family-plot marker is partially covered with rose bushes. There are individual markers as well.

**827. Sontag, John\*** (January 31, 1859–September 3, 1892). His real name was John Contant. He; his brother, George; and Chris Evans, became train robbers in California. He was killed by a sheriff's posse in a gunfight and is buried in Calvary Cemetery in Fresno, California. A small, marble stone bearing an engraved train marks the grave. To locate the grave: enter the cemetery through Calvary Gate and go straight ahead toward the large crucifixion monument. Sontag's grave is on the left, just before reaching the monument.

**828. Sonuk Micco.** See Billy Bowlegs.

**829. Sorbel, Asle Oscar\*** (1859–July 11, 1930). As a boy he turned in the Younger Brothers when they passed the Sorbel farm after their unsuccessful attempt to rob the First National Bank at Northfield, Minnesota. He later received a reward for the act. In order to prevent possible retaliation, all newspaper reports referred to the youngster as Oleson Suborn. The family moved to South Dakota, where Oscar became a veterinarian. He died at Webster, South Dakota, and is buried there in Block 78, Lot 1, of the Webster Cemetery, about one-half mile south of town on the east side of State Road 25. To locate the grave: enter the cemetery from the north gate by turning left at the northern boundary of the cemetery. Go to the second cross-lane. Turn left at the Schmidt marker. The Sorbel plot is near the lane, about two-thirds of the way down the lane. Oscar, his wife, Minnie, and two children are in the Sorbel plot. All graves are marked with pink marble, ground-level stones.

**830. Spalding, Eliza Hart\*** (August 11, 1807–January 7, 1851). She was the wife of the Reverend Henry Spalding, missionary to the Indians of Oregon and Idaho. She was one of the first two white women to cross the Rocky Mountains (the other was Narcissa Whitman). She died in Brownsville, Oregon, but in 1913, her remains were reinterred in the little cemetery at Lapwai, Idaho, where she lies beside her husband. The graves are marked.

**831. Spalding, Henry Harmon\*** (November 26, 1803–August 3, 1874). He was a Presbyterian missionary to the Indians of Oregon and Idaho. Most of his work was with the Nez Percé tribe. After his first wife, Eliza Hart Spalding, died, he married Rachel Smith. Henry died at Lapwai, Idaho, and is buried there beside his wife, Eliza. The graves are marked.

*Left: John Tornow, between
Satsop and Matlock,
Washington.*

*Right: John Sontag,
Calvary Cemetery,
Fresno, California.*

237

**832. Speed, Richard "Dick"*** (December 11, 1867–September 1, 1893). He was a deputy United States marshal who, along with two other deputy United States marshals, was killed in the gun battle between lawmen and Bill Doolin's Gang of outlaws at Ingalls, Oklahoma. He is buried in the Perkins Cemetery at Perkins, Oklahoma. To locate the cemetery and grave: from Highway 177 at the south end of Perkins, take Knipe Street west for 0.2 mile to the cemetery on the right. Enter the cemetery from Knipe Street and go to the second cedar tree on the right. Look past this tree to the right, past the Albright plot. Speed's grave is in the fourth row of graves from the drive. Shrubs grow to the right of the marker, which is a small, upright stone, about 2¹/₂ feet high.

**833. Spencer, Ethan Allen "Al"*** (December 26, 1887–September 20, 1923). He was an Oklahoma and Kansas train and bank robber. Al was killed by a posse in Bartlesville, Oklahoma, and is buried in Ball Cemetery near Nowata, Oklahoma. Dick Gregg, a twenty-four-year-old member of Spencer's gang, and Gregg's mother, Emma L. Gregg, are buried beside him. The three graves are marked and are in the northeast corner of the cemetery. To locate the graves: from Nowata, take US 60 east for about seven or eight miles. Then turn left (north) on Highway 28 for five miles to the cemetery on the right. The graves are in the northeast corner of the cemetery and are marked with large marble headstones.

**834. Spotted Tail*** (circa 1823–August 5, 1881). Spotted Tail was a Brulé Sioux chief. He was killed by another Sioux, Crow Dog, in a dispute on the Rosebud reservation in South Dakota and is buried beside his wife, Julia Black Lodge (1838–May 27, 1913), in the Rosebud Cemetery. The cemetery is on a little hill on the west side of the road just a short distance north of Rosebud. A dirt road leads up to the cemetery. A very tall monument marks Spotted Tail's grave, and a shorter one the grave of his wife.

**835. Spotted Wolf*** (1836–1897). Spotted Wolf was a Southern Arapaho chief and a signer of the Medicine Lodge Treaty. He is buried in the Fort Sill post cemetery at Fort Sill, Oklahoma. There is a marker. A map showing the location of the cemetery can be obtained at the gate.

**836. Standifer, William "Billy"*** (?–October 1, 1902). He was a Texas cowboy who was killed in a gunfight with "Pink" Higgins. Billy was buried at the spot where he fell. Cowboy friends put a red stone marker at his grave. Later J.B. Morrison, who owns the land, put up another headstone and surrounded the grave with a little fence. One way in which to locate the grave: leave the south side of Spur, Texas, on County Road 241. After seven miles, turn left on County Road 1081. About two miles after crossing the Kent County line, watch for the sign on the right (west) to the J.B. Morrison Ranch. Turn right across the cattle guard, which we will call milepost 0.00.

> 0.00—Sign to J.B. Morrison Ranch
> 1.45—cattle guard
> 0.15—ranch house on right
> 0.35—another ranch house on right
> 0.15—ford small stream
> 0.25—road on left but go straight ahead
> 0.25—another road on left; go straight ahead
> 0.20—cattle guard
> 0.30—cattle guard
> 0.75—cross road and cattle guard; go straight ahead
> 0.15—cattle guard
> 0.50—side road right; go straight ahead
> 0.55—stay on same road as it turns right at cattle guard
> 0.15—side road right; go straight ahead
> 0.40—stay on same road as it turns left at cattle guard
> 0.30—side road right; go straight ahead
> 0.45—turn right across cattle guard
> 0.45—small sign on right for the Standifer grave.

Climb the bank on the right, cross the wire fence, and walk about seventy-five yards directly away from the road. Watch for the red headstone surrounded by a small metal fence. All of the roads above are private ranch roads and permission should be obtained from Mr. Morrison, who lives in the first ranch house mentioned in the directions.

**837. Standley, Jeremiah M. "Doc"*** (August 20, 1845–July 8, 1908). Born in Missouri, Standley came with his parents to Ukiah, California, when he was eight years old. Doc spent most of his adult life as a lawman. He survived outlaw bullets only to succumb to a paralyzing injury suffered in a fall down a flight of stairs in Alaska. He died in Portland, Oregon, as he was being brought back to his home in Ukiah. Doc was buried in Ukiah in the Masonic Cemetery in Block Z2, Lot N, SE¼. To locate the cemetery and grave: from North State Street in Ukiah, go west a few blocks on Low Gap Road to the cemetery on the right. Enter the cemetery and drive past the office to Elm Drive. The large, grassed area on the right and beyond Elm is the Standley plot. Many Standleys are here, including Doc's wife, Sarah C. (1851–1913); his father, Harrison (1814–1886); and his mother, Elizabeth (1814–1909).

**838.   Starr, Henry George\*** (December 2, 1873–February 22, 1921). He was a notorious outlaw who robbed stores, banks, and trains. Starr served several long prison sentences. Between prison terms he made a motion picture for former deputy United States marshal Bill Tilghman in which Starr played himself. On February 18, 1921, Starr and two others attempted to rob the bank in Harrison, Arkansas. He was fatally shot by sixty-year-old W.J. Meyers, former president of the bank, and died four days later. He was buried in the Dewey Cemetery at Dewey, Oklahoma. There is no grave marker but his grave is next to his child's, which is simply marked "Baby Star" [sic]. The cemetery is just north of town on the east side of US 75.

**839.   Starr, Myra Belle\*** (February 5, 1848–February 3, 1889; NOTE: Some writers give Febuary 3, 1846, as the date of birth). She was the wife of Sam Starr and a small-time horse thief and consort of outlaws. A previous marriage to Jim Reed had produced two children, Rose Pearl and James Edward. Belle was shot from ambush and killed, probably by Ed Watson, with whom she had quarreled. She is buried near her old home at Younger's Bend a short distance southwest of Porum, Oklahoma. The grave is difficult to find and is on private property. There is an inscribed headstone placed there by the landowner. It replaces the original stone erected by Belle's daughter and destroyed by souvenir hunters. Carved on the stone is the picture of a horse, a bell, and a star.

**840. Starr, Sam\*** (November 24, 1859–December 17, 1886). He was the Cherokee husband of Belle Starr and son of Tom Starr. Sam was shot and killed in 1886 and is buried in the old Starr Cemetery near Briartown, Oklahoma. To locate the cemetery: after crossing the Canadian River going north on Highway 2, go 1.7 miles from the north end of the bridge and turn left (west) on a gravel road for 0.7 mile. Turn right (north) on a poor dirt road for 0.4 mile to the fenced cemetery on the left (the dirt road ends here). Sam's grave is marked by an upright, three-foot marble stone which is inscribed, "Sam Starr, Born Nov. 24, 1859, Died Dec. 17, 1886, Love you are as near me, and not as far, as the round earth is from the farthest star."

**841. Starr, Tom\*** (1813–October 7, 1890). He was a full-blood Cherokee Indian and the father of Sam Starr (husband of Belle Starr). Tom was the leader of the Starr clan and is said to have killed more than 100 men. He is buried in the old Starr Cemetery near Briartown, Oklahoma. To locate the cemetery: see Starr, Sam. Tom's grave is marked by an inscribed, eight-foot, gray marble stone. It is the tallest headstone in the cemetery of some thirty-five graves. The inscription reads, "Tom Starr, Died Oct. 7, 1890, Aged 77 years, Dying is but going home." Other Starrs buried here are: William Starr (March 4, 1844–January 20, 1896); Prost Starr (May 10, 1843–April 24, 1896); Charles R. Starr (October 27, 1849–April 26, 1887); Tom Starr (died February 9, 1900, aged 48 years); Clarissa Starr, wife of Tom (February 8, 1857–February 9, 1922); Joe G. Starr (December 24, 1874–February 15, 1899); and R.P. Middleton (March 7, 1825–May 13, 1887).

**842. Steptoe, Edward Jenner** (circa 1816–April 1, 1865). He was the commanding officer of the expedition which fought in the Battle of Steptoe Butte in Washington State (the battle actually took place some fourteen miles north of Steptoe Butte). In the battle, Colonel Steptoe and his troops were led to safety by a Nez Percé Indian, Chief Timothy. Steptoe resigned from the army and returned to his old home in Virginia, where he suffered a paralytic stroke in the same year and never recovered. He died in Lynchburg, Virginia, and is buried there.

**843. Sternberg, Sigismund\*** (1838–August 1, 1867). He was a lieutenant in the Twenty-seventh Infantry at Fort C.F. Smith in Montana. While in charge of a small group of soldiers detailed to guard a haying party, he was shot through the head and killed by attacking Indians. In commanding the soldiers, he had refused to take cover behind barricades. His men considered him a hero. Sternberg is buried in the Custer Battlefield National Cemetery, Section B, Grave 1226. There is a standard United States military headstone.

**844. Steunenberg, Frank J.\*** (August 8, 1861–December 30, 1905). Born in Iowa, he published newspapers in both Iowa and Idaho. Entering politics, he served in the house of representatives, and in 1896, he was elected governor of Idaho. His two terms as governor were plagued by sheep-cattlemen trouble, as well as labor problems involving the Western Federation of Miners and mine owners. After his retirement from politics, he was assassinated by a bomb explosion at his residence at Caldwell. Harry Orchard was convicted in the killing and sentenced to life in the Idaho state penitentiary. He died there in 1954. Steunenberg is buried in a family plot in Canyon Hill Cemetery on the north side of Caldwell. To locate the cemetery and grave: from downtown Caldwell, take Tenth Avenue north. After passing I-84, the road bends left and becomes Illinois Avenue. Follow Illinois north to the cemetery on the right. The grave is in the northwest quadrant of the cemetery and is marked by one of the largest headstones in that part of the cemetery.

**845. Stevens, Elisha** (April 5, 1804–September 9, 1887). Born in Georgia, he was a plainsman and wagon train leader. He died in 1887 in Bakersfield, California, and is buried there in Union Cemetery. I have been unable to locate a headstone for Stevens. California Landmark Historical Marker 732 stands near the location of Stevens' last home in Bakersfield.

**846. Stokes, Elta\*** (1873–December 8, 1942). He was a small-time robber and outlaw in California. His parents were respectable and well-to-do residents of the state. Stokes served several prison sentences for minor robberies in the Visalia, California, area. His last few years were uneventful, and he died of cancer in 1942. He is buried in the Lamoore Cemetery at Lamoore, California. His grave is in the northeast quadrant of the cemetery and a small, ground-level marker with the inscription, "Elta Stokes—1942" is present. It is southwest of the fairly large Gardoza marker and about forty feet from and just to the south of the six-inch-high, forty-inch-long slab marking the grave of James and Sarah Jones.

847. **Story, Nelson** * (April 4, 1838–March 10, 1926). He was a frontiersman and cattle rancher and became a millionaire and philanthropist. He died in Los Angeles, California, but his body was returned to Bozeman, Montana, and buried in the Sunset Hills Cemetery. There is a very large marker. To locate the cemetery and grave, see Bozeman, John.

848. **Stott, James.** See Bloody Basin Grave Site.

849. **Stoudenmire, Dallas** (December 11, 1845–September 18, 1882). He was a Texas lawman who had fought in the Civil War as a Confederate. He became marshal of El Paso, Texas, in 1881. He killed several men before he was discharged. Trouble with the Manning brothers—Jim, Frank, Doc, and John—led to a fight in which Doc and Jim killed Stoudenmire. Jim shot Stoudenmire through the head. His body was taken to Columbus, Texas, and buried by the Caledonia Masonic Lodge 68 AF and FM of Columbus, Texas. Burial was in the cemetery at Alleyton, Texas, just east of Columbus. At one time a large boulder marked the grave, but it is no longer there, and the exact location of the grave is unknown.

850. **Striding-Along-in-the-Dark "Esse-Too-Yah-Tay"*** (?–April 7, 1878). He was a Comanche leader and guided General Benjamin Grierson to Fort Sill, Oklahoma, in 1868. He is buried on Chief's Knoll in the Fort Sill post cemetery at Fort Sill, Oklahoma. There is a marker.

851. **Stuart, David*** (December 22, 1765–October 18, 1853; NOTE: the year of his birth is variously given as 1765, 1770, and 1773). He was a mountain man and fur trader. Stuart died in Detroit, Michigan, and is buried there in Elmwood Cemetery. There is a marker.

**852. Stuart, Granville*** (August 27, 1834–October 2, 1918). He was a Montana miner and cattleman and led the movement to drive out rustlers. He died at Missoula, Montana, and is buried in Deer Lodge, Montana. His second wife, Allis Belle Brown Stuart (1863–1947), is also buried there, along with other members of the Stuart family. His first wife, Aubony Stockaraka, is buried in the Fort McGinnis Cemetery northeast of Lewistown, Montana, as are her children, Kate and Lizzie. Children Irene and Harry are buried at St. Ignatius. Stuart's grave is a few feet from the small service building in the center of the Deer Lodge Cemetery. There is a bronze plaque on a small granite stone. A shrub partially obscures the plaque.

**853. Stumbling Bear "Set-imkia"*** (1832–March 14, 1903). He was a Kiowa leader. Along with Kicking Bird, he was known as a "peace chief." These two were opposed by Satanta, Satank, Big Tree, and several others. Stumbling Bear was a signer of the Medicine Lodge Treaty. He died of natural causes and is buried on Chief's Knoll in the post cemetery at Fort Sill, Oklahoma. There is a marker.

**854. Sublette, Milton Green** (circa 1801–April 5, 1837). He was a trapper and fur trader. As a result of an injury suffered at the hands of the Apaches, Milton's leg had to be amputated. He died less than a year later, probably of cancer. He is buried in one of the three old cemeteries at Fort Laramie, Wyoming. His grave site has, as yet, not been discovered.

**855. Sublette, Pinckney W.*** (circa 1812–March 1828). He was a fur trapper and mountain man and was a brother of Milton, Solomon, and William Sublette. He was killed by Blackfeet Indians. In 1897, during a lawsuit to determine the disposition of the estate of his brother, Solomon, bones were removed from a grave on Fontenelle Creek near La Barge, Wyoming, and identified as those of Pinckney. These bones were taken to St. Louis, Missouri, and used as evidence of Pinckney's death. They remained in St. Louis more than forty years. When the court finally ordered them returned to Wyoming, they were reinterred July 4, 1936, on the Prairie de la Messe in Sublette County. A pink granite boulder set in concrete marks the site, which is only 0.1 mile from the large monument to Father Pierre Jean (Peter) De Smet.

856. **Sublette, Solomon P.\*** (1815–August 31, 1857). He was a frontiersman, fur trapper, and trader. Solomon died in St. Louis, Missouri, and is buried beside his brother, William, in Bellefontaine Cemetery. A tall granite shaft marks the graves of the two brothers.

857. **Sublette, William Lewis "Bill"\*** (September 21, 1799–July 23, 1845). He was a frontiersman, fur trapper, and trader. Bill was with General William Henry Ashley's expedition to the Northwest in 1823. At one time or another, he was associated with most of the famous mountain men such as David Jackson, Nathaniel Wyeth, Robert Campbell, and Jed Smith. He died in Pittsburgh, Pennsylvania, but his body was returned to St. Louis, Missouri, and buried in Bellefontaine Cemetery beside his wife, Frances S. (1822–1857), and brother, Solomon. A tall granite shaft marks the graves.

858. **Sughrue, Michael "Mike"\*** (February 17, 1844–January 2, 1901). He was a Kansas lawman and the twin brother of Pat Sughrue who was also a lawman. Mike was marshal of Ashland, Kansas, and later became the first sheriff of Clark County, Kansas. He died of natural causes in Ashland and is buried there in the St. Joseph and Highland Cemetery which is east of town on the north side of US 160. To locate the grave: after entering the cemetery, follow the one-way drive until about 200 feet past the stone maintenance building. The grave is on the left side of the drive. There is a single, upright, granite marker for both Mike and his wife, Anna (1858–1936).

859. **Sughrue, Patrick F. "Pat"\*** (February 17, 1844–May 2, 1906). He was a Kansas lawman and the twin brother of Mike Sughrue. Pat died in a fall down an elevator shaft in Topeka, Kansas, and is buried in the Old Calvary Section of Maple Grove Cemetery in Dodge City, Kansas, in Lot 17. His wife and many of the Sughrue children and grandchildren are in the Sughrue plot. The plot is north of the Grand Army of the Republic section and just across the gravel drive beside a very bushy cedar tree. All of the Sughrue markers are ground-level and give only the names.

860. **Sundance Kid.** See Longabaugh, Harry Alonzo.

**861. Sutter, John Augustus\*** (February 28, 1803–June 18, 1880). He was a pioneer and the founder of Sacramento, California. Sutter once owned vast amounts of land in California, and it was at his mill that James W. Marshall discovered gold, leading to the gold rush of 1849. After losing everything, he returned to the East and died in Washington, D.C. John is buried in the Moravian Cemetery in Lititz, Pennsylvania. A flat marble slab covers the grave, which is surrounded by a low cement curb. His wife, Anna Dubeld Sutter (September 15, 1805–January 19, 1881), who was born in Switzerland, lies beside him. John's son, William Alphonse, is buried in Nevada City, California.

**862. Sutton, William "Bill"\*** (October 20, 1846–March 11, 1874). He led the Sutton faction in the Taylor-Sutton Feud in Texas. Bill was killed by Jim Taylor and is buried in Victoria, Texas, in Evergreen Cemetery, which is at Vine and Red River. To locate the grave: enter the cemetery through the Vine Street entrance and immediately turn left and walk to the left-hand fence. Turn right and follow the fence a short distance to the Sutton grave, which is very near the vine-covered fence. Bill's wife, Laura E. Sutton (June 22, 1853–June 29, 1930), and daughter, Willie S. Sutton (August 24, 1874–March 24, 1908), are also buried here, as is Willie's husband, John William Calhoun (August 9, 1868–October 9, 1950). All of the graves are marked.

# T

**863. Tabor, Elizabeth McCourt Doe "Baby Doe"*** (1854–circa March 5, 1935). She married millionaire H.A.W. Tabor after each had divorced earlier spouses. When Tabor's financial empire crumbled, he was left with nothing. Just before he died in 1899, he told Baby Doe to hold on to the Matchless Mine at Leadville, Colorado, believing that the price of silver would rise again in the future. This she did until her own death in 1935, living in poverty in a shack near the mine. She and her husband are buried in Mount Olivet Catholic Cemetery in Denver, Colorado, Section 18, Block 6, Lot 16, Graves 2 and 3. There is a large marble marker. To locate the grave: enter the cemetery through the main entrance from Forty-fourth Avenue on the west side of Denver. Drive straight ahead past the office on the left. Take the next drive to the right and go a short distance. Park. Section 18 is on the left. The graves are near the drive.

**864. Tabor, Horace Austin Warner "Haw"*** (November 26, 1830–April 10, 1899). He was a miner and later a politician. Tabor became a millionaire as a result of his silver mine holdings in Leadville, Colorado. After divorcing his first wife, Augusta Pierce Tabor (1833–1895), he married a young divorcée, Elizabeth McCourt Doe. Sometime after losing his fortune, he developed appendicitis and died shortly thereafter of peritonitis. Tabor and "Baby Doe" are buried in Section 18, Block 6, Lot 16, Graves 2 and 3, of Mount Olivet Cemetery in Denver, Colorado. The graves are marked.

**865. Talahina.** See Rogers, Diana.

**866. Taliaferro, C.G.*** (June 26, 1845–June 1, 1926). He was a member

247

of the posse that captured the men who robbed the bank at Medicine Lodge, Kansas, on April 30, 1884. He is buried in the Medicine Lodge Cemetery. There is a marker.

**867. Ta-moots-tsoo.** See Timothy.

**868. Taylor, Creed\*** (April 10, 1820–December 26, 1906; NOTE: Marjorie Burnett Hyatt's book, *The Taylors, The Tumlinsons And The Feud,* gives Creed's dates as May 20, 1820 and December 29, 1906; his headstone gives the dates indicated above). Taylor fought in the Mexican War and served in the Texas Rangers under Jack Hays. His brother Pitkin, and nephew, Jim Taylor, were killed in the Taylor-Sutton Feud in Texas. He died near the Noxville Community in Kimble County, Texas, not far from Junction City and is buried in the Noxville Cemetery. To locate the cemetery: from US 290, 1.4 miles east of the Kimble County line, turn north on County Road 479. Go about 6.5 miles and turn right on a good gravel road just before reaching Little Devil River. Go 0.5 mile and turn right 0.1 mile to an old shallow creek. Ford the creek and, 0.1 mile beyond, turn right and drive 0.3 mile to the cemetery. Creed is buried beside his wife, Lavinia Amanda (April 23, 1855–March 7, 1903). A tall, brown marble headstone marks Creed's grave, along with a smaller, ground-level, pink marble stone placed at the grave by the State of Texas in 1962. Lavinia's grave is marked by a four-foot-tall, white marble obelisk.

**869. Taylor, H.M. "Muggins"\*** (1830–September 27, 1882). He was an army scout and brought news of the Custer massacre at the Little Bighorn to the outside world. Taylor was a friend of "Liver Eating Johnson." While serving as a deputy sheriff at Billings, Montana, he was shot and killed by a drunken husband, who was beating his wife in a domestic dispute. He is buried in the old Pioneer Cemetery in Billings. This cemetery is at the foot of the eastern end of the mesa which is just across the river north of the city. The grave is marked.

**870. Taylor, Hephzibeth Looker\*** (circa 1790–circa 1841). She was the mother of William, Hardina, Joanna, Creed, Josiah, Pitkin, Rufus, James, Mary Jane, and—by her second husband, Patrick Dowlern—

a son, Joshua Martin Dowlern (born circa 1832). She was born in South Carolina, married Josiah Taylor on October 1, 1807, and went to Texas in 1824. She is buried in the Taylor-Bennett Cemetery near Cuero, Texas. To locate the cemetery: see Taylor, James C.

**871. Taylor, James C. "Jim"\*** (January 15, 1851–December 27, 1875). He was the leader of the Taylor faction in the Taylor-Sutton Feud in DeWitt County, Texas. He shot and killed Bill Sutton in Indianola, Texas, to avenge the murder of his father, Pitkin Taylor. Jim's cousin, Bill Taylor, killed Gabriel Slaughter at the same time. Jim was later killed, along with Mace Arnold ("Winchester Smith") and A.R. Hendricks, at Clinton, Texas, by a group of Sutton adherents led by Sheriff William Weisiger. Jim was probably killed by C.T. "Kit" Hunter. The three slain men, Taylor, Arnold, and Hendricks, are all buried in the Taylor-Bennett Cemetery about two miles south of Cuero, Texas. To locate the cemetery: go south from Cuero on US 87 and take the first paved road to the right beyond the city limits. Continue on this road, which becomes gravel after crossing the railroad tracks, to the fenced cemetery on the left.

**872. Taylor, Josiah\*** (circa 1781–1830). He was born in Virginia and came to Texas in 1812. As a captain of military forces, he took part in the Gutierrez-Magee Expedition to free Mexico from Spain. He fought at La Bahia, Alazan, and Rosales and was wounded seven times in the Battle of Medina. He returned to Texas with his family in 1824 and settled in the Green DeWitt Colony in 1829. Five of his sons fought in the Battle of Salado Creek with Captain John Hays' Company of Texas Rangers during the Mexican invasion of 1842. He is buried in the Taylor-Bennett Cemetery near Cuero, Texas. To locate the cemetery: see Taylor, James C.

**873. Taylor, Pitkin B.\*** (1822–March 1873). He was the father of Jim Taylor and the husband of Susan Cockrum Day Taylor. His parents were Josiah and Hephzibeth Taylor. Pitkin was murdered during the Taylor-Sutton Feud in DeWitt County, Texas, by a group led by Bill Sutton. He is buried in the Taylor-Bennett Cemetery near Cuero, Texas. To locate the cemetery: see Taylor, James C.

874. **Taylor, Rufus P., Sr.**\* (February 5, 1825–October 13, 1854; Note: some sources give November 10, 1824 as the year of his birth). He was the father of Rufus "Scrap" Taylor. He died before the beginning of the Taylor-Sutton Feud and is buried in the Taylor-Bennett Cemetery near Cuero, Texas. To locate the cemetery: see Taylor, James C.

875. **Taylor, Rufus P., Jr. "Scrap"**\* (May 20, 1854–June 21, 1874). He was the son of Rufus P. Taylor, Sr. Scrap was arrested, along with Kute Tuggle and Jim White, on a charge of stealing cattle and placed in jail at Clinton, Texas. A mob broke into the jail and lynched the three boys. Scrap is buried in the Taylor-Bennett Cemetery near Cuero, Texas. To locate the cemetery: see Taylor, James C.

876. **Taylor, Susan Cockrum Day**\* (December 10, 1810–October 1885). She was the wife of Pitkin and the mother of Jim Taylor. Susan is buried beside her husband in the Taylor-Bennett Cemetery near Cuero, Texas. There is a grave marker. To locate the cemetery: see Taylor, James C.

877. **Taylor, William R. "Buck"** (November 1, 1837–December 24, 1868). He was the son of William R., Sr., and Elizabeth Taylor. Buck was killed by the Sutton faction at the beginning of the Taylor-Sutton Feud in DeWitt County, Texas. He is buried in the McCrabb Cemetery at the south end of Stockdale Street in Cuero, Texas, on private property. Buck's father, William R. Taylor, Sr. (February 16, 1811–January 12, 1880); a brother, Creed Taylor (May 28, 1831–July 30, 1855); and two sisters, Martha Ann Taylor McCartney (May 13, 1840–January 25, 1861) and Amanda Taylor Hyatt (September 13, 1850–May 10, 1873), are also buried there.

878. **Ten Bears "Padda-wah-ser-man-oh"**\* (circa 1792–November 23, 1872). He was a Comanche chief and was a signer of the Medicine Lodge Treaty. He is buried on Chief's Knoll in the Fort Sill post cemetery at Fort Sill, Oklahoma. The grave is marked.

879. **Tendoy**\* (circa 1834–May 10, 1907). He was a Lemhi Indian chief who was always a friend to the white man. He died of exposure at

age seventy-three and is buried not far from the Lemhi, Idaho, post office. To locate the grave: from the post office on Highway 28, go east on the Lemhi Pass Road 0.1 mile to a T. Turn right and go 0.2 mile, and turn left up Agency Creek. After 1.5 miles, turn right and cross a cattle guard. Drive 0.5 mile and cross a second cattle guard. Continue ahead and follow the curve 0.2 mile west up to a knoll that overlooks the Lemhi Valley. The large monument of pink sandstone was placed there in 1924 by his white friends.

**880. Terry, David Smith\*** (March 8, 1823–August 14, 1889). Terry is most noted for having killed United States Senator David C. Broderick in a duel brought on by their differences of opinion regarding the issue of slavery. Terry was a supreme court justice of California when the duel took place on September 13, 1859. Broderick died on September 16. During the Civil War, Terry was a colonel in the Texas Cavalry, Confederate States of America. Later he returned to California, where trouble developed between the former judge and Stephen Field, who was a United States supreme court judge. Field hired David Neagle, a former United States marshal, as his bodyguard. The two bitter enemies met in the dining room of the train station at Turlock, California. When Terry rushed to attack Field, Neagle fired two shots, killing Terry instantly. Neagle was later acquitted. Terry is buried in the Stockton rural cemetery in Stockton, California, Section 14. A very tall and elaborate monument marks the Terry plot, which is on the extreme eastern side of the cemetery.

**881. Tettenborn, William Rogers "Russian Bill"\*** (?–January 1, 1881). He was a small-time outlaw in the Southwest and was hanged, along with Sandy King, at Shakespeare, New Mexico. The two are buried at the western edge of the Shakespeare Cemetery in a single grave. There is a grave marker. The cemetery is to the left of the dirt road leading to the ghost town of Shakespeare, which is a short distance south of Lordsburg, New Mexico. Bill was accused of being a horse thief.

**882. Tevis, James Henry "Jim"\*** (July 11, 1835–August 29, 1905). He was a frontiersman and Indian fighter. For a time he worked with the

Butterfield Stage Company before taking up ranching near Mesilla, New Mexico. During the Civil War he joined the Confederate Army and served until the end of the war. He married in 1866, before permanently settling at Bowie, Arizona. Tevis died there and is buried in Desert Rest Cemetery. His wife, Emma Boston Tevis (1845–October 1905), and a child were buried in the Tevis plot. There is a large headstone and the plot is surrounded by a wrought iron fence. The plot is just north of the two rows of cedars and is beside the Olney plot. To locate the cemetery: see Olney, Joseph Graves "Joe."

883. **Tewksbury, Braulia Rivera\*** (?–November 26, 1962). She was the wife of Ed Tewksbury. She died in Globe, Arizona, and is buried there among other relatives in the Tewksbury plot of the Globe Cemetery near the top of the hill. There is no marker for Braulia, but the other graves are marked.

884. **Tewksbury, Edwin "Ed"\*** (?–April 4, 1904). He was the leader of the Tewksbury faction during the Pleasant Valley War in Arizona. After the end of the conflict, he served as a lawman in Globe, Arizona. Ed died there of tuberculosis and is buried in the Globe Cemetery in an unmarked grave. He and his son, James, are buried beside each other but not in the Tewksbury plot where his wife, Braulia, and other family members are buried. Many years after Ed's death, his wife, Braulia, told how her husband had killed Tom Graham. He had been tried for the killing but found not guilty. Members of the Tewksbury family still live in Globe, Arizona. In 1991, Jimmy Tewksbury took me to the Globe Cemetery and pointed out the graves of his father, James, and grandfather, Ed Tewksbury. The graves are on the right, shortly beyond the entrance to the cemetery, and are unmarked but surrounded by a concrete curbing.

885. **Tewksbury, John** (?–September 2, 1887). He was a member of the Tewksbury faction that fought against the Grahams in the Pleasant Valley War in Arizona. He was shot and killed, along with William Jacobs, by Andy Cooper and others in his own yard. Hogs partially ate the bodies while the Grahams held other Tewksbury family

members at bay. They were finally buried near the John Tewksbury home. The graves are unmarked.

886. **Tewksbury, Walter** (1880–May 21, 1945). Walter was a child during the Pleasant Valley War. He died at the Arizona Pioneer Home in Prescott, Arizona, at the age of sixty-five. I have been unable to locate his grave.

887. **Thacker, Jonathan "John"** (1837–January 3, 1913). Thacker served as a sheriff in Nevada and worked many years as a special officer for Wells, Fargo. He died at his home in Oakland, California, and is buried there.

888. **Thomas, Henry Andrew "Heck"*** (January 6, 1850–August 14, 1912). Born in Oxford, Georgia, Thomas spent most of his life as a lawman, including many years as a deputy United States marshal. Thomas, Bill Tilghman, and Chris Madsen were widely known as "The Three Guardsmen." He died as a result of a kidney ailment at his home in Lawton, Oklahoma, and is buried there in Highland Cemetery. A ground-level marker reads, "Henry Andrew 'Heck' Thomas, 1850–1912." To locate the grave: enter the cemetery from the Fort Sill Road through the stone arch main entrance. Go straight ahead to the third driveway. The grave is on the right, just beyond this driveway.

889. **Thompson, Benjamin, "Ben"*** (November 2, 1843–March 11, 1884; NOTE: some sources give his date of birth as November 11, 1842). Born in Knottingley, Yorkshire, England, he became famous as a Texas and Kansas gunman and, at one time, chief of police of Austin, Texas. Prior to that he had served in the Second Texas Cavalry, Confederate States of America. Thompson and King Fisher were ambushed and killed in the Variety Theatre in San Antonio, Texas. The killers are not definitely known. Ben was buried in Oakwood Cemetery in Austin. To locate the grave: enter the cemetery from Navasota. Drive to the office on the left and immediately turn right. Drive until even with a tall, gray monument surrounded by a wrought iron fence on the left. Thompson's grave is just to the right of the fence. A small, two-foot, Confederate States of America military headstone marks the grave.

**890. Thompson, John A. "Snowshoe"\*** (April 30, 1827–May 15, 1876). Thompson delivered mail across the Sierra on skis. He died at Genoa, Nevada, and is buried in the Genoa Cemetery. His wife, Agnes (1821–1915), and only child, Arthur (1868–1879), are beside him. All three graves are marked.

**891. Thompson, John Henry\*** (December 19, 1861–August 2, 1934; NOTE: the headstone gives 1860 as his year of birth). He was sheriff of Gila County, Arizona. He is buried in the Benevolent and Protective Order of Elks section of the Globe Cemetery at Globe, Arizona. This section is enclosed by a wrought iron fence and is to the left of the paved drive, part way up the hill. There is a marker.

**892. Thompson, William "Billy"** (August 28, 1845–circa 1892; NOTE: some sources give July 12, 1841 as the date of his birth). He was a Texas and Kansas gunman and the brother of the more famous Ben Thompson. Billy shot and killed Sheriff Chauncey B. Whitney at Ellsworth, Kansas. After being involved in other trouble, he simply disappeared. Ben's widow, Catherine Thompson, said that Billy was killed in a shootout with three Mexicans, south of Laredo, Texas, and that all four men died.

**893. Thorn, Benjamin "Ben"** (December 22, 1829–November 15, 1905). He was elected sheriff of Calaveras County, California, in 1867 and served in that capacity until 1902. After his retirement that year, he and his wife, Anna Meeks Thorn (December 1, 1837–June 27, 1904), lived in San Andreas, California. He died in San Francisco and is buried in Cypress Lawn Cemetery in Colma, California, in Section G, Plot 435, beside his wife.

**894. Thornhill, James "Jim"\*** (1863–November 7, 1936). He was a friend and sometime member of Butch Cassidy's Wild Bunch. Little is known of his early life; however, his obituary in the November 10, 1936, *Globe* (Arizona) *Record* states that he was a native of Missouri. Pinkerton detective Charley Siringo believed that Thornhill was none other than Frank "Dad" Jackson, a former member of the Sam Bass Gang. Many others were of the same opinion. He was a partner of Kid Curry (Harvey Logan) in a ranch at Landusky,

Montana, and was in Jew Jake's Saloon there when Curry killed Pike Landusky. After disposing of the ranch property, Thornhill moved to Globe, Arizona, where he engaged in the cattle business. He died there and is buried in the Globe Cemetery beside his wife, Lucy (1864–1937). At the time of his death, three of Jim's and Lucy's sons were living: Harvey D., of Globe; George, of Holbrook; and Archie, of El Paso. The graves are near the top of the hill where the one-way drive begins. As you complete the one-way drive circle, the graves are on the left near the drive and are marked by a large, black marble headstone inscribed with names and years of birth and death.

**895. Thurmond, Charlotte "Lottie Deno"*** (April 12, 1844–February 9, 1934). She was a lady gambler who, in her younger days, roamed throughout Texas and the Southwest. She married a gambler, Frank Thurmond, and settled down in Deming, New Mexico, where she died of uremia at age eighty-nine. She was originally from Kentucky. Deno was a psuedonym; she never revealed her maiden name. She and Frank are buried side by side in the Mountain View Cemetery in Deming, New Mexico. Their graves are in the Knights of Pythias section, Row C, Lot 2, and are marked with small marble stones. The location is near the rock wall next to the highway and is across the drive from the flagpole. A large stump is also near the grave.

**896. Thurmond, Frank*** (1840–August 8, 1908). He was born near Atlanta, Georgia, and became the husband of Charlotte Thurmond ("Lottie Deno"). Frank had served in the Confederate Army and had been wounded in battle. In 1881, he and his wife moved to Deming, New Mexico, where he died. He is buried beside his wife in Mountain View Cemetery in Deming. For the location of the grave: see Thurmond, Charlotte.

**897. Tiana.** See Rogers, Diana.

**898. Tibbet, Berton Mills "Bert"*** (1876–June 9, 1939). He was a deputy sheriff in Bakersfield, California, and a brother of George and William Tibbet. Bert killed outlaw Jim McKinney with a shotgun in the Joss House battle in Bakersfield in which lawmen William Tibbet and Jeff Packard were also killed. Bert died in Bakersfield and is buried there in Block 118, Lot 1, in Union Cemetery. There is a marker. Brother George A. Tibbet is buried in another part of the cemetery. The graves are marked.

**899. Tibbet, George A.*** (1857–March 1, 1901). He was a brother of Will and Berton Tibbet and was also a lawman in Bakersfield, California. George is buried in Union Cemetery in Bakersfield. His grave is marked by a tall, white marble monument with four small columns. It is standing adjacent to one of the drives and is beside a large tree.

**900. Tibbet, William M. "Bill"*** (June 20, 1860–April 19, 1903). He was a Bakersfield, California, lawman who was killed by either Jim McKinney or Alfred Hulse in the Joss House battle there. Tibbet was the father of the famous baritone singer and movie star, Lawrence Tibbet, who spelled his name "Tibbett." Bill is buried in Block 132, Lot 3, in Union Cemetery in Bakersfield. There is a large marble marker with the single word, "Tibbet," at the base.

**901. Tilghman, William, Jr. "Bill"*** (September 4, 1854–November 1, 1924). For most of his life he was a Kansas and Oklahoma lawman. Bill, Heck Thomas, and Chris Madsen were known as "The Three Guardsmen" when they served as deputy United States marshals in Oklahoma and Indian territories. Bill is buried in Block 16, Lot 18, Space 1, in Oak Park Cemetery in Chandler, Oklahoma. His wife, Zoe (1881–1964), and a son, Richard L. (1907–1929), are buried beside him. There are ground-level markers for each of the three graves. Bill's parents, William Matthew (1820–1908) and Amanda Shepherd Tilghman (1830–1915), are buried in another part of the cemetery.

**902. Timberlake, James R. "Jim"*** (?–February 19, 1891). He was sheriff of Clay County, Missouri, and spent many years attempting to bring about the downfall of the James-Younger Gang. It is believed that he conspired with Missouri Governor Thomas T. Crittenden in getting Bob Ford to kill Jesse James for the $10,000 reward. Timberlake is buried in Block 89-SE4 of Fairview Cemetery in Liberty, Missouri. There is no marker at the grave site.

**903. Timothy "Ta-moots-tsoo"\*** (1800–1891). He was a Nez Percé Indian who is credited with leading Lieutenant Colonel Edward Steptoe's troops to safety when they faced annihilation at the hands of hostile Indians. He was the father of Jane Silcott, the young Indian girl who led Captain E.S. Pierce to the goldfields in Idaho. Timothy's body was removed from its original grave site and reinterred in Beachview park on the Snake River at Clarkston, Washington. There is a marker. Beachview park is several blocks west of downtown Clarkston, and Timothy's grave is near the river side of the park.

**904. Tisdale, John A.\*** (1855–December 1, 1891). He was a Texan who drove three cattle herds to Kansas. John lived for a time in North Dakota before moving his family to Johnson County, Wyoming. He was a friend of Nate Champion, who was killed by the Invaders during the Johnson County War. Tisdale was ambushed and shot, probably by Frank Canton. No one was ever brought to trial for the murder. He is buried in Willow Grove Cemetery in Buffalo, Wyoming. A large, gray marble stone marks the Tisdale family plot. A smaller stone indicates John's individual grave. The grave is about 150 feet from the entrance gate and slightly to the right.

**905. Tobin, Thomas Tate "Tom"\*** (March 15, 1826–May 15, 1894). Tobin was a Colorado pioneer and mountain man and is credited with tracking down and killing the two outlaw Espinosa brothers. He cut off the heads of the outlaws and brought them back so that he could collect the reward. He is buried in a small cemetery near his ranch, which is now known as Blanca Trinchera. His wife, Maria Pascuala, is buried beside him. In 1985 her headstone was broken into two pieces. A granite monument was placed at Tom's grave in 1937. The cemetery, which is about one mile northwest of Fort Garland, Colorado, is on property that was owned by Malcolm Forbes in 1988. Entrance to the cemetery is very difficult as there are several locked gates and permission must be obtained from an employee of Forbes Enterprises.

**906. Todd, George W.*** (?–October 23, 1864). He was a second lieutenant in the Confederate Cavalry during the Civil War and was a member of Quantrill's Raiders. Todd was killed in battle near Independence, Missouri, and is buried in the Beatty plot in Woodlawn Cemetery in Independence. To locate the grave: from the office, take the drive to the right to the second lane. Turn left on this lane and watch for the large Beatty plot marker on the left. Todd's grave is adjacent to the drive. Some large trees are just beyond the grave. A flat, gray marble marker is inscribed, "George W. Todd, 2nd Lt., Quantrill's Co., Mo. Cav., C.S.A.—Oct. 23, 1864."

**907. Toh-tsee-ah.** See Prairie Flower.

**908. Tolbert, Paden*** (1862–April 24, 1904). Tolbert was an Arkansas lawman and a deputy United States marshal. He led the posse that killed Ned Christie, the renegade Cherokee Indian. Tolbert died of lung congestion at Hot Springs, Arkansas, and is buried in Oakland Cemetery in Clarksville, Arkansas. There is a large, inscribed headstone. To locate the grave: enter the cemetery through the arch. About thirty-five feet beyond the arch, turn left on a grass drive and go about sixty feet to the four-foot obelisk on the left.

**909. Tolby, T.J.*** (1842–September 14, 1875). The Reverend Tolby was a Methodist minister who was assassinated during the Colfax County War in New Mexico. He opposed the "Santa Fe Ring." He is buried in Mountain View Cemetery in Cimarron, New Mexico. There is a large grave marker on the right of the drive, shortly after it enters the cemetery. To reach the cemetery go south on Highway 21 a short distance and turn right on a dirt road at the cemetery sign.

**910. Tolliver, Joseph Melvin "Joe"*** (May 11, 1859–April 13, 1910). He was the son of James Franklin Tolliver and Sarah Rebecca Crouse Tolliver and was born in North Carolina. While living in Brown's Park, Colorado, he took part in the pursuit of Harry Tracy and Dave Lant after Tracy killed posse member Valentine Hoy. On another occasion, after losing a wrestling match to Charles W. Seger, he fatally stabbed Seger with a knife. After leaving Brown's Park, Tolliver went to Vernal, Utah, where he served two terms as marshal of the town. He married Annie Bell Cole and they had several children. Four of them died as infants. One son, David C. Tolliver, was born October 13, 1881, and lived in Vernal until his death December 5, 1968. Joe and his wife are buried in Vernal Memorial Park Cemetery in No. H-112, Lot 4, Spaces 1 and 2. Five of their children are also buried here, and only the graves of the children are marked. Joe was killed when he accidentally shot himself with his new pistol in a Vernal barbershop.

**911. Toponce, Alexander "Alex"*** (November 10, 1839–May 13, 1923). He was born in Belfort, France, but the family came to America in 1846. They lived in Missouri for a time, but Alex ran away from home at age fifteen and went to the Northwest where he spent the rest of his life. He engaged in mining, freighting, and a number of other enterprises including a brief stint as a Pony Express rider. Shortly before his death he wrote a book about his experiences, *Reminiscences of Alexander Toponce: Written by Himself*. Alex died at Ogden, Utah, and is buried there in the Ogden City Cemetery. Beside him are his wife, Katherine Beach Fisher Toponce (1847–1926), and two children, Basil A. (1890–1944) and Jane Fisher Toponce (1891–1947). To locate the grave: from the office drive west to Madison Avenue and turn left to Center Street. Turn right on Center to Sixth Street and turn left. About 150 feet after the turn look for the grave beside the drive on the right. There is a large granite marker.

**912. Tornow, John*** (September 4, 1880–April 16, 1913). When Tornow was placed in a mental hospital by his family at age twenty-nine, he walked away and returned to his former home on the Satsop River near Montesano, Washington. He lived in the wilderness and stole clothing and ammunition from farmers and logging camps. When authorities attempted to arrest Tornow, he reacted violently. An excellent marksman, he killed six men before being killed himself by Giles Quimby. Tornow was buried in a small, remote cemetery between Satsop and Matlock. His parents, Daniel Frederick Tornow (May 29, 1844–August 12, 1909) and Louisa Tornow (January 22, 1838–November 13, 1910), are beside him. To locate the cemetery: from the little town of Satsop, go west on US 12 about one mile to a sign for Matlock on the right. Turn right (north) here for exactly 10.0 miles to the cemetery in a little clearing on the left.

913. **Tracy, Harry** (circa 1874–August 5, 1902). His real name was Harry Severns, and he was born in Wood County, Wisconsin. His criminal career began in the mid-1890s, and he became one of the most dangerous outlaws in the history of the American West. For a while he operated with another outlaw named David Lant. When a posse attempted to arrest them in Brown's Park, Colorado, Tracy shot and killed Valentine Hoy, a posse member. The two were later captured, escaped from the Hahns Peak jail, were recaptured, and again escaped, this time from the Aspen, Colorado, jail. In 1898, Tracy was operating in the Washington-Oregon area with another outlaw named David Merrill. They were captured, tried, and sentenced to long prison terms. They made a sensational escape from the Oregon state penitentiary, leaving three men dead. Tracy later killed Merrill and a number of others as he continued to elude his pursuers. He was finally cornered in a field near Davenport, Washington, by a posse. After receiving two serious wounds, Tracy committed suicide. His body was taken to Salem, Oregon, for burial by prison authorities. His grave was later covered with land fill and then with concrete. Its exact location is unknown. Various items owned by Tracy can be seen at the little Davenport museum.

914. **Travis, Charles Edward\*** (August 9, 1829–1860). He was the son of William Barret Travis of Alamo fame. He was a member of the Texas legislature, a Texas Ranger, and in 1855 was appointed captain of United States Cavalry. He served at Fort Mason, Texas. Travis was dismissed for conduct unbecoming an officer in 1856. He died of tuberculosis at age thirty-one and is buried in the Chapel Hill Masonic Cemetery east of Brenham, Texas. There is a standard United States military headstone.

915. **Travis, William Barret** (August 9, 1809–March 6, 1836). He was born a few miles from Edgefield, South Carolina, but moved to Alabama with his family when he was nine years old. Later he married and became the father of a son and daughter. When his marriage failed, he went to Texas where he practiced law. He fought

with the Texans in their battle for independence from Mexico and rose to the rank of lieutenant colonel. Travis and James Bowie shared command of the defenders of the Alamo until pneumonia felled Bowie, leaving Travis as commander. After a valiant battle, Travis and all of his men fell to the Mexicans. The bodies of the defenders were all piled together and burned.

**916. Troutman, Joanna*** (February 19, 1817–August 1880). She is known as the "Betsy Ross of Texas" because she designed the Lone Star flag. She died in Alabama and was buried there. In 1913, her remains were brought to Austin, Texas, and reinterred in the Texas state cemetery. A large monument, topped by a bronze likeness of Joanna, marks her grave.

**917. Tubbs, Alice.** See Alice Ivers.

**918. Tumlinson, Joseph "Joe"*** (February 16, 1811–November 23, 1874). He was one of the leaders of the Sutton faction during the Taylor-Sutton Feud in DeWitt County, Texas. Joe was the eighth child of John Jackson Tumlinson and Elizabeth Plemmons Tumlinson. He first married Joanna Taylor (1815–1830s), sister to Creed and Pitkin Taylor, on April 2, 1832. They had no children. He later married Elizabeth Newman (1823–1906), and they had the following children: Ann Elizabeth (1842–1923), John J. "Pegleg" (1848–1920), Martha E. "Matt" (1849–?), Sarah Barthena (1851–1930), Rachel Newman (1854–?), and Peter Creed (1855–1936). Joe Tumlinson died at his farm near Yorktown, Texas, and is buried in the Tumlinson family cemetery. To locate the cemetery: from Highway 72 about two miles west of Yorktown, turn north on Highway 952 (Cotton Plant Road). Go 1.6 miles to the Broken Spoke Ranch on the left. The ranch house is about 200 yards from the road, and the cemetery is in a little motte of trees about fifty or seventy-five yards beyond and to the left of the ranch house. Joe's grave has a small fence around it, and the marker can be read. This is private property and permission must be obtained to visit the cemetery. In 1989 cattle were roaming through the little cemetery, and the graves were in poor condition. Most of the headstone were broken and lying down. I was told that the cemetery was cleaned up and fenced in 1991.

**919. Tunstall, John Henry*** (March 6, 1853–February 18, 1878). He was a cattleman as well as a businessman in Lincoln County, New Mexico. Enmity with a faction led by businessmen Lawrence G. Murphy and J.J. Dolan led to Tunstall's murder by a Billy Mathews-led posse of Murphy-Dolan partisans. He was buried behind his store in Lincoln. There is a ground-level marker, but it is probably not at the exact grave location.

**920. Tutt, Davis K. "Dave"*** (1839–July 21, 1865). He was killed in a gunfight with Wild Bill Hickok in Springfield, Missouri. Tutt was first buried in the old Campbell Street Cemetery in Springfield. In 1881, he was moved to the Maple Park Cemetery. He is buried on the north side of the northwest corner of Lot 24, Block 57. His son, David Tutt, is also buried in that plot. There is a marker.

**921. Two Moon*** (April 1847–October 21, 1932). Two Moon was a Northern Cheyenne chief and took part in the Battle of the Little Bighorn. He surrendered to General Nelson A. Miles in April 1877 and later served as a scout for the army. He died on the Tongue River reservation and is buried on a little hill just out of Busby, Montana. A large stone and mortar pyramidal structure holds relics pertaining to Two Moon. A wire fence surrounds this structure and the chief's grave. It can be seen from the east-west highway (US 212). The monument was placed there by W.B. Moncour, a friend.

# U

**922. Upson, Marshal Ashmun "Ash"\*** (November 23, 1828–October 6, 1894). He was the "ghost writer" for Pat Garrett's book on Billy the Kid and held various jobs such as newspaperman and mail carrier in New Mexico and other parts of the Southwest. Ash died at Uvalde, Texas, and is buried in the Uvalde Cemetery in an unmarked grave in Lot 54 between John P. Baker and Will Gibson. Cemetery records show that the plot was obtained from Pat Garrett.

# V

**923. Vance, R. Frank*** (November 7, 1810–January 17, 1912). As a lawman, he served at various times as city marshal, deputy sheriff of Colfax County, New Mexico, and as a member of the New Mexico Mounted Police. Vance was murdered at Cokedale, Colorado. His murderer was never apprehended. Vance is buried in Mountain View Cemetery, which is a short distance south of Cimarron, New Mexico. The grave is on the left of the entrance road. His father and mother, William A. (1838–1914) and Mildred Kingery Vance (1849–1919), are buried beside him.

**924. Vasquez, Louis*** (October 3, 1798– September 5, 1868). Vasquez was a mountain man who died in Westport (now a part of Kansas City, Missouri) or on a farm nearby. He is buried in Woodlawn Cemetery in Independence, Missouri, in the Vasquez family plot. The grave is not marked.

**925. Vasquez, Tiburcio*** (August 11, 1835–March 19, 1875). He was a notorious California outlaw. He was hanged at San Jose, California, and is buried in the Santa Clara Catholic Cemetery. The grave is near the middle of the cemetery. A small palm tree is near the large, upright, granite headstone, which bears Vasquez's name and years of birth and death. The headstone is turned at a forty-five degree angle from that of the other headstones.

**926. Vigil, Juan*** (1886–December 22, 1903). He was a sheepherder who, along with Wiley Berry, was killed by the Booth boys, John and Zack, who were cattlemen. Juan is buried in the Gisela Cemetery at Gisela, Arizona. A small fieldstone inscribed, "Juan

Vigil, 1886–1903," marks his grave, which is about forty feet from the Booth plot. To locate the cemetery: turn east off Highway 87 a few miles south of Payson, Arizona. After about five miles, where the road forks, keep left on a dirt road for 0.7 mile and then turn left for 0.3 mile to the cemetery on a hill to the left. The graves are easily found.

**927. Wade, William Albert "Kid"** (circa 1862–February 8, 1884). He was a member of Doc Middleton's gang of horse thieves in Nebraska and the Dakotas. Wade was captured in Iowa by a posse from Nebraska's Niobrara country and taken to Bassett in Rock County. On the night of February 8, 1884, a mob took him from the building where he was held and hanged him. He was buried on Bassett Hill. To locate the grave: from the junction of US 20 and US 183 in Bassett, go east on US 20 about 0.3 mile. Turn right (south) immediately after passing a large school on the right. Drive up Bassett Hill to a small pull-off on the right. Park and walk southwest to a wire fence. Cross the fence and go to the highest point on the hill. Go south down the hill about 100 yards to an enclosure surrounded by a three-strand, barbed wire fence with a gate. Wade's grave is in the northeast corner of the enclosure and is marked only by two metal stakes in the ground. There are two other graves in the little plot.

**928. Waggoner, Daniel "Dan"** (July 7, 1828–September 5, 1902). He was born in Lincoln County, Tennessee, but moved with his family to Texas in the 1840s. He married Nancy Moore in 1848 and an only child, William Thomas, was born in 1852. Nancy died in the late 1850s and Dan married Scylly Ann Halsell in 1859. He and his son developed the 3D Ranch into one of the largest and finest in Texas. Dan and his second wife are buried in a very large mausoleum on the highest point in Oaklawn Cemetery in Decatur, Texas. Other relatives are nearby.

**929. Waightman, George "Red Buck"** (?–October 2, 1895; NOTE:

266

some writers give his date of death as March 4, 1896). He was a member of the Doolin Gang and was killed by peace officers led by Chris Madsen near Arapaho, Oklahoma. Waightman is buried in the Arapaho Cemetery. For years the grave was marked by only a common brick with "Red Buck" carved on its surface. In 1984, a flat, marble slab the size of a brick, also carrying the words "Red Buck," was placed at his grave, which is in the northeast part of the cemetery and away from the other graves.

**930. Waite, Frederick T. "Fred"*** (September 23, 1853–September 24, 1895). He rode with Billy the Kid's Gang in New Mexico and Texas. Shortly after the end of the Lincoln County War, he returned to his former home in Oklahoma, where he became a respected citizen. He died in Pauls Valley, Oklahoma, and is buried there in the Waite family plot of Pauls Valley Cemetery (the old cemetery just south of town). There is a large headstone with a Woodmen of the World symbol at the top. The Waite family plot is under some trees and is surrounded by a wrought iron fence.

**931. Walker, Joseph Reddeford "Joe"*** (December 13, 1798–October 27, 1876). Born in Tennessee, Walker achieved great fame as a mountain man and explorer. He discovered Yosemite Valley and the giant sequoia trees and was the first to cross the Sierra by way of Walker Pass. Walker died in Martinez, California, and is buried there in Alhambra Cemetery. The grave is on a hill overlooking Suisun Bay northeast of San Francisco and west of Martinez. A large marker gives the history of the old mountain man. The gate to Alhambra Cemetery is locked, but the key may be obtained from the Martinez police department.

**932. Wallace, Marion D.*** (June 19, 1846–December 24, 1888). He was sheriff of Young County, Texas, and was killed by Boone Marlow. Wallace is buried in Oak Grove Cemetery in Graham, Texas. To locate the grave: from Elm Street turn east on Sixth Street to the cemetery entrance. The Wallace graves are in the fifth row back from the cemetery wall on Elm Street and about 100 feet from Sixth Street. A six-foot obelisk marks Wallace's grave. His wife, Mrs. M.D. Wallace (October 12, 1848–June 3, 1915), is beside him. Also in this plot are E.M. Wallace (June 3, 1867–November 23, 1914), Anna L. Wallace (March 7, 1871–May 20, 1911), Thomas E. Wallace (September 25, 1870–March 21, 1946), and Belle Wallace (August 7, 1871–April 19, 1944).

933. **Wallace, Lewis "Lew"**\* (April 10, 1827–February 15, 1905). He was a soldier, a statesman, and a writer. As a soldier, he attained the rank of major general of volunteers during the Civil War. He was later named territorial governor of New Mexico during the latter days of the Lincoln County War and was the author of the literary classic, *Ben Hur*. Wallace died in Crawfordsville, Indiana, and is buried there in Oak Hill Cemetery. There is a very tall monument at his grave.

934. **Wallace, Sidney "Sid"**\* (August 11, 1851–March 13, 1874). He killed at least seven men in revenge for the murder of his father, the Reverend Vincent Wallace, by a gang bent on robbery. Sid was only twelve years old at the time. Wallace was tried and convicted of murder and was hanged by Deputy Sheriff E.A. Kline at Clarksville, Arkansas. He is buried beside his mother, father, a sister, and a brother in Oakland Cemetery in Clarksville. Sid's grave has two headstones. The new one incorrectly gives the month of his birth as May. All the graves are marked and can be pointed out by the cemetery director.

935. **Wallace, William Alexander Anderson "Big Foot"**\* (April 3, 1817–January 7, 1899). For sixty-three years he was a hunter, a scout, an Indian fighter, a soldier, and a Texas Ranger. He died in 1899 and was buried at Bigfoot, Texas. In 1935 the Texas legislature appropriated the money to have his body moved to the Texas state cemetery in Austin, Texas. His grave is at the top of the hill near Stephen F. Austin's and is marked by a large, square, marble marker. He was originally buried in the Devine Cemetery at Devine, Texas.

936. **Waltz, Jacob "The Dutchman"**\* (1810–October 25, 1891). Waltz was of German ancestry and supposedly discovered the Lost Dutchman Mine in the Superstition Mountains of Arizona. He is buried in

the southwest corner of the old city cemetery in Phoenix, Arizona. Waltz is actually buried several feet west of the present grave marker bearing his name.

**937. Ware, Richard Clayton "Dick"\*** (November 11, 1851–June 25, 1902). He was a Texas Ranger and probably fired the shot that killed outlaw Sam Bass. Ware died of heart trouble in Fort Worth, Texas, and is buried in the International Order of Odd Fellows Cemetery in Colorado City, Texas. A marble obelisk marks his grave. There is also an official Texas state historical marker.

**938. Warner, Matt\*** (April 12, 1864–December 21, 1938). He was both an outlaw and a lawman. His real name was Willard Erastus Christiansen, and he was born of Mormon parents at Ephraim, Utah. At one time he rode with the Wild Bunch. Later he was a lawman at Price, Utah. Matt died of natural causes at Price and is buried there in the Price Cemetery. A gray marble stone marks his grave. His wife, Elma Z. Warner (1867–1955), is buried beside him. To locate the grave: enter the cemetery from Sixth East Street and drive to the fourth cross-lane. Turn right and park by the pink marble Harrison obelisk. Follow this row of graves left about ninety feet to the two low, marble headstones of Matt and Elma.

**939. Warren, George\*** (circa 1845–1892). Warren discovered copper at Bisbee, Arizona. He became an alcoholic and spent some time in an insane asylum. Upon his release he returned to Bisbee where he later died of pneumonia. George is buried there in Evergreen Cemetery, which is near the traffic circle and the turn-off for Naco, Arizona. To locate the cemetery and grave: from Bisbee going east on US 80, go three-quarters of the way around the traffic circle and make a sharp right turn. The cemetery is a short distance on the left. A large mine headframe overlooks the cemetery. Turn left into the cemetery; straight ahead is Warren's large, white monument. This is the old Masonic section of the cemetery.

**940. Washakie\*** (circa 1800–February 20, 1900). Washakie was a Shoshone chief and was always a friend to the white man. Supposedly he once killed a Crow brave atop Crowheart Butte and ate part of his heart. He died of natural causes on the Wind River Indian reservation in Wyoming and is buried in the Fort Washakie Indian Cemetery. Some say he may have lived in three different centuries. His grave is near the back (west side) of the cemetery and bears an inscribed marker.

941. **Wassaja "Carlos Montezuma"\*** (1869–1923). Although he was an Indian, he was raised and educated by a white man. Carlos became a well-known and respected surgeon in Chicago. When he became sick and disillusioned, he returned to the Fort McDowell Indian reservation in Arizona, where he died in a wikiup of tuberculosis. His is buried near the center of the Fort McDowell Indian Cemetery. There is a very impressive monument, the largest in the cemetery. To locate the cemetery: turn off Highway 87 at the sign indicating Fort McDowell and drive 4.0 miles to a paved road on the left. Turn left there and drive 0.3 mile. Turn right on a dirt road 0.1 mile to the cemetery. The grave is surrounded by a low fence.

942. **Watie, Stand\*** (December 12, 1806–September 9, 1871). He was a Cherokee leader who had favored selling tribal lands in Georgia, Tennessee, and North Carolina and taking up reservation lands in what would become Indian Territory. During the Civil War he held the rank of brigadier general in the Confederate Army. He is buried in Polson Cemetery in northeastern Oklahoma. The cemetery is best reached by a good gravel road from Southwest City, Missouri. It is two miles northwest of town and is on the Oklahoma side of the state line. There is a large, inscribed granite marker.

943. **Watson, Edward J. "Ed"\*** (November 11, 1855–October 24, 1910). Many believe he killed Belle Starr, with whom he had quarreled shortly before her death. He was tried for the murder but was not convicted. Watson was killed in a fight with several men in Florida and is buried at Fort Myers in the Fort Myers Cemetery on Strickland Lane. His wife, Jane S. Watson (1862–1901), and four of their children are also buried there. To locate the grave: from I-75 at Fort Myers, take Exit 23 and go west on Anderson Avenue. When the road forks, go right on Michigan Avenue Link to Michigan Avenue. When the cemetery appears on the right, watch for an

extremely large banyan tree. Turn right just as the banyan tree is reached. This is Strickland Lane. Drive straight ahead past two cross-lanes. Go about forty-five feet past the second cross-lane. The grave is right beside the drive. Several family members are buried in the Watson plot. All graves are marked.

**944. Wattron, Francis Joseph "Frank"** (February 15, 1861–August 2, 1905). Born in Gasconade County, Missouri, he became sheriff of Navajo County, Arizona. He received great notoriety from his flippantly worded invitation to the hanging of George Smiley, which took place in Holbrook, Arizona, January 8, 1900. Copies of the invitation can be seen in the Holbrook Museum. Wattron died of an overdose of laudanum. He was buried in Los Angeles, California.

**945. Weaver, Phillip N.*** (September 28, 1859–January 19, 1886), **Henry S.*** (August 3, 1860–January 19, 1886), and **Oliver E.*** (March 30, 1863–January 19, 1886). These three brothers were lynched by a large, masked mob in Anthony, Kansas, for seriously wounding Del Shearer. It was believed that Shearer would die, but he finally recovered. A large, ornate marble monument marks their graves in the Anthony Cemetery about one mile west of Anthony on the south side of Highway 44. To locate the graves: turn south off Highway 44 at the east corner of the cemetery and drive to the southeast entrance. On entering the cemetery, look for the large marker just ahead and to the right. Inscriptions on three sides list names, date of death, and ages.

**946. Weaver, Pauline*** (circa 1800–June 21, 1867). He was a mountain man, miner, and explorer and was half Indian. A mountain peak, Weaver's Needle, is named for him. Weaver is buried in the northeast corner of Pioneer Square in Prescott, Arizona. A large boulder bearing a metal plaque marks his grave. He was originally buried with military honors at Camp Verde (then called Camp Lincoln), Arizona. His remains were later taken to San Francisco, California, and in 1929 were returned to Prescott, Arizona, and reinterred at the Sharlot Hall Museum complex on Gurley Street.

**947. Webb, Charles M. "Charley"*** (?–May 26, 1874). He was deputy sheriff of Brown County, Texas, and was killed by John Wesley Hardin. That resulted in a long prison sentence for Hardin. Webb is buried in Greenleaf Cemetery in Brownwood, Texas. To locate the grave: enter the cemetery through the entrance nearest the office. Go past the office to the first paved drive. Turn right and go to the last major lane before reaching the gate. Immediately after passing this lane, look for the very tall Byars monument on the right and under a large oak tree. Webb's three-foot-tall marker, yellowed with age, is a few feet from the Byars monument.

**948. Webster, Alonzo B.*** (?–1887).  A native of New York, he resided in Hays, Kansas, before moving to Dodge City with his wife, Amanda, in 1872. Webster operated a combination saloon and gambling house and also a drugstore. He served three terms as mayor of Dodge City, two terms in the early 1880s and again in 1886. Trouble between Webster and the Luke Short-W.H. Harris faction, operators of the Long Branch Saloon, led to the formation of the Dodge City Peace Commission composed of Wyatt Earp, Bat Masterson, and other friends of Short and Harris. Webster died of pneumonia in 1887 and is buried in Maple Grove Cemetery at Dodge City. His grave is marked by a standard United States military headstone indicating his service as a corporal in Company C, First Michigan Cavalry. The grave is in the west Grand Army of the Republic section, Block 63, Lot 3. It is not far from the cemetery office and near a large Bond gray marble headstone which is turned at a ninety-degree angle to the other headstones. Webster was first buried in Prairie Grove Cemetery and later moved to Maple Grove.

**949. Wells, Henry*** (March 3, 1881–October 31, 1963).  Born in Virginia, he went to Missouri at age sixteen. He moved to Indian Territory, where he worked as a cowboy until he joined a gang of outlaws and began robbing banks. Wells was captured after a robbery attempt in 1916 and spent five years in prison, where he met Al Spencer, Henry Starr, Silas Meigs, and other outlaws. After his release from prison, he returned to robbing banks with Meigs and Spencer. After several of his cohorts were killed, Wells retired as an outlaw and lived out a quiet life in Oklahoma. He died in Bartlesville, Oklahoma, and is buried there in White Rose Cemetery. The grave is in Block 1 and is in the fifth row of graves, about thirty feet from a large "tree trunk" type Woodmen of the World headstone marked Bruce. There is a small, ground-level marker for Henry Wells.

950. **West, Jesse J.**\* (January 8, 1863–April 19, 1909). He was a Texas and Oklahoma cattleman who, along with rancher J.C. Allen, was arrested for having hired "Killing Jim" Miller to murder Gus Bobbitt, an influential rancher of Ada, Oklahoma. Also arrested were Miller and Berry Burrell. The four men were taken from jail by a band of vigilantes said to be friends of Bobbitt, carried to an unused barn, and lynched. After their deaths, Allen and West were taken to Mobeetie, Texas, for burial in the old Mobeetie Cemetery. Tall, "tree trunk" type Woodmen of the World monuments mark their graves, which are side by side in the northeastern part of the cemetery.

951. **West, Richard "Little Dick"**\* (1865–April 8, 1898). He was a member of the Bill Doolin Gang of bank and train robbers. In 1897, after Doolin's death, he joined the Jennings Gang. West was killed by a posse led by Bill Tilghman and Heck Thomas not far from Guthrie, Oklahoma, and is buried in Summit View Cemetery in Guthrie. There is a marker. The grave is about 200 feet to the left of a toolshed. Several other outlaws are buried in the immediate vicinity.

952. **Wheeler, Harry Cornell**\* (July 23, 1875–December 17, 1925). At one time Wheeler was head of the Arizona Rangers. He died in Bisbee, Arizona, and is buried there in Evergreen Cemetery, which is near the traffic circle and the turn-off for Naco, Arizona. To locate the grave: upon entering the cemetery, go to the large, white, Warren monument straight ahead. The Wheeler grave is a few feet west of that monument. The large, gray marble marker is easily seen. The grave is in Section G. Wheeler's daughter, Jesse Wheeler Adams, is buried beside him.

953. **White Bear.** See Satanta.

954. **White Bull**\* (1834–1910). He was a Northern Cheyenne chief who

took part in the Platte River Bridge battle near present-day Casper, Wyoming. White Bull also took part in the Custer battle at the Little Bighorn. He surrendered to Colonel Nelson A. Miles and later became a scout for Miles. After serving as a trial judge for many years, he died of natural causes on the Cheyenne Indian reservation at Lame Deer, Montana. He is buried in the Lame Deer Cemetery, and his grave is marked by a wooden marker, which was lying on the ground when I visited the grave in 1990.

955. **White, Gideon Shields "Cap"**\* (1842–September 3, 1914). White was a deputy United States marshal under Judge Isaac Parker and took part in the battle that led to the death of Ned Christie, a Cherokee Indian renegade. He died while visiting his brother-in-law at La Veta, Colorado, and is buried in the La Veta Cemetery. There is a white marble, United States military headstone. To locate the grave: enter the cemetery and go left to the last lane. Turn right to the grave, which is beside the first large tree on the left. His grave marker is inscribed, "Gideon S. White, Co. C, 1 Tenn. Cav."

956. **White, James "Jim"**\* (1828–1880). He was born in Missouri and served in the Confederate Army. He became one of the greatest of the buffalo hunters, first in Texas and then in Montana. He was shot in the head and killed by an unknown assassin. His partner found his body several days later. White was originally buried in a hayfield on the Irvy Davis Ranch near the mouth of Shell Canyon in Montana. On May 22, 1979, his remains were reinterred at Old Trail Town just west of Cody, Wyoming. There is a large marker.

957. **Whitehill, Harvey Howard**\* (September 2, 1837–September 8, 1906). He was sheriff of Grant County, New Mexico, when Billy the Kid, his mother, and stepfather were living in Silver City. Harvey served several terms as sheriff. He died in Deming, New Mexico, but his body was returned to Silver City, New Mexico, for burial in the Masonic Cemetery there. To locate the cemetery and grave: from Highway 90, take Broadway to the courthouse and turn left (south) for about one mile. The Masonic Cemetery is on the left (east) side of the road. Enter the cemetery at the north entrance (a gravel drive) and follow the curve to the right. The grave is on the

left of the lane, about 100 feet beyond the curve. There is a large, marble marker. His wife, Harriett M. (1841–1895), and several relatives are buried in the plot.

**958. Whitman, Marcus*** (September 4, 1802–November 29, 1847). He was a Congregational missionary to the Cayuse Indians and founded a mission at Waiilatpu, which is near present-day Walla Walla, Washington. Whitman; his wife, Narcissa; and some dozen others were murdered in an uprising of the Cayuses. They are buried at Waiilatpu in marked graves.

**959. Whitman, Narcissa Prentiss*** (March 14, 1808–November 29, 1847). She was the wife of Marcus Whitman and, like her husband, was a missionary to the Indians of the northwest. She and Eliza Spalding were the first two women to cross the Rocky Mountains. With her husband, she was a victim of the Cayuse uprising in which some fourteen people lost their lives. Narcissa is buried beside her husband at Waiilatpu in a marked grave.

**960. Whitmer, David*** (January 5, 1805–January 25, 1888). He was one of the "Three Witnesses" to the Book of Mormon. He died at Richmond, Missouri, and is buried there in City Cemetery, which is west of town on Highway 10. There is a marker. To locate the grave: there are three very narrow entrances to the cemetery from Highway 10. Enter through the easternmost entrance and go to the top of the hill. The grave is on the left of the drive as it curves to the left. Across the lane on the right-hand side of the curve is the grave of Robert Ford, the man who killed Jesse James.

**961. Whitney, Charley S.*** (April 19, 1890–November 13, 1968). He was an outlaw who also used the name, Frank S. Taylor, and was originally from Cokeville, Wyoming. He died in Hot Springs, Montana, and is buried in the Whitefish Cemetery in Whitefish, Montana. Very large, glass-covered boards stand in each section of the cemetery, showing the location of graves by name.

**962. Whitney, Chauncey Belden*** (March 31, 1842–August 18, 1873). He served as marshal of Ellsworth, Kansas, and later was elected sheriff of Ellsworth County. As a scout with George Alexander "Sandy" Forsyth's expedition, he had taken part in the Battle of Beecher Island against a group of Cheyennes led by Chief Roman Nose. Whitney was shot and killed by a drunken Billy Thompson, brother of the more famous Ben Thompson, at Ellsworth, Kansas. He was given a Masonic burial in the Ellsworth Cemetery south of town. The grave is in the extreme southwest part of the cemetery, only a few feet from the road. There is a large marble headstone.

963. **Whitney, Hugh** (1888–October 25, 1950). He and his brother, Charlie, were outlaws who originally came from Cokeville, Wyoming. He died in Saskatoon, Saskatchewan, and is buried there in Woodlawn Cemetery in an unmarked grave.

964. **Wickenburg, Johannes Henricus "Henry"**\* (November 21, 1819–May 1905; NOTE: the marker on the grave incorrectly gives the year of his birth as 1820; his baptismal certificate gives November 21, 1819, as his birth date). He discovered gold at Wickenburg, Arizona, in 1863. He committed suicide by shooting himself with an old pistol and is buried on the south side of Wickenburg between Mesquite and Jefferson streets. The grave, which is covered by a concrete slab, is reached by a gravel street.

965. **Willard, Alexander Hamilton**\* (August 24, 1778–March 6, 1865). He was a member of the Lewis and Clark Expedition. In 1807, he married Eleanor McDonald of Shelbyville, Kentucky. They had twelve children, five daughters and seven sons, one of whom was named Lewis and another Clark. The family lived in Missouri, Wisconsin, and California. Willard is buried in the Franklin Cemetery at Franklin, California, a few miles south of Sacramento. There is a marker.

966. **Willingham, Caleb Berg "Cape"**\* (April 8, 1853–January 18, 1925). He worked as a cowboy and a range detective and was the first sheriff of Oldham County, Texas. Cape was later foreman of the Turkey Track Ranch near the historic Adobe Walls battleground in the Texas panhandle. He spent his later years in the cattle business in New Mexico and as cattle commissioner in El Paso, Texas. He

died at Ajo, Arizona, in 1925 and is buried in the Ajo Cemetery, Block 2, Lot 5. To locate the grave: enter the cemetery from First Street and go to the third cross-lane. Turn left to the second cross-lane. Turn left. The small, marble marker is on the left, a few feet from the corner. It is inscribed, "C.B. Willingham," and is shaded by a small mesquite tree.

**967. Willis, Ann Bassett "Queen Ann"\*** (May 12, 1878–May 8, 1956). After the deaths of her parents, she ran cattle in Brown's Park, Colorado. Doris Karren Burton, in her book, *Queen Ann Bassett: Alias Etta Place,* suggests that the two were the same person. Ann died in Leeds, Utah, and was cremated. Later her husband, Frank Willis, had her ashes buried in the Bassett Cemetery on the hill just west of the old Bassett Ranch beside her sister Josie and other relatives. There is a marker.

**968. Willis, Frank\*** (December 11, 1883–July 16, 1963). He was the husband of Queen Ann Bassett of Brown's Park, Colorado. Frank is buried on the hill about 100 yards above and to the west of the Bassett Cemetery near the old Bassett Ranch. He asked not to be buried in the Bassett Cemetery because he was not a church member. There is a marker.

**969. Willow, Edwin L.\*** (1864–January 25, 1925). He was the city marshal of Bakersfield, California, when he killed Percy Douglass in 1897. Douglass was attempting to enter a woman's room against her wishes. Douglass was a known killer and had served a prison sentence. Willow later became fire chief and served as such for ten years. He died of pneumonia in 1925 and was buried in Union Cemetery in Bakersfield, Main Section, Block 843, Lot 5. An impressive, flat marker covers his grave, which is very near that of Douglass. To locate the grave: drive past the office to the back (east) of the cemetery. Turn left on this easternmost lane and look for three palm trees which seem to grow from a common root system. Stop. Look toward the office from the three palms. About forty feet away is the flat stone covering the Willow grave. A marker with the word "Rest" is beside Willow.

**970. Wilson, Billy.** See Anderson, David L.

**971. Wilson, William "Billy."** See Bloody Basin Grave Site.

**972. Wilson, Jack.** See Wovoka.

**973. Wilson, Vernon "Coke"** (May 1, 1857–September 13, 1892). At one time he was a member of the Texas Rangers. Later he served as a deputy United States marshal and as a special investigator for the Southern Pacific Railroad. In 1892, he went to California to aid in the manhunt for the outlaws John Sontag and Chris Evans. As a member of the posse attempting to arrest the pair at the Evans farm, Wilson was shot and killed instantly by Sontag, who fired a shotgun through a window of the house. Wilson's body was returned to Tucson, Arizona, and was buried in the old Tucson Cemetery. When the bodies from that cemetery were removed and reinterred in Evergreen Cemetery, the exact site of his grave was lost.

**974. Winema "Toby Riddle"\*** (circa 1846–February 18, 1920). She was the Modoc Indian wife of Frank Riddle and the cousin of Captain Jack. Toby frequently served as an interpreter, as did her husband. Both were in the tent when Captain Jack shot and killed General Edward R.S. Canby under a flag of truce. She died in Oregon and is buried in the Chief Schonchin Cemetery in a marked grave. To locate the cemetery: see Schonchin, "Old Chief."

**975. Winslow, Henry Francis\*** (January 14, 1863–February 3, 1954). Henry was a Texas Ranger. He is buried in the Voca Cemetery near Brady, Texas; a low, granite stone marks his grave. The Voca Cemetery is about thirteen miles southeast of Brady on a paved road a short distance from Highway 71. The grave is in the northeast part of the cemetery.

**976. Wohrle, John Anton\*** (November 1845–August 10, 1875; NOTE: On his enlistment papers, John spelled his name "Wohrle," but other spellings are used. On his headstone, his name is spelled "Whorlie." All papers in his wife's government pension file, copies of which were obtained from the National Archives, use the spelling "Whorle." The pension application is also signed "Hellena Whorle"). John enlisted in the Union Army at Cleveland, Ohio, on January 27, 1864, and served in Troop B, Third Regiment, United States Cavalry for exactly three years. He carried the rank of corporal when he was discharged at Fort Craig, New Mexico. He went to Mason, Texas, and on August 5, 1872, he and Hellena Geistweidt (originally "Helene") were married by Conrad Pluenneke, pastor of the Methodist Episcopal Church at Willow Creek, Mason County, Texas. A son, William D. Wohrle, was born on January 9, 1876. Hellena (called "Lena") had previously suffered a miscarriage brought on by stress due to the violence in the county. While serving as deputy sheriff of Mason County, John was shot in the back of the head and killed by Scott Cooley. Cooley had blamed Wohrle for the death of a friend, Tim Williamson, during the early days of the Mason County War. Cooley took John's scalp and carried it for some time thereafter. A marker on the west side of Mason stands at the site of Wohrle's death. He is buried in the Gooch Cemetery just east of town. To locate the grave: turn north from Highway 29 on the east side of town to the cemetery, on the left. Drive to the second entrance and turn left (west) into the cemetery. The grave is on the left, just beyond the entrance, and is behind and to the left of the large, pink marble, Bickenbach marker. A small, United States military headstone indicates his grave.

**977. Wood, George B.*** (May 21, 1853–August 18, 1881). He was born in Owen Sound, Canada, but went to Kansas in the 1870s. Wood was shot and killed by Charlie Davis in an argument over one of the inmates of Wood's Red Light Saloon and brothel, the latter operated by Wood's wife, Mag. Davis was captured and served a prison sentence. Wood was buried in the Caldwell Cemetery at Caldwell, Kansas. A massive headstone, shared by Fred Kuhlman, who was also murdered, was placed at the grave site by Mag Wood. The huge stone is on the east side of the lane leading south from the flagpole. To reach the cemetery: drive north from Caldwell on Main Street (State Road 49). Turn left on Avenue G, just beyond the water tower, to the cemetery. The flagpole can be seen from the maintenance building.

**978. Woods, James*** (?–September 12, 1861). Along with David C. McCanles and James Gordon, Woods was killed by Wild Bill

Hickok and possibly others at Rock Creek Station near present-day Fairbury, Nebraska. He was originally buried in the Rock Creek Station Cemetery. Later his remains, along with those of McCanles, were removed to the cemetery at Fairbury. There is a ground-level marker.

979. **Woolsey, King S.*** (circa 1832–June 30, 1879). He was a rancher and Indian fighter of Arizona, and at one time he owned a large ranch near Gila Bend, Arizona. He is buried in the Old City Cemetery in Phoenix, Arizona. There is a large marker in the southwestern part of the cemetery.

980. **Wootton, Richens Lacy "Uncle Dick"*** (May 6, 1816–August 22, 1893). Born in Virginia, he became a mountain man, a trapper, and a buffalo hunter and acted as a scout and guide for the army. In 1865, Wootton built a toll road over Raton Pass on the Colorado-New Mexico line; he operated it for many years. He is buried in the Trinidad Catholic Cemetery in Trinidad, Colorado, Lot 29, Section 4, Grave 2. There is a marker.

981. **Worcester, Samuel Austin*** (January 19, 1798–April 20, 1859). The Reverend Worcester was a missionary to the Cherokee Indians in Oklahoma. He founded the Park Hill mission and established the first Cherokee newspaper. Worcester died near Park Hill and is buried in the Worcester mission cemetery along with his first wife, Ann (1800–1840), and second wife, Erminia (1802–1872). The cemetery is one-quarter mile southeast of the Murrell Mansion. The graves are marked by obelisks surrounded by an iron fence.

982. **Wovoka "Jack Wilson"*** (circa 1856–September 20, 1932). He was a Paiute Indian and lived in the southern part of Nevada's Mason Valley. Wovoka developed the Ghost Dance ritual which spread throughout the Indian tribes of the West and eventually led to the massacre at Wounded Knee, South Dakota. He is buried under the name of "Jack Wilson," a name given to him by the white Wilson family with whom he lived. He is buried in the Schurz Indian Cemetery at Schurz, Nevada. In 1979 there was a marker bearing the name "Jack Wilson."

983. **Wratten, George Medhurst*** (January 31, 1865–June 23, 1912). He was a scout and interpreter for the army and was a good friend of Geronimo. In 1909, he was trampled by a horse in a corral accident and suffered from the effects until his death some three years later. Wratten is buried in the Fort Sill post cemetery at Fort Sill, Oklahoma. A large, red granite stone marks his grave. It is some distance south of the grave of Quanah Parker.

984. **Wright, Alfred*** (March 4, 1788–March 31, 1853). The Reverend Wright was a missionary to the Choctaw Indians in Oklahoma. He founded the Wheelock Academy, which is about one mile from Millerton, Oklahoma. South of the academy site is the Wheelock Mission Church, and nearby is the mission cemetery where Wright is buried. There is a marker.

985. **Wright, Robert "Bob"*** (September 2, 1840–January 4, 1915). He was the son of Robert M. Wright and was a Dodge City, Kansas, pioneer and businessman. Bob is buried in Maple Grove Cemetery a short distance west of Dodge City. There is a marker.

986. **Wright, Robert M.*** (1801–1872). He was a Kansas pioneer and the father of Robert Wright. He died at Dodge City, Kansas, and is buried there in Maple Grove Cemetery, Block 8, Lot 26, Grave 3.

987. **Wyatt, Nathaniel Ellsworth "Zip"** (1863–September 7, 1895). He also used the name "Dick Yeager." He was a member of the Bill Doolin Gang of bank and train robbers. Using a .40–70 single-shot Winchester, Ab Poak shot Wyatt on August 4, 1895, near Sheridan, Oklahoma. Wyatt died some thirty-four days later in the Garfield County jail. He was buried in the pauper's cemetery south of Enid, Oklahoma.

988. **Wyeth, Nathaniel Jarvis** (January 29, 1802–August 31, 1856). Born in Massachusetts, he became a fur trader in the Northwest. Although he built Fort Hall in Idaho and Fort William at the mouth of the Willamette River, most of his enterprises met with little success. He died at his old home in Cambridge, Massachusetts, and was buried there.

**Y**

**989. Yantis, Oliver "Ol"\*** (August 11, 1868–November 30, 1892). Yantis was a member of the Bill Doolin Gang. He was shot at the home of his sister by a posse made up of Chalkley Beeson, George Cox, Tom Hueston, and Hamilton B. Hueston. He was taken to a doctor in Orlando, Oklahoma, and died a few hours afterward. His sister had the body taken to Mulhall, six miles south of Orlando, and buried in the Rose Lawn Cemetery. The cemetery is a short distance east of Highway 77 and about a mile south of town. There is a three-and-one-half-foot, inscribed marble obelisk. The grave is about twenty-five feet from a wire-enclosed plot and just north of a large, gray marble headstone with a cross on top.

**990. Yeager, Dick.** See Wyatt, Nathaniel Ellsworth "Zip."

**991. Yellow Bear\*** (1842–1887). Yellow Bear was an Arapaho chief. He is buried on Chief's Knoll in the Fort Sill military cemetery at Fort Sill, Oklahoma. There is a marker.

**992. York, William H.\*** (circa 1835–March 1873). York was a medical doctor, and during the Civil War he was an assistant surgeon, Fifteenth United States Infantry. He was killed by the "Bloody Benders" at their roadhouse near Cherryvale, Kansas. His brother, Colonel A.M. York, started an investigation which led to the demise of the Benders. After York's body was uncovered in the Benders' backyard, it was taken to Independence, Kansas, and buried in Mount Hope Cemetery. There is a small United States military headstone. To locate the grave: enter the cemetery at the mausoleum and drive straight ahead on the paved drive to the first cross-drive.

About forty feet beyond this cross-drive, on the right and adjacent to the drive, is the grave site.

**993.  Young, Brigham\*** (June 1, 1801–August 29, 1877).  After the death of Joseph Smith, founder of the Mormon Church, Young led the Mormons to Utah where they founded Salt Lake City.  On December 27, 1847, he became the second president of the Mormon Church. He had twenty-seven (some say twenty-nine) wives and fathered fifty-seven children.  He died in 1877, possibly of arsenic poisoning, and is buried in the little Young Cemetery at Salt Lake City.  A wrought iron fence surrounds the grave.  Several of his wives are also buried in his plot.

**994.  Young, Ewing\*** (circa 1792–February 15, 1841).  He was an Oregon pioneer.  He had trapped and explored throughout the Southwest before going to Oregon in 1834.  Young became a successful rancher there before his death from stomach problems.  A large, round oak tree grows over his grave and bears a bronze marker.  There is a wooden historical marker on a stone monument beside Highway 240, 3.2 miles northwest of Newberg, Oregon.  The large oak tree can be seen from this point, about one-quarter mile to the east.  Access by car is difficult.  A few hundred yards south of the marker, a poor dirt road once led to the grave site.  It is now impassable.

**995.  Younger, Bursheba Fristoe\*** (1816–1870).  She was the mother of the Younger boys, Cole, John, Jim, and Bob.  Her husband was Colonel Henry W. Younger, who was killed by Union soldiers during the early days of the Civil War.  Bursheba is buried beside three of her sons, Cole, Jim, and Bob, in the northeast part of Lee's Summit Cemetery at Lee's Summit, Missouri.  The four graves are near Highway 291, which passes the cemetery on the east side.  All of the graves are marked.

**996.  Younger, James "Jim"\*** (January 15, 1848–October 19, 1902). He was a member of the James-Younger Gang of train and bank robbers. Jim was badly wounded and captured following the attempt to rob a bank in Northfield, Minnesota.  He was imprisoned but was paroled in 1901. Disappointed, some say because he was not allowed to marry a woman he loved, he committed suicide in 1902. Others say the love story is pure fiction. Jim is buried beside his mother and two brothers, Cole and Bob, in the northeast part of Lee's Summit Cemetery. The grave is marked. To locate the grave: see Younger, Bursheba Fristoe.

**997. Younger, John*** (1851–March 16, 1874). He was a member of the James-Younger Gang and was killed in a gunfight by a Pinkerton detective, Captain Louis J. Lull. In the fight, John killed deputy Ed B. Daniels and wounded Lull. Younger was buried in the old Yeater Cemetery at Chalk Level and Osceola roads near Roscoe, Missouri. The grave is at a forty-five degree angle to the other graves, and for many years was marked only by a metal rod driven into the ground at the head. An inscribed granite stone was placed at John's grave in 1991. There is also an inscribed stone marker at the site of the gunfight beside a dirt road a few miles away. To locate the cemetery and grave: from Highway 13 just north of Osceola, Missouri, take County Road B 4.2 miles west. Turn right (north) on a gravel road for about one mile to a sharp curve to the left. At the curve, turn right (beside a farmhouse) to the cemetery entrance. Enter the gate and walk about two-thirds of the way across the cemetery. Look right to the large marker bearing the name "Dark." Younger's grave is a little beyond and to the right of that marker.

**998. Younger, Rebecca*** (March 20, 1826–November 28, 1850). She is buried in St. Charles Borromeo Cemetery at St. Charles, Missouri. The cemetery is west of Blanchette Park, which is at Randolph and Chestnut streets. An inscribed marble stone marks the grave site. Although the stone indicates that Rebecca was the wife of the famous outlaw, Cole Younger, of Missouri, that is obviously in error. She died when Cole was only six years old.

**999. Younger, Robert "Bob"*** (October 29, 1853–September 16, 1889). He was a member of the James-Younger Gang and was wounded and captured following the attempt to rob a bank at Northfield, Minnesota. Bob was sentenced to life imprisonment. He died of tuberculosis in prison at Stillwater, Minnesota. He is buried in the

*Thomas Coleman Younger, James "Jim" Younger, Robert "Bob" Younger, and Bursheba Fristoe Younger, Lee's Summit Cemetery, Lee's Summit, Missouri.*

*John Younger, Yeater Cemetery, Osceola, Missouri.*

family plot in Lee's Summit Cemetery in Lee's Summit, Missouri. His mother, Bursheba, and two of his brothers, Cole and Jim, are buried in the same plot. Each of the four graves is marked. For the location of the cemetery and grave: see Younger, Bursheba Fristoe.

**1000. Younger, Thomas Coleman "Cole"\*** (January 15, 1844–March 21, 1916). He was a member of the James-Younger Gang. Near the end of the Civil War he had been an officer in Quantrill's Raiders. Cole was wounded and captured, along with his brothers, Jim and Bob, following an attempt to rob a bank at Northfield, Minnesota. He was sentenced to life imprisonment at Stillwater penitentiary but was paroled on July 10, 1901. In 1903, he returned to Missouri and lived at Lee's Summit until his death. He is buried in Lee's Summit Cemetery, along with his mother, Bursheba, and two of his brothers, Jim and Bob. There are two markers at Cole's grave, one of them a Confederate States of America military headstone.

# Z

**1001. Zepko-ett.** See Big Bow.

# Appendices

# Appendix I

## Westerners' Graves by State

### Alabama

Burrow, Reuben Houston "Rube"

### Alaska

Reid, Frank

Smith, Jefferson Randolph
    "Soapy"

### Arizona

Behan, John Harris "Johnny"
Berry, George C.
Berry, Wiley
Blevins, Charles
Blevins, Sam Houston
Bloody Basin Grave Site
Booth, John
Brady, Patrick W. "Pat"
Breakenridge, William M. "Billy
Brewer, Richard M. "Dick"
Christian, William "Black Jack"
Claiborne, William Floyd
Clanton, Joseph Isaac "Ike"
Clanton, Newman Haynes
Clanton, Phineas "Phin"
Clanton, William H. "Billy"
Cummings, Mary K. "Big Nose
    Kate Elder"
Daniels, Benjamin "Ben"

Earp, Warren
East, James Henry "Jim"
Fly, Camillus S.
Free, Mickey
Gabriel, J.P. "Pete"
Gildea, Augustine Montague
    "Gus"
Glaspie, Robert M. "Bob"
Graham, John
Graham, Thomas "Tom"
Graham, William
Hadji Ali "Hi Jolly"
Hamblin, Jacob
Herron, Anna May
Howell, Amazon C.
Jeffords, Thomas J. "Tom"
Kempton, Martin R.
Kinney, John William Young
Kitchen, Peter "Pete"

Manning, Frank
Manning, George Felix "Doc"
McLaury, Robert Frank
McLaury, Thomas "Tom"
Middleton, Harry
Milton, Jefferson Davis "Jeff"
Old, William "Billy"
Olney, Joseph Graves "Joe"
Owens, Commodore Perry
Phy, Joseph "Joe"
Pickett, Thomas "Tom"
Power, John Grant
Power, Thomas J., Jr. "Tom"
Reed, Pearl
Reed, Rose Pearl
Reynolds, Glenn
Rhodes, John (Tewksbury)
Rhodes, Mary Ann Crigger
   Tewksbury
Ringo, John "Johnny"
Roberts, James F. "Jim"
Roberts, Mose
Rose, Albert "Al"
Schieffelin, Edward L. "Ed"

Shanley, Edward P.
Shibell, Charles A.
Sieber, Albert "Al"
Sisson, Thomas "Tom"
Slaughter, John Horton
Smith, Henry
Tevis, James Henry "Jim"
Tewksbury, Braulia Rivera
Tewksbury, Edwin "Ed"
Tewksbury, John
Tewksbury, Walter
Thompson, John Henry
Thornhill, James "Jim"
Vigil, Juan
Waltz, Jacob "The Dutchman"
Warren, George
Wassaja (Carlos Montezuma)
Wattron, Frank J.
Weaver, Pauline
Wheeler, Harry
Wickenberg, J.H. "Henry"
Willingham, Caleb Berg "Cape"
Wilson, Vernon Coke "Vic"
Woolsey, King S.

## Arkansas

Maples, Daniel "Dan"
McConnell, Edward Taylor
   "Bud"
Parker, Isaac Charles
Powers, John Hall

Reed, Nathaniel "Texas Jack"
Rusk, David Vance "Dave"
Sarber, John Newton
Tolbert, Paden
Wallace, Sidney "Sid"

## California

Antrim, William H.
Aten, Ira
Barter, R.H. "Rattlesnake Dick"
Beaver, Oscar
Cushman, Pauline

Dalton, Littleton
Dalton, William Marion "Bill"
Douglass, Percy
Earp, James Cooksey "Jim"
Earp, Morgan

Earp, Newton Jasper
Earp, Nicholas Porter
Earp, Virginia Ann Cooksey
Earp, Wyatt Berry Stapp
Edwards, Adelia Douglas Earp
French, John William "Peter"
Godey, Alexis
Goodyear, Miles Morris
Gridley, Ruel
Hays, John Coffee "Jack"
Herron, James "Jim"
Hulse, Alfred "Al"
Kidder, Jefferson Parish "Jeff"
Kosterlitzky, Emelio
Lassen, Peter
Lay, William Ellsworth "Elzy"
Manning, James "Jim"
Marshal, James Wilson
Mason, Barney
McKinney, Andrew
McKinney, James "Jim"
Morse, Harry Nicholson
Packard, Thomas Jefferson "Jeff"
Parkhurst, Charley Darkey

Rath, Charles "Charley"
Rynning, Thomas H. "Tom"
St. John, Silas
Scott, Walter Ellsworth "Death
   Valley Scotty"
Seng, Marvin B.
Serra, Junipero
Shea, Cornelius "Con"
Simpson, Raymond "Ray"
Sontag, John
Standley, Jeremiah M. "Doc"
Stevens, Elisha
Stokes, Elta
Terry, David Smith
Thacker, Jonathan "John"
Thorn, Benjamin "Ben"
Tibbet, Berton Mills "Bert"
Tibbet, George A.
Tibbet, William M. "Bill"
Vasquez, Tiburcio
Walker, Joseph Reddeford "Joe"
Willard, Alexander Hamilton
Willow, Edwin L.

## Colorado

Autobees, Charles
Bain, George
Bassett, Eb
Bassett, Elizabeth
Bassett, Josephine "Josie"
Bene (Beni, Reni), Jules
Bent, William W.
Blachley, Andrew T.
Born, Henry "Dutch Henry"
Chew, William
Chivington, John Milton
Clarke, James "Jim"

Cody, W.F. "Buffalo Bill"
Cook, David J. "Dave"
Dart, Isom
Day, Barney B.
Dean, Thomas J.
Duggan, Martin "Matt"
Faber, Charlie
Farnham, Ethan Allen
Farr, Edward J. "Ed"
Holliday, John Henry "Doc"
Horn, Thomas "Tom"
Hoy, Harold "Harry"

Hughes, Bella Metcalf
Hurley, Thomas J. "Tommy"
Jarvie, John
Kreeger, Louis Michael "Lew"
Law, George
Leroy, William "Billy"
Logan, Harvey "Kid Curry"
Lowe, Benjamin "Ben"
Mayer, Frank H.
McCarty, Thomas "Tom"
McCarty, William "Bill"
Meeker, Nathan Cook
Mills, John G.
Modena, Mariano
Neiman, Charles Willis "Charley"
Omohundro, J.B. "Texas Jack"
Ouray

Packer, Alfred (Alferd)
Packer Victims Gravesite
Pearce, "The Kid"
Pfeiffer, Albert H.
Riley, John Henry
Sampson, Cassius "Cash"
Shirley, James "Jim"
Shores, Cyrus Wells "Doc"
Tabor, Elizabeth McCourt Doe
Tabor, H.A.W. "Haw"
Tobin, Thomas Tate "Tom"
White, Gideon Shields "Cap"
Willis, Ann "Queen Ann"
Willis, Frank
Wootton, Richens Lacy "Uncle Dick"

## Delaware

Carlisle, William "Bill"

## Florida

Hutchinson, William H.

Watson, Edward "Ed"

## Georgia

Miner, William "Bill"

## Idaho

Colgate, George
Craig, William
Hall, Maggie "Molly B'Dam"
Lawyer (Chief)
Orchard, Harry

Silcott, Jane "Indian Jane"
Spalding, Eliza
Spalding, Henry Harmon
Steunenberg, Frank J.
Tendoy (Chief)

## Illinois

Bassett, Herbert
Smith, Hyrum

Smith, Joseph

## Indiana

Bass Family Cemetery
Boone, Squire, Jr.
Bratton, William C.
Canby, Edward Richard Sprigg
Lucas, Orrington "Red"
Reno, Frank

Reno, John
Reno, Simeon
Reno, William
Shields, John
Short, Charles Edward "Ed"
Wallace, Lewis "Lew"

## Iowa

Floyd, Charles
Keokuk (Chief)

McMillen, Frank
O'Day, Thomas "Tom"

## Kansas

Baldwin, Lucius M.
Beeson, Chalkley M.
Bell, Hamilton "Ham"
Broadwell, Richard L. Dick"
Brown, Charles G.
Brown, Charles J.
Brown, George S.
Brown, Henry Newton
Bull, Hiram C.
Coffee, Gideon H. "Gib"
Comstock, William "Billy"
Connelly, Charles T.
Cormack, Charles H. "Charley"
Cubine, George B.
Custer, Thomas "Tom"
Dalton, Emmett
Dalton, Franklin "Frank"
Dalton, Gratton "Grat"
Dalton, James Lewis
Dalton, Robert "Bob"
Durfey, Jefferson "Jeff"
Ellis, Abraham "Bullet Hole"
Flatt, George W.
Grover, Abner T. "Sharp"
Hanks, Romulus "Rome"

Hardesty, R.J.
Hodges, Benjamin "Ben"
Hollister, Cassius M. "Cash"
Hoover, George M.
Jones, John Stykes
Julian, J.E. "Ed"
Kelley, James H. "Dog"
Kloehr, John Joseph
Kuhlman, Fred
Lane, James Henry "Jim"
Lytle, O. Vernon
McCanles, William Monroe
Marshall, John E. "Curly"
Masterson, Edward J. "Ed"
Masterson, James P. "Jim"
Mathewson, William
Meagher, Michael "Mike"
Morrow, David "Prairie Dog
   Dave"
Nation, David
Nixon, Thomas Clayton "Tom"
Olive, Isom Prentice "Print"
Olive, W. Prentice "Willie"
Payne, David L.
Power, William Todd "Bill"

Rand, Theodore P.
Rath, Ida Ellen
Rising, Don Clarence
Rudd, William L.
Shadley, Lafayette "Lafe"
Smith, Thomas James "Bear
    River Tom"
Sughrue, Michael "Mike"
Sughrue, Thomas "Tom"

Weaver, Henry S.
Weaver, Oliver E.
Weaver, Philip N.
Whitney, Chauncey Belden
Wood, George B.
Wright, Robert
Wright, Robert M.
York, William H.

## Kentucky

Boone, Daniel
Boone, Rebecca Bryan
Hite, Clarence

Hockensmith, Clarke L.
Martin, R.A.C.
Osborne, John E.

## Louisiana

Bunch, Eugene F.

## Maryland

Mullan, John

## Massachusetts

Wyeth, Nathaniel Jarvis

## Michigan

Stuart, David

## Minnesota

Ames, Jesse
Gerard, Frederic Francis

Heywood, Joseph Lee
Pitts, Charlie

## Mississippi

Hobgood, Edward S. "Curnell"

## Missouri

Anderson, William T. "Bloody
    Bill"

Ashley, William Henry
Askew, Daniel H.

Austin, Moses
Bassett, Charles E.
Benson, John W.
Bent, George
Bent, John
Bent, Robert S.
Bent, Silas
Benton, Thomas Hart
Berry, James "Jim"
Biddle, Thomas
Bingham, George Caleb
Bonneville, B.L.E.
Boone, Nathan
Bridger, James "Jim"
Bugler, Henry
Cabanne, Jean Pierre, Sr.
Campbell, Robert
Cerre, Michael Sylvestre
Chiles, James M. "Jim Crow"
Chouteau, Auguste Pierre
Chouteau, Jean Pierre "Pierre the Younger"
Chouteau, Pierre, Jr.
Clark, Meriwether Lewis
Clark, William
Clements, Archibald "Arch"
Colter, John
Cowdery, Oliver
Cummins, James Robert "Jim"
Daugherty, Roy "Arkansas Tom Jones"
De Smet, Peter John
Doniphan, Alexander William
Dripps, Andrew
Edwards, John Newman
Ford, Charles Wilson "Charley"
Ford, Robert Newton "Bob"
George, Hiram J. "Hi"

George, John Hicks
Griffin, B.G.
Harris, William H.
Henry, Andrew
Hildebrand, Samuel "Sam"
Hunt, Wilson Price
James, Alexander Franklin "Frank"
James, Jesse Woodson
Jarrette, John L.
Kearney, Stephen Watts
Lee, Robert "Bob"
Leonard, Zenas
Lisa, Manuel
Logan, Loranzo "Lonny Curry"
Maddox, George
Majors, Alexander
Massie, William Rodney
Miller, Clelland D. "Clell"
Mossman, Burton
Nation, Carry Amelia Moore
Peacock, James
Price, Sterling
Provost, Etienne
Quantrill, Kate King
Russell, William Hepburn
Samuel, Archie Peyton
Samuel, Reuben
Samuel, Zerelda Cole James
Sarpy, Peter A.
Seabourn, Joseph C.
Shannon, George "Peg Leg"
Sheets, John W.
Shepherd (Shepard), Oliver B.
Shepherd, George Washington
Sublette, Solomon P.
Sublette, W.L. "Bill"
Timberlake, James R. "Jim"

Todd, George W.
Tutt, David K.
Vasquez, Louis
Whitmer, David
Younger, Bursheba Fristoe

Younger, James "Jim"
Younger, John
Younger, Rebecca
Younger, Robert "Bob"
Younger, T.C. "Cole"

## Montana

Beidler, John X.
Bozeman, John
Comstock, Henry Thomas Paige
Cruse, Thomas "Tommy"
Curly
Dull Knife
Dunn, John Boggs
Fairweather, William H. "Bill"
Fetterman, William Judd
Gallager, Jack
Helm, Boone
Kelly, Luther Sage "Yellowstone
  Kelly"
Kohrs, Conrad

Landusky, Powell "Pike"
Lane, George "Clubfoot George"
Little Wolf
Logan, John "John Curry"
Lyons, Hayes "Haze"
Plenty Coups (Chief)
Ravalli, Antonio
Reno, Marcus Albert
Sternberg, Sigismund
Story, Nelson
Stuart, Granville
Taylor, H.M. "Muggins"
Two Moon (Chief)
Whitney, Charley S.

## Nebraska

Crazy Horse (Chief)
Crittenden, John Jordan
Culbertson, Alexander
Currie, G.S. "Flat Nose George"
Fontenelle, Logan
Garnier, Baptiste "Little Bat"
Hoy, Valentine
Ketchum, Ami
McCanles, David Colbert
Milner, Moses Embry "California
  Joe"

Mitchell, Luther H.
North, Frank
North, Luther
Oatman, Lorenzo
Sandoz, Jules Ami "Old Jules"
Sandoz, Mari Susetta
Shonsey, Michael "Mike"
Wade, William Albert "Kid"
White Bull
Woods, James

## Nevada

Bowers, Lemuel S. "Sandy"
Davis, J.L. "Diamondfield Jack"

Lamb, Selah Graham
Logan, Thomas W.

Longstreet, Andrew Jackson
 "Jack"
Monk, Henry "Hank"

Ormsby, William
Thompson, John A. "Snowshoe"
Wovoka (Jack Wilson)

## New Mexico

Adamson, Amanda E. Clements
Adamson, Carl
Arny, William Frederick
Arnold, Philip
Aubry, Francois X.
Baca, Cipriano
Baca, Elfego
Baca, Saturnino
Beaubien, Charles H.
Beckwith, Robert "Bob"
Bell, James W.
Bent, Charles
Bockius, Amanda Jane
Bowdre, Charles "Charley"
Bowman, Mason T. "Mace"
Brown, Frederick H.
Carson, Christopher H. "Kit"
Catron, Thomas "Tom"
Chisum, James
Clements, Joseph Hardin "Joe"
Clements, May Myrtle
Coe, Frank
Coe, George
Cooney, James C.
Cox, William Webb "Bill"
Crockett, David, II "Davy"
Dolan, James Joseph
Fornoff, Frederick "Fred"
Fountain, Albert Jennings
Fraker, Charles L.
Galusha, Jandon R.
Garrett, Patrick F.J. "Pat"
Griego, Juan Francisco "Pancho"

Harkey, Daniel R. "Dee"
Hindman, George
Johnson, William H.
Ketchum, Samuel "Sam"
Ketchum, Thomas "Black Jack"
King, Sandy
Lambert, Fred
Lambert, Henry (Henri)
Latham, James V.
Lee, Oliver Milton
Lilly, Benjamin Vernon "Ben"
Llewellyn, Wm. Henry Harrison.
Lucero, Felipe
Matthews, Jacob Basil "Billy"
Maxwell, Lucien Bonapart
Maxwell, Pedro "Pete"
McCarty, Henry "Billy the Kid"
McHughes, James H. "Jim"
McKinney, Thomas Christopher
 "Kip"
McSween, Alexander A.
Murphy, Lawrence Gustave
O'Folliard, Thomas "Tom"
Olinger, Robert A. "Bob"
Patron, Juan Batista
Peppin, George Warden "Dad"
Poe, John William
Robert, Sallie Chisum
Roberts, Andrew L. "Buckshot"
"Russian Bill" (W.R. Tettenborn)
Rynerson, W.L.
Salazar, Yginio
St. Vrain, Ceran

Scarborough, George A.
Scott, William "Bill"
Sieker, Edward Armon "Ed"
Thurmond, Charlotte "Lottie
    Deno"

Thurmond, Frank
Tolby, T.J.
Tunstall, John Henry
Vance, Frank
Whitehill, Harvey Howard

## New York

Custer, George Armstrong
Mackenzie, Ranald Slidell

Masterson, Bartholomew "Bat"
    (William Barclay)

## North Dakota

"Bloody Knife"

Dills, Jefferson

## Ohio

Collins, Caspar Wever
Oakley, Annie

Quantrill, William Clarke
Rich, Charles Henry "Charlie"

## Oklahoma

Ballew, D.M. "Bud"
Big Bow (Chief)
Big Tree (Chief)
Billy Bowlegs
Black Beaver
Black Kettle
Blake, William "Tulsa Jack"
Bobbitt, Allen Angus "Gus"
Boudinot, Elias
Brown, Neal
Bruner, Hickman "Heck"
Canton, Frank
Chapman, Amos
Chihuahua
Chisholm, Jesse
Christie, Ned
Clark, Benjamin "Ben"
Clifton, Charles Daniel "Dyna-
    mite Dick"

Colcord, Charles "Chuck"
Crittenden, E.C. "Zeke"
Crittenden, Richard "Dick"
Dalton, Julia Johnson
Doolin, William "Bill"
Duck, Bluford "Blue"
Dunn, Bill "Bee"
Elliot, Joel
Garrett, Buck
Geronimo
Goldsby, Crawford "Cherokee
    Bill"
Gotebo (Chief)
Guerrier, Edmond "Ed"
Haines, Wiley Green
Hart, Lawson "Loss"
Hennessey, Patrick "Pat"
Herron, Alice I.
Higley, Brewster, III

Houston, Sequoyah
Houston, Temple Lea
Hueston, Thomas J. "Tom"
Kicking Bird (Chief)
Ledbetter, James Franklin "Bud"
Little Raven (Chief)
Loco (Chief)
Long, Crockett
Lynn, Wiley U.
Madsen, Christopher "Chris"
Mangus (Chief)
Newcomb, George "Bitter Creek"
Parker, Cynthia Ann
Parker, Quanah (Chief)
Pierce, Charlie
Proctor, Ezekiel "Zeke"
Pryor, Nathaniel Hale "Nate"
Queteon (Chief)
Raidler, William "Little Bill"
Reed, Edward "Eddie"
Ridge, John
Ridge, Major
Rogers, Diana (Tiana)
Ross, John
Satank (Chief)

Satanta (Chief)
Sitting Bear (Chief)
Speed, Richard "Dick"
Spencer, Ethan Allen "Al"
Spotted Wolf (Chief)
Starr, Henry George
Starr, Myra Belle
Starr, Sam
Starr, Tom
Striding-Along-In-The-Dark
Stumbling Bear (Chief)
Ten Bears (Chief)
Thomas, Henry Andrew "Heck"
Tilghman, William, Jr. "Bill"
Waightman, George "Red Buck"
Waite, Frederick T. "Fred"
Watie, Stand
Wells, Henry
West, Richard "Little Dick"
Worcester, Samuel Austin
Wratten, George Medhurst
Wright, Alfred
Wyatt, Nathaniel Ellsworth "Zip"
    (Dick Yeager)
Yantis, Oliver "Ole"

## Oregon

Applegate, Jesse
Barlow, Samuel K.
Barlow, William
Captain Jack
Charbonneau, Jean Baptiste
Craigie, James
D'Autremont Brothers
Decre, Phillipe
Earp, Virgil
Evans, Christopher "Chris"
Heddon, Cyrus

Holladay, Benjamin "Ben"
Joseph "Old Chief"
Laframboise, Michael
Lee, Jason
LeJuenneuse, Jean Baptiste
McLoughlin, John
Meek, Joseph Lafayette "Joe"
Ogden, Peter Skene
Rivet, Francois
Schonchin "Old Chief"
Schonchin John

Snipes, Benjamin "Ben"
Tracy, Harry

Winema
Young, Ewing

## Pennsylvania

Sutter, John Augustus

## South Dakota

Ash, Benjamin "Ben"
Big Foot (Chief)
Bisonette, John P.
Bissonette, Joseph
Bordeaux, James "Jim"
Bullock, Seth
Cannary, Martha Jane "Calamity Jane"
Gall (Chief)
Hickok, James Butler "Wild Bill"
Hollow Horn Bear (Chief)
Ivers, Alice "Poker Alice"
Maxwell, Electa B.

McCall, John "Jack"
Nelson, John Young
Nolin, Charles
O'Hara, Moses "Mose"
Phillips, James "Scotty"
Pourier, John "Big Bat"
Red Cloud (Chief)
Sitting Bull (Chief)
Smith, Henry Weston "Preacher Smith"
Sorbel, Asle Oscar
Spotted Tail (Chief)

## Tennessee

Bullion, Laura
Crockett, Pauline "Polly"
Crockett, Rebecca Hawkins

Jackson, David E.
Lewis, Meriwether
Maledon, George I.

## Texas

Allee, Alfred Young
Allee, Alonzo Rolland
Allen, J.C.
Allison, Robert Clay
Armstrong, John Barclay
Arnold, Mason "Mace"
Arrington, George Washington (John C. Orrick, Jr.)
Austin, Stephen Fuller
Baird, Moses "Mose"

Baker, Cullen Montgomery
Baker, Joseph
Ballard, Charles Littlepage
Bass, Samuel "Sam"
Baylor, George Wythe
Bean, Roy
Bean, Samuel "Sam"
Becknell, William
Bee, Hamilton P.
Bigford, George

Bockius, James Monroe "Doc"
Boren, Henry
Boren, Israel
Bostick, Sion Record
Bowie, James "Jim"
Boyce, Reuben H.
Briant, Elijah S. "Lige"
Brown, James M. "Jim"
Bryant, Charles "Black Face
   Charley"
Bryant, Robert Edward "Ed"
Bullis, John Lapman
Burnett, Samuel Burk
Bussell, Richard "Dick"
Byars, Noah T.
Campbell, George
Carson, Moses Bradley
Carver, William Todd "Bill"
Chisum, John Simpson
Clark, John Rufus
Clements, Emanuel Mannen
Clements, James "Jim"
Clements, John Gibson "Gip"
Clements, Mannie, Jr.
Clements, Mary Ann
Coe, Phillip H. "Phil"
Coldwell, Neal
Connell, Edward Fulton "Ed"
Cooley, Scott
Courtright, Timothy Isaiah "Long
   Haired Jim"
Crawford, William "Bill"
Crockett, David "Davey"
Crockett, Elizabeth
Cunningham, James
Dixon, William "Billy"
Dorsey, Frank
Duval, John Crittenden

Fairchild, Olive Ann Oatman
Fall, Albert Bacon
Fannin, James Walker
Fisher, John King
Ford, John Salmon "Rip"
Fransel, August
Frazer, George A. "Bud"
Gillett, James Buchanan "Jim"
Gillett, James S.
Goff, Thomas Jefferson "Tom"
Goodnight, Charles
Gressett, Susan T.
Grimes, Ahijah W. "Hi"
Hall, Leigh "Lee"
Hanks, Camillo "Deaf Charley"
Hardin, John Wesley
Hardin, Joseph "Joe"
Harmonson, G. Frank
Henderson, Howard
Hendricks, A.R.
Higgins, John Calhoun Pinckney
   "Pink"
Hobek, "Ole"
Hoerster, Daniel
Houston, Samuel "Sam"
Houston, Samuel, Jr. "Sam"
Hughes, John Reynolds
Ikard, Bose
Johnson, Gerry
Johnston, Albert Sidney
Jones, Frank
Jones, John B.
Kilpatrick, Ben "The Tall Texan"
Kilpatrick, Daniel Boone
Lamar, Mirabeau Buonaparte
Larn, John
Lee, Daniel W.
Lee, Elizabeth

Lee, Robert "Bob"
Lehman, Herman
Lewis, Elmer "Kid"
Lewis, William Winslow "Will"
Long, Jane
Longley, James Stockton "Jim"
Longley, William Preston "Wild
  Bill"
Loving, Oliver
McCormick, Elizabeth "Frenchy"
McDonald, William Jesse "Bill"
McKinney, Charles Brown
McNelly, Leander H.
Milam, Benjamin Rusk "Ben"
Miller, James B. "Killing Jim"
Miller, Sarah Francis "Sallie"
Mooar, J. Wright
Mooar, John Wesley
Nevill, Charles L.
Norfleet, J. Frank.
Olive, James "Jim"
Olive, Julia Ann Brashear
Olive, Thomas Jefferson "Jeff"
Outlaw, Baz (Bass)
Parmer, Allen H.
Parmer, Susan James
Peacock, Lewis
Pierce, Abel Head "Shanghai"
Pierce, William Hartwell
Pleasants, Henry Clay
Potter, Andrew Jackson
Pridgen, Oscar Fitzgerald
Rash, Madison M. "Matt"
Rayner, Hamilton Polk
Riggs, Barney K.
Roberts, Daniel Webster "Dan"
Roberts, Ollie L.
Rose, Louis Moses

Royal, Andrew Jackson
Sapp, Emory Eran
Scurlock, Josiah Gordon "Doc"
Selman, John Henry
Selman, John Marion
Seguin, Juan Nepomuceno
Short, John Luke
Slaughter, Gabriel Webster
  "Gabe"
Smith, Erastus "Deaf Smith"
Standifer, William "Billy"
Stoudenmire, Dallas
Sutton, William "Bill"
Taylor, Creed
Taylor, Hephzibeth Looker
Taylor, James C. "Jim"
Taylor, Josiah
Taylor, Pitkin
Taylor, Rufus P., Jr. "Scrap"
Taylor, Rufus P., Sr.
Taylor, Susan
Taylor, William R. "Buck"
Thompson, Benjamin "Ben"
Thompson, William "Billy"
Travis, Charles Edward
Travis, William Barret
Troutman, Joanna
Tumlinson, Joseph "Joe"
Upson, Ash
Waggoner, Daniel
Wallace, Marion D.
Wallace, William Alexander
  Anderson "Big Foot"
Ware, Richard Clayton "Dick"
Webb, Charles M. "Charley"
West, Jesse J.
Winslow, Henry Francis
Wohrle, John Anton

## Utah

Biddlecomb, Joseph "Joe"
Connor, Patrick Edward
Ewing, Jesse
Gentles, William
Gunnison, John William
Hanks, Charles R. "Charley"
Harris, Martin
Lee, John Doyle
Maxwell, C.L. "Gunplay"
Parker, Ann C. Gillies
Parker, Maxmillian
Preece, Thomas William "Billy"
Rockwell, Orrin Porter
Seger, Charles W.
Slade, Joseph Alfred "Jack"
Tolliver, Joseph Melvin "Joe"
Toponce, Alexander "Alex"
Warner, Matt (Willard Erastus Christiansen)
Young, Brigham

## Virginia

Crawford, Emmett
Miles, Nelson Appleton
O'Neill, William Owen "Buckey"
Pike, Albert
Sheridan, Philip Henry "Phil"
Steptoe, Edward Jenner

## Washington

Glispin, James "Jim"
Joseph "Young Chief"
Timothy (Chief)
Tornow, John
Whitman, Marcus
Whitman, Narcissa Prentice

## Washington, D.C.

Fitzpatrick, Thomas "Broken Hand"

## West Virginia

Gass, Patrick

## Wyoming

Angus, William Galispie "Red"
Averill, James "Jim"
Baker, James "Jim"
Bazil
Bernard, Hiram "Hi"
Boswell, Nathaniel Kimball "N.K."
Cahill, T. Joe
Champion, Ben
Champion, Dudley
Champion, Nathan D. "Nate"
Coble, John C.
Crouse, Charles "Charley"
Hazen, Joseph "Joe"

Hesse, Fred George S.
Hickman, William Adams "Wild Bill"
Irvine, William C. "Billy"
Johnston, John "Liver Eating"
Jones, Orley E. "Ranger"
Lathrop, George
LeFors, Joseph S. "Joe"
Manning, Charles
Maxwell, Ella "Cattle Kate"
Middleton, David C. "Doc"
"Mother Featherlegs"
Nickell, William "Willie"
Parrott, George "Big Nose"

Phillips, John "Portugee"
Pike, George
Punteney, Walter "Walt"
Ray, Nicholas "Nick"
Richey, Ann "Queen Ann"
Sacajawea
Slaughter, John "Johnny"
Smalley, Edwin J. "Ed"
Sublette, Milton Green
Sublette, Pinckney W.
Ten Sleep Mass Grave
Tisdale, John A.
Washakie (Chief)
White, James "Jim"

## Canada

Whitney, Hugh

# Appendix II

## Outlaw Gangs, Feudists, Texas Rangers, and Other Groups

### Arizona Rangers

Kidder, Jefferson Parish "Jeff"
Mossman, Burton

Old, William "Billy"
Wheeler, Harry

### Billy the Kid Gang

Anderson, David L. (Billy Wilson)
Bowdre, Charles "Charley"
Brown, Henry Newton
McCarty, Henry "Billy the Kid"

O'Folliard, Thomas "Tom"
Pickett, Thomas "Tom"
Scurlock, Josiah G. "Doc"
Waite, Frederick "Fred"

### Brown's Park Bunch

Bassett, Eb
Bassett, Elizabeth
Bassett, Herbert
Bassett, Josephine "Josie"
Bernard, Hiram "Hi"
Chew, William
Crouse, Charles "Charlie"
Dart, Isom
Ewing, Jesse

Hoy, Harold "Harry"
Hoy, Valentine
Jarvie, John
Rash, Madison M. "Matt"
Seger, Charles W.
Willis, Ann ("Queen Anne" Bassett)
Willis, Frank

307

## Dalton-Doolin Gang

Blake, William "Tulsa Jack"
Broadwell, Richard L. "Dick"
Bryant, Charles "Black Face Charley"
Clifton, Charles Daniel "Dynamite Dick"
Dalton, Emmett
Dalton, Gratton "Grat"
Dalton, Robert "Bob"
Dalton, William M. "Bill"
Doolin, William "Bill"
Dougherty, Roy "Arkansas Tom Jones"
Dunn, Bee
Newcomb, George "Bitter Creek"
Pierce, Charlie
Powers, William "Bill"
Raidler, William "Little Bill"
Waightman, George "Red Buck"
West, Richard "Little Dick"
Wyatt, Nathaniel Ellsworth "Zip" (Dick Yeager)
Yantis, Oliver "Ol"

## Dodge City, Kansas, Bunch

Bassett, Charles E.
Beeson, Chalkley
Bell, Hamilton Butler "Ham"
Brown, Neal
Daniels, Benjamin F. "Ben"
Earp, Wyatt Berry Stapp
Hardesty, R.J.
Harris, William H.
Hodges, Benjamin "Ben"
Holliday, John Henry "Doc"
Hoover, George M.
Julian, J.E. "Ed"
Kelley, James H. "Dog"
Masterson, Edward John "Ed"
Masterson, James P. "Jim"
Masterson, Bartholomew "Bat" (William Barclay)
Mather, David "Mysterious Dave"
Morrow, David "Prairie Dog Dave"
Nixon, Thomas Clayton "Tom"
Rath, Charles
Short, John Luke
Sughrue, Patrick "Pat"
Tilghman, William, Jr. "Bill"
Webster, Alonzo B.
Wright, Robert

## Fur Trade

Ashley, William Henry
Baker, James "Jim"
Beaubein, Charles H.
Bent, Charles
Bent, George
Bent, Robert S.
Bent, William W.
Bisonette, Joseph
Bonneville, B.L.E.
Bordeaux, James "Jim"
Bridger, James "Jim"
Cabanne, Jean Pierre, Sr.

Campbell, Robert
Carson, Christopher H. "Kit"
Cerre, Michel Sylvestre
Chouteau, Auguste
Chouteau, Jean Pierre
Chouteau, Pierre, Jr.
Colter, John
Craig, William
Craigie, James
Culbertson, Alexander
Dripps, Andrew
Fitzpatrick, Thomas "Broken Hand"
Goodyear, Miles
Henry, Andrew
Hunt, Wilson Price
Jackson, David E.

Laframboise, Michel
Leonard, Zenas
Lisa, Manuel
McLoughlin, John
Meek, Joseph Lafayette "Joe"
Ogden, Peter Skene
Provost, Etienne
St. Vrain, Ceran
Sarpy, Peter A.
Stuart, David
Sublette, Milton
Sublette, Pinckney W.
Sublette, Solomon P.
Sublette, William Lewis "Bill"
Vasquez, Louis
Walker, Joseph R. "Joe"
Young, Ewing

## Indian Leaders

Big Bow
Big Foot
Big Tree
Billy Bowlegs
Black Beaver
Black Kettle
Boudinot, Elias
Captain Jack
Chihuahua
Christie, Ned
Crazy Horse
Curly
Dull Knife
Fontenelle, Logan
Gall
Geronimo
Gotebo
Hollow Horn Bear
Joseph "Old Chief Joseph"

Joseph "Young Chief Joseph"
Keokuk
Kicking Bird
Little Raven
Little Wolf
Loco
Mangus
Ouray
Parker, Quanah
Plenty Coups
Queton
Red Cloud
Ridge, John
Ridge, Major
Ross, John
Satank
Satanta
Schonchin "Old Chief"
Schonchin John

Sitting Bear
Sitting Bull
Spotted Tail
Spotted Wolf
Striding Along In The Dark
Stumbling Bear
Ten Bears

Tendoy
Two Moon
Washakie
Watie, Stand
White Bull
Wovoka (Jack Wilson)
Yellow Bear

## James-Younger Gang

Cummins, James Robert "Jim"
Ford, Charles W. "Charley"
Ford, Robert N. "Bob"
James, Alexander Franklin
    "Frank"
James, Jesse Woodson
Miller, Clelland, D. "Clell"

Pitts, Charlie
Younger, James "Jim"
Younger, John
Younger, Robert "Bob"
Younger, Thomas Coleman
    "Cole"

## Johnson County War and the Cattleman-Homesteader Conflict

Angus, William G. "Red"
Averill, James "Jim"
Canton, Frank
Champion, Dudley
Champion, Nathan D. "Nate"
Garrett, Buck
Hesse, Fred G.
Horn, Thomas "Tom"

Irvine, William C. "Billy"
Jones, Orley E. "Ranger"
LeFors, Joseph S.
Maxwell, Ella "Cattle Kate"
Nickell, William "Willie"
Ray, Nick
Shonsey, Michael "Mike"
Tisdale, John A.

## Lee-Peacock Feud

Boren, Henry
Boren, Israel
Lee, Daniel W.
Lee, Elizabeth

Lee, Robert "Bob"
Peacock, Lewis
Pierce, William Hartwell

## Lewis and Clark Expedition

Bratton, William E.
Charbonneau, Jean Baptiste

Clark, William
Colter, John

Decre, Phillipe
Floyd, Charles
Gass, Patrick
LeJeunneuse, Jean Baptiste
Lewis, Meriwether
Pryor, Nathaniel "Nate"

Rivet, Francois
Sacajawea
Shannon, George, Jr. "Pegleg"
Shields, John
Willard, Alexander Hamilton

## Lincoln County War

Beckwith, Robert "Bob"
Bell, James A.
Bowdre, Charles "Charley"
Brady, Patrick William "Pat"
Brewer, Richard "Dick"
Brown, Henry Newton
Coe, Frank
Coe, George
Dolan, James Joseph
Garrett, Patrick Floyd "Pat"
Hindman, George
Johnson, William H.
Kinney, John William Young
Mason, Barney
Matthews, Jacob Basil "Billy"

McCarty, Henry "Billy the Kid"
McSween, Alexander A.
McSween, Susan Barber
Murphy, Lawrence Gustave
Olinger, Robert A. "Bob"
Peppin, George Warden "Dad"
Pickett, Thomas "Tom"
Riley, John Henry
Roberts, Andrew L. "Buckshot"
Rynerson, W.L.
Salazar, Yginio
Scurlock, Josiah G. "Doc"
Tunstall, John Henry
Waite, Frederick "Fred"
Wallace, Lewis "Lew"

## Mason County War

Baird, Moses "Mose"
Clark, John Rufus
Cooley, Scott

Hoerster, Daniel
Wohrle, John Anton

## Miners and Mining

Comstock, Henry P.T.
Cruse, Thomas "Tommy"
Fairweather, William H. "Bill"
Marshall, James Wilson
Schieffelin, Edward L. "Ed"
Sutter, John Augustus

Tabor, Horace Austin Warner
  "Haw"
Waltz, Jacob "The Dutchman"
Warren, George
Wickenburg, J.H. "Henry"

## New Mexico Mounted Police

Baca, Cipriano
Fornoff, Fred
Galusha, Jandon R.

Lambert, Fred
McHughes, James H. "Jim"
Vance, Frank

## Pleasant Valley War (Graham-Tewksbury Feud)

Blevins, Andy (Andy Cooper)
Blevins, Charles
Blevins, Sam Houston
Bloody Basin Gravesite
   Scott, James
   Stott, James "Jim"
   Wilson, William "Billy"
Glaspie, Robert M. "Bob"
Graham, John
Graham, Thomas "Tom"
Graham, William

Middleton, Harry
Rhodes, John (Tewksbury)
Rhodes, Mary Ann Crigger
   Tewksbury
Roberts, James F. "Jim"
Roberts, Mose
Rose, Albert "Al"
Tewksbury, Braulia Rivera
Tewksbury, Edwin "Ed"
Tewksbury, John
Tewksbury, Walter

## Quantrill's Raiders

Anderson, William T. "Bloody
   Bill"
Benson, John W.
Clements, Archibald "Archie"
George, Hiram J. "Hi"
George, John Hicks
Hildebrand, Samuel "Sam"
Hockensmith, Clarke L.
James, Alexander Franklin
   "Frank"

James, Jesse Woodson
Jarrette, John L.
Maddox, George
Parmer, Allen H.
Quantrill, William Clarke
Shepard, Oliver B.
Shepherd, George Washington
Todd, George W.
Younger, Thomas Coleman
   "Cole"

## Ranching

Burnett, Samuel Burk
Chisum, John Simpson
Coble, John C.
French, Peter
Goodnight, Charles
Hesse, Fred G.

Irvine, William C. "Billy"
Kitchen, Peter "Pete"
Kohrs, Conrad
Loving, Oliver
Maxwell, Lucien Bonapart
Pierce, Abel Head "Shanghai"

Shea, Cornelius "Con"
Slaughter, John Horton
Snipes, Benjamin "Ben"
Story, Nelson

Stuart, Granville
Tisdale, John A.
Waggoner, Daniel
Woolsey, King S.

## Scouts (Military)

"Bloody Knife"
Chapman, Amos
Clark, Benjamin "Ben"
Comstock, William "Billy"
Cormack, Charles H. "Charley"
Dixon, William "Billy"
Free, Mickey
Garnier, Baptiste "Little Bat"
Godey, Alexis
Grover, Abner T. "Sharp"
Guerrier, Edmund "Ed"
Jeffords, Thomas J. "Tom"
Kelly, Luther Sage "Yellowstone Kelly"

Mathewson, William
Milner, Moses Embry "California Joe"
North, Frank
North, Luther
Omohundro, John Baker "Texas Jack"
Pourier, John Baptiste "Big Bat"
Sieber, Albert "Al"
Taylor, H.M. "Muggins"
Tobin, Thomas Tate "Tom"
Weaver, Pauline
Wratten, George Medhurst

## Taylor-Sutton Feud

Arnold, Mason "Mace"
Bockius, James Monroe "Doc"
Hendricks, A.R.
Pleasants, Henry Clay
Slaughter, Gabriel W. "Gabe"
Sutton, William "Bill"

Taylor, James C. "Jim"
Taylor, Pitkin B.
Taylor, Rufus P., Jr. "Scrap"
Taylor, William R. "Buck"
Tumlinson, Joseph "Joe"

## Texas Rangers

Allee, Alfred Young
Allee, Alonzo Rolland
Armstrong, John Barclay
Arrington, George Washington
Aten, Ira
Ballard, Charles Littlepage
Baylor, George Wythe

Bigford, George
Bryant, Robert Edward "Ed"
Coldwell, Neal
Connell, Edward Fulton "Ed"
Cunningham, James
Ford, John Salmon "Rip"
Frazer, George A.

Gildea, Augustine Montague "Gus"
Gillette, James Buchanan "Jim"
Gillette, James S.
Goff, Thomas Jefferson "Tom"
Grimes, Ahijah W. "Hi"
Hall, Leigh "Lee"
Hays, John Coffee "Jack"
Henderson, Howard
Hughes, John Reynolds
Jones, Frank
Jones, Gerry
Jones, John B.
Latham, James V.
Lewis, William Winslow "Will"

McDonald, William Jesse "Bill"
McNelly, Leander H.
Milton, Jefferson Davis "Jeff"
Nevill, Charles L.
Outlaw, Baz (Bass)
Pridgen, Oscar Fitzgerald
Roberts, Daniel Webster "Dan"
Rudd, William L.
Scott, William "Bill"
Sieker, Edward Amon "Ed"
Slaughter, John Horton
Wallace, William Alexander Anderson "Big Foot"
Ware, Richard Clayton "Dick"
Winslow, Henry Francis

## The Tombstone, Arizona, Bunch

Behan, John "Johnny"
Berry, George C.
Breakenridge, William Milton "Billy"
Claiborne, William Floyd "Billy"
Clanton, Joseph Isaac "Ike"
Clanton, Newman Haynes "Old Man"
Clanton, Phineas "Phin"
Clanton, William H. "Billy"
Cummings, Mary K. "Big Nose Kate Elder"
Earp, James Cooksey "Jim"
Earp, Morgan

Earp, Virgil Walter
Earp, Warren
Earp, Wyatt Berry Stapp
Fly, Camillus
Holliday, John Henry "Doc"
Howell, Amazon C.
Leslie, Frank "Buckskin Frank"
Masterson, Bartholomew "Bat" (William Barclay)
McLaury, Robert Frank
McLaury, Thomas "Tom"
Ringo, John "Johnny"
Schieffelin, Edward L. "Ed"
Slaughter, John Horton

## The Wild Bunch

Bullion, Laura
Carver, William Todd "Bill"
Currie, George Sutherland "Flat
   Nose George"
Hanks, Camillo "Deaf Charley"
Kilpatrick, Ben "The Tall Texan"
Lay, William Elsworth "Elzy"
Lee, Robert "Bob"
Logan, Harvey "Kid Curry"
Longabaugh, Harry Alonzo
   "Sundance Kid"
McCarty, Thomas "Tom"
O'Day, Thomas "Tom"
Parker, Robert Leroy "Butch
   Cassidy"
Punteney, Walter "Walt"
Thornhill, James "Jim"
Warner, Matt

# Index

All index numbers refer to items, not to pages.

# C

# E

# H

# N

# O

**P**

# S

# U

Upson, Marshal Ashmun "Ash": 922

# V

Valentine, Ed: 10
Vance, Mildred Kingery: 923
Vance, R. Frank: 482, 923
Vance, William A.: 923
Van Deventer, Len H.: 265
Vasquez, Louis: 924
Vasquez, Tiburcio: 925
Victorio: 518
Vigil, Juan: 79, 108, 789, 926
Vincent, "Tip": 665

# W

Wade, William Albert "Kid": 927
Waddell, W.B.: 562
Waggoner, Daniel "Dan": 928
Waggoner, Nancy Moore: 928
Waggoner, Scylly Ann Halsell: 928
Waggoner, William Thomas: 928
Wagner, Jack: 575
Waightman, George "Red Buck": 929
Waite, Frederick "Fred": 930
Walker, Joseph Reddeford "Joe": 931
Wallace, Anna L.: 932
Wallace, Belle: 932
Wallace, E.M.: 932
Wallace, Lewis "Lew": 932
Wallace, Marion D.: 381, 932
Wallace, Mrs. M.D.: 932
Wallace, Sidney "Sid": 544, 934
Wallace, Thomas E.: 932
Wallace, Vincent: 934

Wallace, William Alexander Anderson "Big Foot": 935
Walters, "Broncho Bill": 336
Waltz, Jacob "The Dutchman": 936
Ware, Richard Clayton "Dick": 937
Warner, Elma Z.: 938
Warner, Matt (Willard Erastus Christiansen): 938
Warren, George: 939
Washakie: 940
Wassaja (Carlos Montezuma): 941
Watie, Kilakeena "Buck": 115
Watie, Stand: 115, 730, 731, 748, 942
Watkins, Rody: 523, 535
Watson, Edward J. "Ed": 839, 943
Watson, Ella: 28
Watson, Jane S.: 943
Wattron, Francis Jospeh "Frank": 944
Weaver, Henry S. "Hank": 945
Weaver, Oliver E.: 945
Weaver, Pauline: 946
Weaver, Phillip N., Jr.: 945
Webb, Alex: 19
Webb, Charles M. "Charley": 378, 379, 947
Weber, E.P.: 267
Webster, Alonzo B.: 948
Webster, Amanda: 948
Weisiger, William: 16, 871
Wells, Henry: 949
Wesley, John: 133
West, Jesse J.: 7, 596, 950
West, Richard "Little Dick": 951
Westfall, William H.: 556
Wheeler, Ben F.: 133
Wheeler, Harry Cornell: 633, 952
White, Gideon Shields "Cap": 955
White, James "Jim": 875, 956
White Bull: 954
Whitehill, Harriett M.: 957

**Y**

**Z**

# The Author

Jim Browning's interest in the Old West began more than fifty years ago. Since then he has traveled and done research extensively throughout the United States, Canada, Mexico, and Central America. He estimates that he has driven more than 250,000 miles and taken more than 34,000 color slides of old forts, ghost towns, grave sites, and weapons owned by famous outlaws and lawmen. His other book, *The Western Reader's Guide*, was also published by Barbed Wire Press.